Desire and Infinity
in W. S. Merwin's Poetry

Desire and Infinity in W. S. Merwin's Poetry

FENG DONG

Louisiana State University Press

Baton Rouge

Published by Louisiana State University Press
lsupress.org

W 上 海 外 语 教 育 出 版 社
外教社 SHANGHAI FOREIGN LANGUAGE EDUCATION PRESS

Licensed for sale in the United States of America only.

Designer: Barbara Neely Bourgoyne
Typeface: Arno Pro

Cover image: istockphoto.com/Punnarong

Several chapters of this book have been published in peer-reviewed journals. The author thanks
the reviewers and editors for lending their expertise. An earlier version of chapter 2 appeared
in *Concentric: Literary and Cultural Studies* 41.2 (2015): 143–70, published by National Taiwan
Normal University. An earlier version of chapter 3 appeared in *NTU Studies in Language and
Literature* 35 (2016): 63–95, © 2016 NTU Press and National Taiwan University. A shorter version of chapter 4 appeared in *College Literature: A Journal of Critical Literary Studies* 45.1 (2018):
106–33, © 2018 Johns Hopkins University Press and West Chester University of Pennsylvania.

Library of Congress Cataloging-in-Publication Data
Names: Feng, Dong, author.
Title: Desire and infinity in W. S. Merwin's poetry / Feng Dong.
Description: Baton Rouge : Louisiana State University Press, [2021] | Includes bibliographical
    references and index.
Identifiers: LCCN 2021018537 (print) | LCCN 2021018538 (ebook) | ISBN 978-0-8071-7611-5
    (cloth) | ISBN 978-0-8071-7685-6 (pdf) | ISBN 978-0-8071-7686-3 (epub)
Subjects: LCSH: Merwin, W. S. (William Stanley), 1927–2019—Criticism and interpretation.
Classification: LCC PS3563.E75 Z66 2021 (print) | LCC PS3563.E75 (ebook) |
    DDC 811/.54—dc23
LC record available at https://lccn.loc.gov/2021018537
LC ebook record available at https://lccn.loc.gov/2021018538

for Ayin

TO W. S. MERWIN

A man
sat by the side of a river
listening to the turning of the wheel
only there was no wheel to turn
he just sat there listening
day and night passed
the first light of dawn
traveled through the green trees
he looks up at the unnamed sky
waiting for
the alien blessing
to come

CONTENTS

ACKNOWLEDGMENTS

I am grateful to my advisor, Prof. Yang Jincai, in the English Department of Nanjing University, whose inspiration and academic acumen greatly contributed to the first draft of this book. I also thank Zhang Ziqing, Qian Jiaoru, and Jeffrey Gray for initiating me into the study of English literature and, particularly, American poetry. I thank Bob Riggle for his rigorous, even "cruel," methodology on academic writing—it worked for me. My friends Scott Alexander Jones, Thomas Eisenbeiser, and Sun Dong read parts of the manuscript and offered invaluable advice. I am enormously indebted to the anonymous reviewer's comments that have greatly expanded my critical horizon on many issues. I thank James W. Long and Neal Novak, editors at the Louisiana State University Press, for their support and encouragement every step of the way. I am grateful to Stan Ivester for the copyediting and Jo-Ann Parks for the index. Finally, I thank Susan Stewart and Jean-Michel Rabaté, truly my mentors in literary study and poetry criticism.

in the Furnace" from *The First Four Books of Poems*. Copyright © 1952, 1954, © 1956, and 1960 by W. S. Merwin. Excerpts from "The Saint of the Uplands," "December Night," "The Dream Again," "The Herds," "How We are Spared," "Midnight in Early Spring," "Separation," and "To the Rain" from *The Second Four Books of Poems*. Copyright © 1963, 1967, 1970, 1973 by W. S. Merwin. Excerpts from "Still Morning," "By the Avenue," "No," and "To Paula in Late Spring" from *The Shadow of Sirius*. Copyright © 2008 by W. S. Merwin. Excerpts from "The Flight," "Kore," "Islands," and "Sunset Water" from *Flower & Hand: Poems 1977–1983*. Copyright © 1977, 1983 by W. S. Merwin. Excerpts from "To the Lightning" and "To Grief" from *Present Company*. Copyright © 2007 by W. S. Merwin. All reprinted with the permission of The Permissions Company LLC on behalf of Copper Canyon Press, coppercanyonpress.org.

"Travelling West at Night" from *The River Sound: Poems* by W. S. Merwin, copyright © 1999 by W. S. Merwin. Used by permission of Alfred A. Knopf, an imprint of the Knopf Doubleday Publishing Group, a division of Penguin Random House LLC. All rights reserved.

"The Moment of Green," "Cinchona," "The Palms," and "Field Mushrooms" from *Travels* by W. S. Merwin, copyright © 1992 by W. S. Merwin. Used by permission of Alfred A. Knopf, an imprint of the Knopf Doubleday Publishing Group, a division of Penguin Random House LLC. All rights reserved.

"Vixen," and "Hölderlin at The River" from *The Vixen: Poems* by W. S. Merwin, copyright © 1995 by W. S. Merwin. Used by permission of Alfred A. Knopf, an imprint of the Knopf Doubleday Publishing Group, a division of Penguin Random House LLC. All rights reserved.

"Anniversary on the Island," "Late Spring," "The Sound of the Light," "Waking to the Rain," and "Memory" from *The Rain in the Trees* by W. S. Merwin, copyright © 1988 by W. S. Merwin. Used by permission of Alfred A. Knopf, an imprint of the Knopf Doubleday Publishing Group, a division of Penguin Random House LLC. All rights reserved.

"The Saint of the Uplands," "December Night," "The Dream Again," "End of Summer," "Lemuel's Blessing," "The Judgment of Paris," and "Separation" from *The Second Four Books of Poems* by W. S. Merwin, copyright © 1993 by W. S. Merwin, Copper Canyon Press, used by permission of The Wylie Agency LLC.

"Islands" and "Sunset Water" from *Flower & Hand: Poems 1977–1983* by W. S. Merwin, copyright © 1997 by W. S. Merwin, Copper Canyon Press, used by permission of The Wylie Agency LLC.

"On the Subject of Poetry," "Two Paintings by Alfred Wallis," "The Iceberg," "The Bones of Palinurus Pray to the North Star," "Sailor Ashore," "Proteus," "Leviathan," "Sea Monster," "White Goat, White Ram," "The Passion," "Saint Sebastian," and "December: Of Aphrodite" from the *The First Four Books of Poems* by W. S. Merwin, copyright © 2000 by W. S. Merwin, Copper Canyon Press, used by permission of The Wylie Agency LLC.

"To the Lightning" and "To Grief" from *Present Company* by W. S. Merwin, copyright © 2005 by W. S. Merwin, Copper Canyon Press, used by permission of The Wylie Agency LLC.

"Hunger Mountain" and "Marietta" from *The Book of Fables* by W. S. Merwin, copyright © 2007 by W. S. Merwin, Copper Canyon Press, used by permission of The Wylie Agency LLC.

"Still Morning," "By the Avenue," "No," and "To Paula in Late Spring" from *The Shadow of Sirius* by W. S. Merwin, copyright © 2008 by W. S. Merwin, Copper Canyon Press, used by permission of The Wylie Agency LLC.

ACKNOWLEDGMENTS

"The Color They Come To" from *The Moon Before Morning* by W. S. Merwin, copyright © 2015 by W. S. Merwin, Copper Canyon Press, used by permission of The Wylie Agency LLC.

ABBREVIATIONS

BF   *The Book of Fables* (2007)
CW   *Conversations with W. S. Merwin* (2015)
EE   *The Ends of the Earth: Essays* (2004)
FC   *The Folding Cliffs: A Narrative* (1998)
FF   *The First Four Books of Poems* (2000)
FH   *Flower & Hand: Poems 1977–1983* (1997)
FI   *Finding the Islands* (1982)
GT   *Garden Time* (2016)
LU   *The Lost Upland: Stories of Southwest France* (1992)
MB   *The Moon Before Morning* (2015)
MV   *The Mays of Ventadorn* (2002)
P   *The Pupil* (2001)
PC   *Present Company* (2005)
RM   *Regions of Memory: Uncollected Prose, 1949–82* (1987)
RS   *The River Sound* (1999)
RT   *The Rain in the Trees* (1988)
SD   *Summer Doorways: A Memoir* (2005)
SF   *The Second Four Books of Poems* (1993)
SS   *The Shadow of Sirius* (2008)
ST   *Selected Translations 1948–2011* (2015)
T   *Travels* (1993)
UO   *Unframed Originals: Recollections* (1982)
V   *The Vixen* (1996)

Desire and Infinity
in W. S. Merwin's Poetry

INTRODUCTION

A modern disciple of high Romanticism, with all its remoteness, ghost-
liness, shadows, dreams, fantasies, ecstasies, and nostalgia, William
Stanley Merwin (1927–2019) claims a unique status in the contemporary literary scene of the United States. Despite his concern for and
involvements with major social issues such as the anti–Vietnam War
movement, protests against nuclear arms, and the environmental movement starting back in the 1960s, Merwin's writings have maintained
another dimension beyond immediate US social realities. To readers
accustomed to urban lyrics, Merwin's poetry may sound anachronistic,
for much of it does not refer to the current postindustrial consumer
society; rather, Merwin sings of skylarks and nightingales in the remote
villages of southern France, where he lived intermittently for years, or
of the fauna and flora of Majorca and Maui. Like the migrant birds he
loves and writes about, Merwin himself has traveled extensively during
his life, from New Jersey, where he grew up, to Portugal, Spain, France,
England, Greece, Mexico, and finally to Hawaii. He has lived in Hawaii
for his last forty years. Like the Knights Templar of the Middle Ages
seeking the Holy Grail, Merwin over his entire poetic career exhibits a
strong and persistent spiritual quest for the distant, the transcendent,
and the infinite. His unquenchable spiritualism puts him in the same
camp as such poets as P. B. Shelley, W. B. Yeats, and Friedrich Hölderlin.
In the age of mechanical reproduction of artworks, Merwin's writings
have curiously retained that aura associated with the enchantment of
words and fascination with origins.

Merwin can be described as a post-Romantic in that he has de-romanticized Romanticism; he keeps the basic gesture of Romantic transcendence while discrediting both Byron's self-aggrandizement and Whitman's appropriation of nature. Merwin also questions the grand narratives of equality, freedom, and brotherly love, which constitute the ideal of human emancipation since the French Revolution. Indeed, in the 1960s Merwin's poetic vision was so bleak and apocalyptic that he was in the paradoxical position of being considered either the most Romantic or the most anti-Romantic of contemporary poets. Robert Pinsky, after reading "Whenever I Go There" in *The Lice* (1967), cries that it "embodies an extreme Romanticism: a pursuit of darkness, of silence" (94), while Thomas B. Byers, reading the same book and comparing it with the poems of Walt Whitman, concludes that "Merwin not only disbelieves the Romantic position but finds it immoral and destructive" (*What I Cannot Say* 88–89).[1] The controversy points to the inherent contradiction between Merwin's deconstructive voice and what Laurence Lieberman calls "a sustained inner urgency" (qtd. in Folsom and Nelson 10), a poetic yearning for what is "higher" than the experiential world.[2]

The problematics of transcendence and historicity in Merwin's poetry have long perplexed his critics. Reviewing *The Lice* in 1967, Laurence Lieberman hastened to crown Merwin the poet-prophet by announcing that the book "has perfectly captured the peculiar spiritual agony of our time" (qtd. in Perloff 122). Now it has become commonplace to consider Merwin's poems from the 1960s to be dark, sparse, and pessimistic, because the historical time did not seem particularly hopeful for poets. Lieberman's praise actually demotes Merwin to a "representative poet" of a certain historical condition, inexorably pinning him down by historical repercussions. Although Merwin admits that "it was possible for [*The Lice*] to be considered as a reflection of its historical context," he soon adds that "readers continue to share with us something of history that is not strictly historic" (*SF* 1, 2). It seems that what concerned Merwin then was not just the process of national history but the end of history—eschatology, the "coming of extinction," as one of his prophetic poems in *The Lice* is titled.[3]

Cary Nelson, commenting on another typical poem, "Beginning," in *The Moving Target* (1963), says, "It is an eschatology of origins; it binds the course of history to a single core of emptiness" (107). Dismantling the master narrative of history as progress and enlightenment, Merwin presents the final impasse of man's age-old hegemonic control over each other and over the natural world, calling for a spiritual journey into "the white plain / under the white sky" (*SF* 218), a pre- or post-historical site where "its beginning is a true origin—an end" (Nelson 107). Thus, Merwin had gone further than any "spiritual agony" to the "No Man's Land," to the kernel of history that is ahistorical, where spiritual agony is largely swallowed up by the biblical pre-creational chaos. Reading *The Lice* along with Merwin's mythopoeic poems of the 1950s helps to clarify Merwin's continuous effort to break out of man's anthropocentric obsession with *his own story*. In *W. S. Merwin the Mythmaker* (1986), Mark Christhilf finds that "Merwin often describes the present in images suggesting the mythical apocalypse: things are falling, broken, ending" (24); Merwin's transcendental vision is thus bound up with the prophesied end of human history.

Not every critic is ready to credit Merwin's apocalypse. After laying bare the elaborate metrical devices in several exemplary 1960s poems of Merwin, Marjorie Perloff dismisses Merwin as a "fastidious poet, whose gift is perhaps less for revelation than for delicate resonance" (142). Merwin was indeed "fastidious" in his early discursive poems such as "Dictum: For a Masque of Deluge," "East of the Sun and West of the Moon," "Leviathan," and "Grandmother Dying," in which he was working more with dramatic invention than poetic reduction. To characterize *The Moving Target* or *The Lice* as "fastidious" on the mere ground of metrics, however, is to mistake Merwin's built-in sense of meter (Merwin started writing regular hymns at the age of five) for the ostensible manipulation of the poetic process, something Merwin highly suspected in the 1960s and eventually abandoned after the 1970s. The innate poetic resonance does not handicap Merwin's transcendental reverie but enhances its enchantment. Revelation need not exclude resonance.

Harold Bloom, less enthusiastic than Lieberman and more lenient than Perloff, dictates in a half-sympathetic and half-condescending tone that "Merwin's predicament . . . is that he has no Transcendental vision, and yet feels impelled to prophesy" (14). What Bloom has in mind is the Emersonian transcendentalist, a self-confident, optimistic eyeball viewing the whole phenomenal world. Merwin's dark defeatism in *The Moving Target* and *The Lice* obviously does not fit into this paradigm. Therefore, Bloom considers Merwin incapable of "a belief in an influx of light and power," and the light Merwin presents is "wholly meaningless" (16). However, one is tempted to read Merwin in the opposite direction and argue with Bloom as to the meaning of the adjective "meaningless." Jarold Ramsey, commenting on *The Lice*, observes that "the speaker ultimately looks beyond man to a natural world as desolate as T. S. Eliot's vision of the end," yet what Merwin opens up is more like a "posthuman world" than a wasteland (32). What Bloom has overlooked or misrecognized is exactly this "beyond" emphasized by Ramsey. Merwin's transcendental vision is "meaningless," not because it is too dark or despairing, as Bloom finds, but because it has crossed the border of human signification and passed into a psychotic state in which the naive dichotomy of optimism and pessimism no longer applies. The vision is more pathological than historical.

Like the German Romantic poet Friedrich Hölderlin, Merwin often perceives human reality from a nonhuman or divine vantage. Charles Molesworth notices that in Merwin "all human projects are seen through a lens of oblivion or transcendence that renders details insignificant and turns hope into something furtive and numbing" (153). Molesworth, however, is reluctant to recognize that, for Merwin, hope does not reside in other humans (or even a personal God), but in what is other than the human, although Merwin's poems would grow more "human-friendly" (more affirmative of human values) after the mid-1970s. The numbness of hope testifies to the need of a more radical understanding of hope, for Merwin's is another kind of hope, which is not *for* or *of* humans, but largely *without* humans. It is the No One's hope. In this sense, Merwin has radicalized the (im)possibility of poetic language to signify the alternative modes of being: the encounters with the monstrous, the inanimate, and the undead—what is *beyond* hope or remedy.

All these characteristics of Merwin differ significantly from nineteenth-century American Transcendentalism, which Harold Bloom espoused and used as a yardstick for contemporary poetry. Unlike Emerson or Whitman, Merwin cherishes neither patent love for fellow humans nor any optimistic view of human perfectibility.[4] Merwin's stance is more critical and deconstructive. Merwin *does* believe in "the influx of light and power," and his works in the 1980s and afterward would override this judgment of Bloom's. This "light and power," however, should not be equated with the Emersonian idealism that proposes an autonomous subject fully capable of absorbing the object without leaving any remainder, but with a radical revelation from the infinite Other that cannot be properly subjectivized through both theoretical and poetic discourses. For Merwin, it is presumptuous to regard ego as the Whole, the unity of the pieces of the external reality as supposed by Emerson. Human ego cannot completely transcend itself in a mystic unity with the divine, the holy, or the infinite; it remains irreducibly distant from what draws it despite its epiphanies and approximations—or what Cary Nelson calls the "inaccessible proximity" (107). Even though Merwin exhibits a strong tendency of transcendence, it is inaccurate to characterize him as a "transcendentalist" with all its Emersonian halo of self-confidence, for in the Merwinian world, the proximity between self and Other, desire and object, humanity and nonhumanness simultaneously produces a sense of distance and loss.

The bulk of Merwin's poetry from *A Mask for Janus* (1952) up to *Garden Time* (2016), despite many transformations of poetic style, voice, and motif, manifests a desire that does not call for fulfillment but circles around the Infinite. Merwin's desire for infinity largely differs from American Transcendentalism in that the lyrical subject manifests certain symptoms such as anxiety, amnesia, obsession, euphoria, and hallucination before the infinite Other. Throughout his poetic career Merwin seems to maintain a transferential relationship with the deified

Other. I will narrate Merwin's Pilgrim's Progress, which indefatigably seeks what Emmanuel Levinas calls "the holiness of the holy" (qtd. in Derrida, *Adieu* 4) in both sacred and secular spheres. By positing a kind of fleeting divinity, not only religious but also existential, in the Other, Merwin stages an endless query that retroactively produces its own object-cause. Merwin's controversial apocalyptic vision in the 1960s can be read as an eruption of his psychoneurotic transgression that intensified in the 1960s but had already been latent in the 1950s and continued onto the 1970s and 1980s. More importantly, Merwin's vision is accompanied by an urgent decision for separation to open new existential and ethical grounds outside the given social order. Different from Allen Ginsberg who howls before a spiritless civilization, Merwin not only transgresses present reality but also establishes potential or alternative realities through the medium of enchanted verbal movements, as he wrote in the 1950s: "We became / The eyes of sleep that chased receding fires / Through the bodiless exile of a dream," and "We seek a new dimension for the world" (*FF* 11). The receding, beckoning fires and the new dimension of the world would herald Merwin's lifelong pursuit of a radical poetic reality outside any given historical conditions.

This book elucidates the problematics of desire and infinity in Merwin's poetry from a dialogue between psychoanalysis and post-Heideggerian philosophy. I borrow the formulation of desire/drive from the French psychoanalyst Jacques Lacan and the Lacanian theorist Slavoj Žižek. Lacan incorporates structuralism into Sigmund Freud's concept of "unconscious wish," proposing that "desire is neither the appetite for satisfaction nor the demand for love, but the difference that results from the subtraction of the first from the second, the very phenomenon of their splitting (*Spaltung*)" (*Écrits* 276). Desire (*désir*) is a product of separation, of "splitting" between instinctual need (*besoin*) that can be satisfied and unconditional demand (*demande*) that cannot. Desire points to the desire of the Other when the infant first perceives that (m)Other's desire is directed elsewhere and tries to fill in that lack by asking, "What does she desire?" Replacing the desire for mother with the Name-of-the-Father, the infant enters the Symbolic (*symbolique*) of signifiers and language (the big Other, as opposed to the imaginary/ mirrored other)—"that foreign language that we are born into and must learn to speak if we want to articulate our own desire" (Homer 70). In its articulation, desire is inextricably woven into the network of words and sentences, as Lacan famously claims: "[Desire] is not so much a pure passion of the signified as a pure action of the signifier" (*Écrits* 253). Generated by the abyssal desire of the (m)Other, the subject's own desire hides and slides in the network of metaphors, metonymies, and references, seeking temporary satisfaction in the very hindrance it meets.

There is, however, something that cannot be properly symbolized by signifiers and language—the Real (*réel*), which includes the objects of desire (*das Ding, objet petit a*), unconscious fantasies, ecstatic enjoyments (*jouissance*), and libidinal drives. The relationship between the Real and reality is a reversed one: the Real is more real than reality in that it, being psychic, provides the authentic cause for human actions. The Real not only resists the erosion of symbolic reality but also constitutes the kernel of the latter, for what has been excluded from the surface of reality is what truly organizes this reality and constitutes its representational framework.

Lacan specifically develops the concept of *das Ding*, the Thing, in *Seminar VII* (1959–60) as "the absolute Other of the subject," which "one is supposed to find again . . . as something missed" (52). Subject is caught up in an endless circle of *déjà vu* because "one doesn't find it, but only its pleasurable associations"; "It is in this state of wishing for it and waiting for it that, in the name of the pleasure principle, the optimum tension will be sought" (*Seminar VII* 52). Thus the Thing, what Žižek terms "the non-sensical, pre-ideological kernel of enjoyment" (*Sublime* 124), is not a tangible entity but the traumatic void within the Symbolic, functioning as the phantasmal/inaccessible object of desire by drawing the subject's libidinal cathexes around it. One is compelled to touch the Real without touching it; every encounter with the Real (*tuché*) is a missed encounter (*Seminar XI* 52). Lacan's theory points out the fundamental and ontological alienation in the formation of human subjectivity. In his revolutionary interpretation of Sophocles's tragedy *Antigone*, Lacan puts forward his ethics as "not to compromise one's desire" (*ne pas céder sur son désir*). To work through one's desire to the end, to disavow the mandate of the Symbolic and thus to objectify oneself as the Real, becomes a viable ethical choice under the incessant domestication of desire by educators and academies (*Seminar VII* 324).

Merwin's poetry is exactly characterized by a devotional gesture apropos of the traumatic Thing and an uncompromised drive to surpass the Name-of-the-Father and its corollaries such as the system of signification, language, and intersubjective network. The poetic signifiers seem to point to a central void, a nondiscursive field in subjectivity which manifests only "pleasurable associations" of the Thing but not the Thing itself. In his endless wishing and waiting for the phantasmal object to emerge from the void, Merwin hopes to capture the remnants/traces of the Other through the poetic form. The spirituality as well as the spectrality of Merwin's poetry corresponds to the poet-speaker's infinite proximity to the posited object rather than its direct attainment. Writing under the weight of ecological crises, Merwin's "pale" words around the loss of the Thing rather expose earth as a planet that is already hollowed out, emptied of languages and species.[5] In the Anthropocene era, Merwin's poetics of devotional proximity rather tests how far we can go with a radically altered environment and to what extent the holy, the transcendent, can still be constitutive of humanness.

In order to fully describe the libidinal economy of Merwin's quest for the hallowed object, I employ the concept of "infinity" in post-Heideggerian philosophy, which overlaps much with the Lacanian Real. In *Totality and Infinity: An Essay on Exteriority* (1969), Emmanuel Levinas rewrites Heidegger's being-there (*Dasein*) by emphasizing both the corporeality and alterity of the existent. In this book, Levinas launches a war against totality by positing the "radical separation between the same and the other," so that one can be "at home with oneself," coiling in his solipsistic contentment and enjoyment (*Totality* 36, 37). But unlike other sentient beings such as the animals, this egoistic existent uniquely harbors the Cartesian "idea of the Infinite" to the degree that this idea "overflows the thought that thinks it," and infinity is nothing but this dynamic process of "overflowing" (25).[6] Infinity is "produced in the improbable feat whereby a separated being . . . contains in itself what it can neither contain nor receive by virtue of its own identity" (27). For Levinas, the idea of infinity could be incarnated in the absolute Other (*Autrui*), the Stranger, "who disturbs the being at home with oneself" (39). As the exteriority of the Other, the infinite overflows the interiority of the self, drawing the self out of itself by bringing forth a traumatically inassimilable otherness. The cognizing self cannot have an adequate notion of what infinity is, and this "non-adequation," as Levinas expounds, would define infinity proper (27). So far, we may have noticed that the Levinasian infinity strongly correlates with the Lacanian Real in that both breach the totality of historicized realities and both have an incarnation in a tangible entity which, being nonidentical, carries an excess of signification over itself.

For Levinas, desire is always the desire for the invisible, the infinite, and similar to Lacan, Levinas strictly differentiates desire from need that can be well satisfied. The Levinasian desire works like a metaphysical impulse that relates to the high, the noble, and the good (*Totality* 34–35), as it yearns not for symbolic recognitions but for the non-understandable Stranger, the face of the Other which can be approximated but whose meaning cannot be thoroughly decoded by the self. In fact, desire and infinity can be synonymous in Levinasian discourse. "Desire 'measures' the infinity of the infinite":

> The term we have chosen to mark the propulsion, the inflation, of this going beyond is opposed to the affectivity of love and the indigence of need. Outside of the hunger one satisfies, the thirst one quenches and the senses one allays, exists the other, absolutely other, desired beyond these satisfactions, when the body knows no gesture to slake the desire, where it is not possible to invent any new caress. This desire is unquenchable, not because it answers to an infinite hunger, but because it does not call for food. This desire without satisfaction hence

takes cognizance of the alterity of the other. It situates it in the dimension of height and of the ideal, which it opens up in being. (Levinas, *Collected* 56)

Levinas therefore shares with Lacan a similar formulation of desire as desire without satisfaction: human desire can be pictured as an encircling around the sublime height, the ideal, or the Lacanian Thing, which is "sublime" too in that it functions as the inaccessible object of representation. The dynamism of *propulsion* and *inflation* indicates the restless movements of desire/drive in an organism,[7] as the form of desire could hardly hold its content—desire always overflows and decenters itself. In this framework, the essence of desire/drive consists of a dynamic process of "going beyond" the self toward an infinite Other who passes through the finite and leaves traces of its withdrawal.[8] Merwin seems to yearn for a non-categorizable entity that is ex-timate to the subject—both inside and outside it.[9] This essential dynamic of propulsion/withdrawal interestingly aligns Merwin's poetry with the notion of "hyperobject" in recent ecological studies. Hyperobjects, according to Timothy Morton, are "massively distributed in space and time relative to humans," "occupy[ing] a high-dimensional phase space that results in their being invisible to humans for stretches of time" (*Hyperobjects* 1). Throughout his career Merwin is attentive to these higher dimensions of space-time phasing in and out of worldly appearances.

Typically, after reading a Merwin poem, readers may find that it has said nothing substantial but left a haunting sense of absent traces ringing in their ears, or, to use Charles Molesworth's words, Merwin's works "achieve a kind of exhaustion and fullness by pointing on to some yet greater emptiness" (150). Bloom complains that Merwin's poetry is "bare of true content" (16), and Helen Vendler, reviewing Merwin's prose book *Miner's Pale Children* in 1970, advises him to "eat something, anything, to cure his anemia" (233). Bloom and Vendler refuse to acknowledge that the task for poetry, however, is not to present a tangible and substantial content but to wrap up silence in the minimal number of words, like Roland Barthes's "mode négatif" (*Le degré* 56). Robert von Hallberg considers Merwin's diction in *The Lice* as having "severely narrowed the range of the language: simple, concrete words took on new power when he refused the syntactic structures that elaborate complexity" (140). It's true that poetry does not represent but evokes, as the Black Mountain poet Charles Olson would term it, "kinetics" of the open form (1054). To describe the poetic process as kinetics (from Greek *kinēsis:* movement) reveals the psychological mechanism of post-Romantic transcendence as Lacanian pulsion or Levinasian propulsion. Poetry carries with it a phantasmal inner force that constantly breaches its own form. It aims to create ambience instead of substance.

Merwin's work resembles a reflexive apparatus of powerfully cathected echoes that imitate the ghostly circulation of desire and drive. Merwin writes in "On Open Form" (1969) that poetry comes from "an unduplicatable resonance, something that would be like an echo except that it is repeating no sound" (*RM* 299). Altieri likewise perceives Merwin's poems from the 1960s as an "elaborate system of echoes" (178), and Lieberman says pretty much the same concerning *The Lice:* "It is as though the voice filters up to the reader like echoes from a very deep well" (qtd. in Folsom and Nelson 10). These echoes, like narcissistic desires, endeavor to capture the silent vestiges left by the infinite after it has passed or shot through the finite form. However, it is inadequate to describe Merwin's characteristics within the dialectic of absence and presence, as many Merwin critics are fond of doing.[10] Is not poetry itself a presence through absence, since it leaves so many blanks on the white paper? Is not the core of a poem a spectral presence, generating words while simultaneously resisting words, like the Lacanian Real or the Levinasian Stranger? Merwin has banished "true content" and substantial references from his poems because for him poetry functions exactly by tour, retour, and detour, by encircling, circumscribing, circumventing something invisible, untouchable, and even incomprehensible to common reason. This is not to repeat the cliché that poetry speaks something unspeakable but to work or force through that unspeakability per se.

In his 1954 poem "On the Subject of Poetry," Merwin allegorizes the poetic process as desire of/for the Other. I quote the poem in full because it encapsulates Merwin's lifelong endeavor to understand alterity:

I do not understand the world, Father.
By the millpond at the end of the garden
There is a man who slouches listening
To the wheel revolving in the stream, only
There is no wheel there to revolve.

He sits in the end of March, but he sits also
In the end of the garden; his hands are in
His pockets. It is not expectation
On which he is intent, nor yesterday
To which he listens. It is a wheel turning.

When I speak, Father, it is the world
That I must mention. He does not move
His feet nor so much as raise his head
For fear he should disturb the sound he hears
Like a pain without a cry, where he listens.

I do not think I am fond, Father,
Of the way in which always before he listens
He prepares himself by listening. It is
Unequal, Father, like the reason
For which the wheel turns, though there is no wheel.

I speak of him, Father, because he is
There with his hands in his pockets, in the end
Of the garden listening to the turning
Wheel that is not there, but it is the world,
Father, that I do not understand. (*FF* 109)

This poem from Merwin's early phase serves as an entrance into the labyrinth of the poet's longtime hysteria in relation to the inherent otherness of world and reality. The dialectic of desire is laid out on several levels. First of all, the concept of the "world," qua the infinite Other, eludes the grasp of the speaker's Cartesian cogito. In many of his poems, Merwin consistently confesses a certain kind of Socratic ignorance in face of external reality, or, as he said in a 1981 interview, "humility before phenomenal things" (*RM* 336). His poetics is that of "not knowing" (unconscious): "I think a real poem comes out of what you don't know. You write it with what you know, but finally its source is what you don't know" (*RM* 335). The essence of the phenomenal world—the mystery of space-time—is infinitely withdrawn from the poet's perspective, and what poetry can do is, spectrally, recapture the traces of the fleeting alterity of the world, or Morton's "high-dimensional phase space." Poetry "must mention" the world it fails to *understand* (to withstand and withhold), to *com*prehend or en*com*pass, since poetry is nothing but this roundabout astonishment before the order of things. Second, the "man" in the poem, the mirrored other, is a "psychotic" poet par excellence: he excessively ponders on the turning of a nonexistent or phantasmal wheel that functions as Lacanian Thing by organizing his/Merwin's libidinal economy, which is realized in the poem as the cathected movement of words without definite references. Finally, the speaker in the poem can be seen as entering into a transferential relationship with the Father, acting out his confusions before this enigmatic Other. The whole poem is thus a staging of a guilty ego's anxious confession before an omniscient God-Other. It presents no solid content but a dreamlike movement of desire around an invisible kernel—the wheel of fate that only the poet can see.

In *A History of Modern Poetry: Modernism and After* (1987), David Perkins subsumes Merwin, together with Robert Bly, James Wright, Galway Kinnell, and Gary Snyder, under the chapter title "Against Civilization," admitting that "[Merwin] is included in this chapter partly because he would be less appropriate in any other" (556). Perkins's reluctance reveals that Merwin's style is largely sui generis. Early Merwin was certainly vaguer than Wright and Bly and more ultraphenomenal, more apocalyptically fantastic, although all of them were heavily influenced by European surrealism. Perkins comments that after 1970 the "haunting cadences" of Merwin have continued into "quasi-philosophical lyrics of a vague, musing, moody description" (582). Although sharing the same melancholic moodiness with Bly and Wright, Merwin's personae are more disoriented and more anonymous. For Christopher Beach, however, among the Deep Imagists, Merwin would come closer to Mark Strand and Charles Simic who work toward a "surrealist mode" than to Bly, Wright, Kinnell, and Snyder who remain committed to a "realist or descriptive aesthetic" (179–80). Beach's classification has pulled Merwin away from the "descriptive aesthetic" because of the Merwinesque elusiveness—that "harvest pallor" (*SF* 103).

Under the influences of European surrealism and Asian Zen poetry, Merwin distrusts and therefore tries to avoid conscious control over the poetic process. He aims at the free play of creative forces without claiming any aim, achieving a sort of Kantian purposefulness without purpose. Merwin's poems are therefore not a conglomerate of related or disparate details, like the imagistic/objectivistic works since Ezra Pound and W. C. Williams, but an animated, haunting movement of "naked" words that strives for the infinite/indefinite realm. Details in "On the Subject of Poetry" contain such nonidentity that the readers are tempted to ask: What is the relationship between the man listening to the "wheel" and the "world" that the speaker tries in vain to understand but "must mention"? The conjunctions ("but," "because") fail to function on the semantic level, appearing fortuitous and nonsensical, as they confusingly explode the infinite distances between self and Other, poetry and world. Other textual details of the poem also fail to give readers substantial information concerning the topoi of self and world; instead, they weave out an enigma in their incessant *versus:* turning, returning, circumscribing, and circumventing.

Merwin's sustained inner urgency, his dreamlike encounter with psychic realities, and his quest for the traces of the Other have already drawn full critical attentions. In *Poetry as Labor and Privilege* (1991), Edward Brunner comes several times to the theme of desire and infinity in Merwin's works; commenting on Merwin's early poems of the bestiary, he says, "To delight in its mystery is a strength Merwin associates with describing creatures that escape his understanding. Even as it sets a limit to our knowledge, it compels us to imagine its infinity" (44). To read Merwin from the sole perspective of mythology, as Mark Christhilf does in *W. S. Merwin the Mythmaker* (1986), is to neglect the deeper psychic and philosophical suppositions underlining Merwin's project, which stages the myth of origin in an obsessional manner that invites both a Lacanian and a Levinasian reading. The unknown dimension of the world at once magnetizes, energizes, and paralyzes Merwin. This circulation concerning infinity corresponds to a pathological compulsion mixed with anxiety, disorientation, and even horror rather than pure delight. Brunner continues to say, "[The sea poems] reveal that we are all brushed by the unknown and that we all guard ourselves against a direct encounter with it by rehearsing details that deflect our attention" (*Poetry* 63). The necessary guarding, deflecting, and rehearsing before the Real initiate the dialectical circulations of desire that manifest by tour, retour, and detour of poetic energy. In the epilogue of his book Brunner theorizes that Merwin actually interacts with two worlds: the "orderly" world of institution and its opposite, "which cannot have a single name, which unfolds equidistantly through time and space and seems riddled with exceptions" (287). For Merwin, the second world might be taken as an infinite one, since it has not been defined/confined by human language and intention: it is exceptional.

If early Merwin criticism revolved upon deconstructive stylistics (absence, silence, alienation, disembodied voice, and so forth),[11] myth and mythology, apocalyptic vision, Heideggerian disclosure,[12] and Merwin's ambivalent relation with the United States,[13] recent studies have recognized him as a pioneer of eco-poetry. Much of the eco-criticism on Merwin appeared in the late 1990s. While keeping an eye on *The Lice* (1967), *The Carrier of Ladders* (1970), and *Writings to an Unfinished Accompaniment* (1973), in which environmental concern lurks behind a fragmented syntax, eco-critics mainly focus on Merwin's works after he moved to Hawaii in the late 1970s: *The Compass Flower* (1977), *The Rain in the Trees* (1988), *Travels* (1993), and *The Vixen* (1996), in which Merwin writes luxuriously about fauna and flora, pleading for the ultimate infinity of nature.

For example, in *From Origin to Ecology: Nature and the Poetry of W. S. Merwin* (1999), Jane Frazier identifies Merwin's experimentation of free verse in 1963 with his first ecological awakening: "As a result and as a reason for this move to freer form, Merwin has discovered a poetic place for himself—the wandering, alienated poet of the modern age has found a 'home' within the ecosystem and a tangible entity whose cause he can espouse for global betterment" (15). Whether Merwin, the "alienated poet of the modern age," really found a home in this ecosystem or whether this home is an imaginary construction is still open to question—Merwin is "darker" than one initially thinks. According to Sean Joseph McDonnell, Merwin might have turned to Nature in order to "escape the narcissistic/omnipotent position that has dominated his work" (7). Nature writing embodies an attempt to break what Levinas calls the "coiling of self," to reach out to the Other that cannot be reduced to any homogeneity. In a book published in the same year, *Sustainable Poetry: Four American Ecopoets* (1999), Leonard Scigaj likewise considers Merwin's final settlement in Maui as the "event" leading to Merwin's "new environmental esthetic" (178). Scigaj has painstakingly narrated Merwin's deep involvements in Hawaiian history and its ecosystem in *The Rain in the Trees, Travels,* and *The Vixen,* arguing that Merwin's poetic language "refreshes the essential relation of human consciousness to the other of nature" (182). Reading Merwin from the double perspective of Heidegger's philosophy of language and Merleau-Ponty's phenomenology of perception, Scigaj locates Merwin's ecologic concerns within the dialectics of words and things, separation and identification, body and world. Scigaj opposes Charles Altieri's "poetics of absence" (and also Marjorie Perloff's "antireferential" stance) by developing a poetics of what he calls "*référance*" (35–81). His phenomenological and historicist reading of Merwin's later work, however, does not investigate the poet's psychic fantasies in those historical narratives.

Other notable eco-criticism on Merwin includes Carl Clifton Toliver's "W. S. Merwin and the Postmodern Environment" (1997), Jeanie S. Dean's "Re-seeding the Burnt Wasteland" (2001), J. Scott Bryson's "Between the Earth and Silence" in his seminal book *The West Side of Any Mountain: Place, Space, and Ecopoetry* (2005), and Aaron M. Moe's "Learning My Steps" from *Zoopoetics: Animals and the Making of Poetry* (2014). These studies have accentuated Merwin's critique of anthropocentrism, his humility before what is "other-than-human beings" (Toliver 3), his "concern about the destruction of nature" (Dean 81), his "place-making commitment" based on "a harmonization of place and space" (Bryson 101, 109), and "the interrelationship between biological and linguistic extinction" in Merwin's entire oeuvre (Moe 100). Eco-criticism could not have missed what is obvious in Merwin, for the poet himself has been an active environmentalist—since the late 1970s Merwin has planted a thousand trees in Maui, among which some are endangered species, and it is no exaggeration to call him a "poet-planter" as Aaron Moe did (95). As early as 1958, in a manifesto, "Ecology, or the Art of Survival," Merwin had predicted that the modern, self-destructive society could only survive "under circumstances so artificial, restricted and neurotic as to resemble captivity" (*RM* 204). Half a century later, Merwin's worry has proven to be true: We do find ourselves uncomfortable in an increasingly restricted, artificial, unbalanced, and *uncannily disastrous* world. Part of Merwin's poetic power thus comes from his magic vision into the future.

Although Merwin's investment in nature is profound, portraying him solely as an eco-poet, as done by Scigaj, Bryson, and others, still raises questions. Considering the astonishingly diverse aesthetic and spiritual influences (Romanticism, European Surrealism, Zen Buddhism, Deep Image, Pound, Eliot, Graves) that have come into the making of such a Protean poet as Merwin, any single dominant consciousness seems problematic. It's like calling René Char a Resistance poet or Paul

Celan a Holocaust poet—both have more dimensions than being a representative poet for a group of writers or a historical period. As a poet, Merwin would be wary of any -isms. Basically, what a poet does is never equivalent with what his or her poetry says, although these two aspects are never separate. Different from naming which seeks a stable, if not permanent, relationship with things, poetry rather estranges one's rapport with the world. It not only lights up things but darkens them as well. It filters, separates, distorts, and remakes, leaving residues after interpretation. Poetry "touches on all that is unrealized" (*RM* 300). Thus, theoretically, Merwin has to be many kinds of poet before becoming an eco-poet, in a journey of poetic metamorphosis.

The evolution of eco-critical thinking has complicated Merwin's involvement with nature. Whereas early eco-criticism regards nature as the conferrer of a transcendental meaning (advocating a harmonious bond with nature, sustainable development, and so forth), recent discussions have come to question the very makeup of Nature itself. Timothy Morton, in his provocative *Ecology without Nature: Rethinking Environmental Aesthetics* (2007), punctures environmentalists' fantasy by pointing out: "Putting something called Nature on a pedestal and admiring it from afar does for the environment what patriarchy does for the figure of Woman" (5). To release ecological thinking from such an idealization of Nature, Morton suggests the idea of ambience, or "the stuff that generates seductive images of 'nature'" (68). In a radical gesture to "deconstruct" nature, Morton continues to fathom the weird and depressive objectivity of human's environment in later books *Hyperobjects* (2013) and *Dark Ecology* (2016). For Morton, ecological thinking, or what he calls "ecognosis," will be "Knowing in a loop—a weird knowing," because whenever and wherever we reflect on the ecosystems, we are already caught in a circle of causality, "the spool of fate" (*Dark Ecology* 5). Morton's loop/spool brings us back to Merwin's wheel in "On the Subject of Poetry," where a man, a proto-poet, obsessively listens to the ever-turning wheel "that is not there." Both present an encounter with that which endlessly, invisibly, turns and returns, a strange binding of deep time and human time.

My project, however, is not to continue with an eco-critical reading of Merwin's work but to provide a psychoanalytical/philosophical ground for such a reading. Through an elucidation of the essential dynamic in Merwin's work, I want to plant the seed for more fruitful discussions within the current field of eco-criticism.[14] Whereas a Romantic conceives of soaring skylarks and wandering clouds as his own imago, Merwin finds in nature the ever-receding vestiges of what is older than self/ego. He seldom evokes nature without resorting to an impersonal origin where his libidinal fixation seeks its optimum satisfaction. In this sense, Merwin has pushed eco-criticism to a new frontier by eroticizing nature as the alien love object "caught in the throat" of the subject. For Merwin, Nature becomes both the stage and the protagonist of fantasies, through which the self's obsessional devotion to the infinite is fully unleashed. Rather than being scientifically measurable, nature in Merwin's work is categorically heterogeneous, traumatic; every encounter with nature is also a nonencounter that leaves a sense of loss and remorse.

My discussion of Merwin's pursuit for the infinite largely follows a chronological order, together with Merwin's evolving sense of poetry as a vehicle of desire and drive. The first chapter presents an analysis of Merwin's early texts with an emphasis on the sea poems and animal poems within a Freudian-Lacanian framework. In *A Mask for Janus* (1952) and *The Dancing Bears* (1954), Merwin frequently assumes a psychotic ballad tone that informs a libidinal urge to transgress the limitations of the Symbolic. The pathological symptoms continue in *Green with Beasts* (1956) and *The Drunk in the Furnace* (1960), in which Merwin records his entry into the traumatic core of the Symbolic: the Lacanian Real. Merwin's imagination is largely directed toward the Other, which is horribly fascinating. The sea monsters Merwin evokes incarnate the object-cause of desire: a massive, direful, and spectral presence outside the sociohistorical order. The domestic animals that Merwin portrays—dogs, rams, goats, horses, cockerels, and so forth—all share the same characteristic of inscrutability and symbolize what precedes and escapes human utterance.

The second chapter explores the substitution of the anonymous Other for the Judeo-Christian Other in Merwin's early and middle period. Abandoning the univocal salvation theme in Christian theology after the onset of the Vietnam War, Merwin has come to envision redemption in a vast, anonymous wilderness. The urge of apocalypse paves the way for new existential and ethical grounds outside the existing social order. The poet's spirit disavows the Symbolic for an exodus into the ultraphenomenal. This spirit is not only Hegelian/negative but also Levinasian/alternative; foreclosing the existing social order, it attempts to open a new dimension in the interval between humanity and divinity. Although the dark, sparse poems of Merwin in the 1960s were partly the products of the historical process, what Merwin sought then was an alterity beyond historicity. Merwin's poems of the 1960s also attest to a decisive change in style and voice; he now strengthened the anti-rhetorical, anti-ornamental strain that had been only latent in his earlier work. The elliptical style disrupts the smooth functioning of language, revealing Merwin's anxious desire to capture the object of divinity that eludes Judeo-Christian thematization.

The third chapter treats Merwin's transformation from severity to corporeality in *The Compass Flower* (1977) and *The Rain in the Trees* (1988), both of which witness Merwin's immersion in the life-world as a being of enjoyment. Blending the sensual, the natural, and the spiritual, Merwin's love poetry successfully conjures up what Lacan terms the "Other jouissance" in order to circumscribe the paternal function and its delimitation on the loving subject. This chapter traces Merwin's erotic mode back to *The Dancing Bears* and then reads its full outburst in *The Compass Flower* and *Finding the Islands* (1982) in light of psychoanalytical and philosophical formulations of alterity. Merwin's love poetry follows the tradition of the troubadours in the Middle Ages in its conventional portrait of the female as elusive and enigmatic. In the fantasy of love, the male speaker seems able to enjoy union with the beloved woman, although in most cases she appears distant and heterogeneous, sublimated as the Lacanian object or the Levinasian Stranger. Merwin's later works are increasingly characterized by the problematic combination of nature and Eros and the subsequent eroticization of flora in *The Rain in the Trees* and *Travels*: the poet fantasizes about nature and women, confusing them so as to diffuse Eros into infinite cosmos. In a reading that overlaps much with recent ecofeminism, Merwin's love/ nature poetry is revealed as a testimony of the structural difference or non-adequation between man and nature rather than their harmonious coexistence.

The last chapter examines the recurrent and polysemic image of the sunlight and its underside darkness in Merwin's later writings such as *Opening the Hand* (1983), *The Rain in the Trees* (1988), *The Vixen* (1996), *Present Company* (2005), *The Shadow of Sirius* (2008), *The Moon Before Morning* (2015), and *Garden Time* (2016). Sunlight represents the transient object that prompts Merwin to contemplate time, origin, grief, and death. Apparently, Merwin's grief from *The Lice* (1967) onward points to the decimation of the earth and the impotence of language to articulate the loss of species. Yet more implicitly, certain psychic mechanisms—for example, involuntary memory and libidinal fixation—underlie much of his later writings and make them only darkly "green." Merwin's father complex plays a crucial role in the formation of the sunlight imagery, as the sun, according to Freud's study on psychosis, symbolizes paternal authority. Largely foreclosing the Name-of-the-Father in search of fluidity and infinite realizations, Merwin has incurred a strong sense of guilt through the years, which finally erupts into a poetry of endless mourning through nature writing. To overcome grief, Merwin evokes ancestral origins and memory traces from childhood; his yearning for anonymous origins to surpass the paternal function summarizes his lifelong pursuit of the infinite Other outside the socio-symbolic order.

1

ALL THE UNCOVENANTED
TERROR OF BECOMING

Merwin's Early Encounter with the Real

From the very beginning of his poetic career, Merwin was obsessed with what W. B. Yeats calls the "horrible splendour of desire" (196). In *A Mask for Janus* (1952) and *The Dancing Bears* (1954), we witness how Merwin struggles with the fixed poetic form in order to articulate, as well as imitate, the truth and movement of desire. In *Green with Beasts* (1956) and *The Drunk in the Furnace* (1960), however, we wonder at Merwin's close-up delineations of the vehicles of desire, the biblical and domestic animals that simultaneously embody and resist human signification, the foghorn and icebergs that warn sailors of the imminent danger and fascinate them by its false look. One conspicuous feature of these early texts is the lack of specific reference to outer sociohistorical facts, as if Merwin, being concerned with the landscapes of human mind, were writing completely from his intricate psyche, where reality and fantasy intermix. Merwin's traveling poems during this period therefore do not give the impression of a certain locale but register a diffused allegorical purport. The sailings, long and short, resemble the Odyssean journey loaded with temptations and hardships, as the sea poems also evoke the traumatic unrealness of the kernel of the Symbolic, an all-engulfing void. Merwin the eternal traveler of the mind went into the heart of wilderness and was saved there by some mysterious power testified by faith alone: "For from the very hunger to look, we feed / Unawares, as at the beaks of ravens" (*FF* 156). Many of Merwin's poems from the first three books share the Dantean trilogy of *Inferno, Purgatorio,* and *Paradiso;* like the biblical Job, Merwin's speaker must go through the maddening ordeal of symbolic death before he can see the light of Providence and be thus redeemed or reborn.

While Sean Joseph McDonnell sees the tension between "a rejection of the social realm and a need for the kind of stability society may offer" as the motif of Merwin's first three books (9), I would argue that the "stability" Merwin finds in the 1950s does not reside in society or community but in fluidity and transgression, which have been deeply implanted in Merwin since childhood. Merwin was at home when he was largely out of home; his métier lies exactly in portraying the inner- and ultraphenomena before which the subject is magnetized and paralyzed. These early texts present a developing pattern from high-toned, half-mad ballads to calmer meditations on desire and disaster, language and signification. Merwin dallies with an impossible combination of delicacy and violence, probing alternative realities that escape the existent sociohistorical process.

THE FIRST CLEAVAGE AND ITS CONCUSSIONS

To begin with, I will present a biographical reading in order to sketch out the constitutive elements of Merwin's early mythical style, which has been elaborated upon by critics.[1] Indeed, Merwin's curiosity for the phenomenal world and his desire to explore the distant and the transcendent can be traced back to his early childhood. Growing up in a Presbyterian minister's family with a reticent mother and a "prohibitive" father, Merwin in his early years assumed a bohemian and rebellious posture, less fiery than Arthur Rimbaud perhaps but equally conspicuous (Merwin was later to write "Rimbaud's Piano" to show his sympathy).[2] When Merwin was born in 1927, the family lived in Union City, New Jersey, where the Hudson River was busy with traffic. While his father wrote his sermons in his study, Merwin the small boy "knelt on the blue velvet cushion on the window seat, gazing out through the leaded panes, or through the open casements . . . watching the river, without a word, utterly rapt in the vast scene in front of [him]": the vast scene of roaring trains, busy ferries, "puffs of steam," "whistles and horns," "the distant sounds," and as a child he "was seeing something that [he] could not reach and that would never go away" (*SD* 28). Merwin in his childhood was thus seduced by the fleeting image of water and what it symbolizes: immersion and fluidity. In spite of, or rather because of, his parents' severe warnings, Merwin attempted to get close to the water, the symbol of flux, fluidity, travels, and phantasmagoria. At the age of fourteen, Merwin strategically researched the public library of Scranton, Pennsylvania, and built his first boat with his ten-cents-a-week allowance, naming it Zephyr (30–33).

Merwin's libidinal attachment to fluidity in early childhood persists into his young adulthood, only in a slightly varied form. Setting Rimbaud and Shelley as his ideal ego, the imaginary other he attempted to identify with, Merwin in college adopted the posture of the wandering artist, occupying himself with random reading, sailing, and horse riding. His nonconformist behavior might have incurred bad feelings from some of the faculty at Princeton University, as he later admitted: "I read far outside the assignments, and often on wild tangents, forgetting the assignments themselves. . . . I must have been exasperating to most of my professors" (*SD* 36). Merwin reminisces that some of the Princeton faculty could not tolerate his Thoreauvian disobedience and wanted to dismiss him when he was "busy being Shelley" (*RM* 190). Merwin stayed at Princeton, however, largely due to the efforts of his mentor, Richard Blackmur, who appreciated his talent and irregularity. Blackmur himself exemplified a bohemian artist: a self-made critic who did not have a degree and whose presence at Princeton was suspected by his colleagues. Indeed, Blackmur held "an ethic of fierce devotion to an art in a philistine society" (*RM* 190) and defined, much to Merwin's own exhilaration, the basic characteristic of a critic and a reader as "a house waiting to be haunted" (*SD* 45). This *fierce* and *haunting* sense of art and poetry is perhaps what influenced Merwin most in subsequent years.

If Blackmur struck Merwin as a paradigm of the wandering scholar, the confessional poet John Berryman, Blackmur's assistant at the time, came to influence Merwin for his highly emotive use of poetic language. Berryman worked like a mentor for Merwin at Princeton, constantly offering him "a cluster of new names in [his] head to be tracked down" and spurring him to "find the fire in them," as Merwin later assimilated much of Berryman's own "intense, unremitting, and fierce" poetic language into his first book of poems, *A Mask for Janus* (*SD* 45). Berryman's unconditional devotion to poetry also stunned young Merwin: for Berryman, poetry was "a matter of life and death," and he "cared about it more than he did about anyone's ego, including his own" (*SD* 44). In a belated poem to Berryman from the 1980s, Merwin celebrates his credo of passion:

> He said the great presence
> that permitted everything and transmuted it
> in poetry was passion
> passion was genius. . . . (*FH* 156)

Derived from the Latin *passio,* passion first means divine suffering, and then it denotes a certain libidinal fixation; therefore, passion, by definition, is a curious mixture of both pleasure and pain. For Berryman and Merwin, passion enters poetry as the highly cathected movement of words; the poetic process is initiated and sustained by passion, a psychic movement that dictates what is to be written and maybe also how it is written. The transformative power of poetry, contra New Criticism, does not originate in a deliberate deployment of the poetic form such as irony, tension, balance, and rhythm, but in a sustaining and haunting undercurrent of desire for incantations, invocations, and enchantments. Berryman's own work, *The Dream Songs* (1969), bears this out, whereas in Merwin, the "great presence" of passion would take a more devious and spectral path.

Merwin's spiritual growth in early years clearly follows a centrifugal pattern: persons and things he came into contact with broadened his mind and strengthened his devotion to art and poetry, until he could no longer endure the symbolic restrictions from family and institution. In 1948, at the age of twenty-one, Merwin quit his graduate study in Romance language at Princeton University and sailed for Europe with an utterly unknown future, with his "youth and inexperience" and a "vertiginous sensation" due to "complete lack of money" (*SD* 3). Like most idealistic young poets influenced by Shelleyan Romanticism, in his early twenties Merwin avowed that "I did not know what I would do for a living, and even more strangely I took it for granted that I would not know, for a while" (*RM* 194–95). Sailing for a new world seems all that matters. The first breach of one's socio-symbolic framework proves permanent, and all Merwin's later work would endlessly rehearse that first act of decision, of cutting oneself off from that which preexists the individual.

The desire for fluidity, bohemianism, and poetic passion (suffering) suffuses many of Merwin's early poems that exhibit a strong urge to break off the socio-familial relationship and reach into the domain of contingency and pure ecstasy. From *A Mask for Janus* to *The Drunk in the Furnace,* despite their conspicuous formalism, Merwin constantly resorts to the emotive, irregular, and pathological trends in poetry. The efforts are impersonated in some half-insane figures, as Merwin dramatizes the traumatic calling of the Other in the vein of Keats's "La Belle Dame sans Merci" and Tennyson's "The Lady of Shalott." In "Ballad of John Cable and Three Gentlemen," the first ballad in *A Mask for Janus,* the protagonist, John, spellbound by some vague calling, came all the way to "a gray river / Wide as the sea" and received an anti-Althusserian interpellation from the mysterious Other incarnated in "three dark gentlemen" who were already waiting for him there (*FF* 18). The three men invited John to board the boat, but John hesitated out of consideration for his sister, wife, and mother, to whom his familial duty was bound. Under the devilish persuasion that his service to family was not indispensable and his departure not insufferable, John was finally "carried / On the dark river; / Not even a shadow / Followed him over. // On the wide river / Gray as the sea / Flags of white water / Are his company" (*FF* 21). Abandoning his family, John, similarly to John the Baptist, was baptized by the water that had completely erased his personal history. Christhilf reads the ballad as the destined calling of an artist: "The gentlemen represent the Muse, for they want Cable to accompany them to a place that is clearly Byzantium" (4). This Yeatsian reading actually has overlooked the biographical allusion to Merwin's grandfather John Otto, who had worked on the Allegheny River as a pilot for many years, and his family could hardly understand this irregular profession (Hix, *Understanding* 109). This is why the three gentlemen in the poem exhorted John Cable to "follow the feet . . . / Of your family, / Of your old father / That came already this way" (*FF* 18).

Though there's strong temptation to read John's unreasonable departure as the physical, real death that his paternal ancestors had all succumbed to, the ballad lays bare another type of death: the symbolic death that places the subject in the limbo between the living and the dead—what Žižek calls "the undead" (*Žižek Reader* 279). Cutting off his ties with fellow humans, John the Prodigal Son enters the "far side" without a "shadow" (*FF* 21), exactly going through the "subjective destitution" formulated by Lacanian psychoanalysis.[3] John, if not dead, becomes a living ghost, "the ash that walk[s]" ("Blind William's Song," *FF* 24), a subject without corporeality in a posthuman landscape of "gray" river and "white water." The three gentlemen, in contradistinction to T. S. Eliot's three magi heralding the birth of Christ, represent the Mephistophelean Other who brings destruction to one's personal past. They seem to uncannily possess that omniscient knowledge of the subject's (John Cable's) desire but stand in utter mystery themselves, refusing to be known. The whole poem stages John's/Merwin's desire to break the tender fetters of family for an utterly unknown and even dangerous future. John did not struggle so much with Devil's temptation as with himself, with his own imagined, paranoiac socio-symbolic status. Moonstruck by an unnamable urge to welcome this Other who came over "seven hills" and "the last tree" (*FF* 18), John suddenly realized that his roleplaying in the family was but a fantasy, which he later traversed by deciding to leave "his poorly mother," "his wife at grieving" and "his sister's fallow." This is John's psychic one-man war. In this reading, John

Cable could be readily identified with one of the three gentlemen, just as Dr. Faust is already part of Mephistopheles. Shedding one's fantasy of a stable, fully constituted self, the mythic "dark river" that John felt drawn to works here as the object of man's unsatisfiable desire for, not the Beckettian, absent Other, but the Goethean, devilish Other—the "guide in the journey toward the mythic consciousness" (Guy 420).

This poem is highly autobiographical in that Merwin himself has come to be the Prodigal Son who left his family for an utterly unknown future and who, as R. M. Rilke says, "was learning to love, learning so laboriously and with so much pain" (113). In order to grow into a bohemian bard like Rimbaud or Baudelaire, Merwin could do no better than renounce the city of his birth, New York, as "Ruin / My city," and proclaim, "I would never have thought I would be born here" (*SF* 52). Contrary to Whitman, who, in Ed Folsom's reading, embodies "the absorptive and appropriating American attitude," Merwin holds a more critical attitude toward "things American" (231). Unlike Whitman, Merwin incorporates radical self-alienation into the construction of his own identity, but the effect of "breaking up" with the United States and all its symbolic ties proves definitely double: it enables the poet to explore the exotic, the Other, while it has also permanently altered his consciousness of what home is. While Merwin exhibits a strong tendency of wandering and the resultant yearning for home, home itself has become more and more abstract, fictive, and even metaphysical. In a 1958 essay, "Flight Home," Merwin expressed this "loss" of home after spending several years in Europe: "The first shock of maturity: a realization that home, where you grew up and belonged—belonged with and without your own volition—no longer exists" (*RM* 179). What Merwin returned to each time in frequent travels was not his physical home, his origin or ancestors, which he took to be already lost, but this symptomatic act of returning itself. It is exactly because home and origins were lost in the first place that Merwin feels compelled to evoke them again and again in his writings. Edward Brunner, who is among the most sympathetic critics of Merwin, likewise observes that "the only genuine home is this aura of homelessness within which we live" (*Poetry* 65).

Despite similar motivations, this scenario should not be reduced to another version of "on the road," of the restless rebellion of the US youth during the 1960s, as if traveling away were a panacea for all personal and social ills. The compulsion to split away, to leave, to travel elsewhere like troubadours in the Middle Ages, has a more ontological and constitutive significance for Merwin as well as for the modernists like T. S. Eliot and Ezra Pound. Apart from the desire to experience exotic landscapes and cultures, poets, compared with others, have a more astute awareness of the abyss of subjectivity, the void lying at the very heart of human endeavors. All their works are an attempt to give a voice to the otherwise mute emptiness as the Real, a visible contour to the chimera of human desire that hides in the network of language.

In "The Prodigal Son," Merwin details the traumatic event or the "primal scene" of the son's home-leaving in a haunting and somewhat psychotic vision. The poem begins with an observation on the semblance or emptiness of time and space:

> . . . the semblance of afternoon
> Was all the surface that shimmered there, even
> The dust shining and hanging still, the dusty
> Carob trees and olives gleaming, all hung
> Untouchable and perfect, as in its own
> Mirage. (*FF* 158)

The luminous setting corresponds not to Heidegger's disclosure of being but to a peculiar psychic state when the subject has crossed over the border of signification to confront the heart of meaninglessness. Under the quiet, shiny surface of homely objects lies a death of all signifieds: "And between / There and the ruled shade of this white wall / There is nothing." The tabula rasa of the world qua the embedded Real is the emptiness of ego suffered by a mourning subject. In "Mourning and Melancholia" (1917), Freud asserts that "mourning is commonly the reaction to the loss of a beloved person," and while "people are reluctant to abandon a libido position," they keep "holding on to the object through a hallucinatory wish-psychosis" (*Penguin Freud Reader* 310–11). "Follow[ing] / The departing image of a son beyond / Distance into emptiness" (*FF* 159), the old man in the poem has unwittingly replaced the loss of the love object with the loss of the world itself, which only engenders endless hallucinations:

> For emptiness is lord of his hollow house,
> Sits at his side at table, devouring,
> Shows him from room to room, for all faces
> Of loss.... (*FF* 160)

Under such unbearable lightness of nonbeing, the father suffers severe perceptual disorders—he projects inner loss to outside reality, producing symptom formations that would alleviate anxiety. In this poem, Merwin's protagonist, who has lost his son, seems to derive traumatic jouissance from the very loss.

The poet-speaker's determination to get away from home and the subsequent melancholia are truly symptomatic, as the act of decision brings not only trauma but also ecstasy, though the resultant journey may not be a felicitous one. The son, who has severed his ties with his family in pursuit of some unknown future, in a twist of irony, suffers from that future. Unable to integrate the meanings of radical Otherness, the son, as Merwin continues to narrate in the poem, beholds the same hallucinatory emptiness in the distant land as his father at home has gone through:

> ... a mirage
> Merely in which he had no part, a strange
> Vista made of familiar pieces caught
> In an odd light in a mirror, an image
> Of emptiness out of a restive daydream
> Gone wrong at home; unreal, if he could turn
> The mirror, open his eyes. (*FF* 161)

Through this much-commented lavish play of the mirror image,[4] Merwin creates an echolalic labyrinth that upsets the sense of both reality and self-identity, placing readers in the uncanny zone between homeliness and foreignness, the Symbolic and the Real.

The paradox of alterity is that the self can never fully absorb it—no matter how ardently one follows and approaches it. If cleavage leaves a permanent concussion in the father's psyche, it does the same in the son's, perhaps more deeply and traumatically. The alien landscape may be delightful at first but soon turns out to be depressive and, finally, horrifying. In another poem "Anabasis (I)," the travelers left their homes and marched into a non-site, as it were, that was both internal and external, physical and psychic, familiar and strange:

> Exhausted leaves, suspended, through
> The distant autumn do not fall,
> Or, fallen, fired, are unconsumed,
> The flame perduring, the still
> Smoke eternal in the mind. (*FF* 5)

Suffering the "perduring" consumption of desire for the new world, the speaker enumerates one after another the disastrous effects of this compulsive journey:

> We fled a saeculum what sick repose
> But woke at morning where the fever burned
> . . .
> We have half-waked to hear the minute die
> And heard our minds that, waiting toward the east,
> Embraced the seed and thought of day, and we
> Were by the pool of dark the crouched beast. (*FF* 9–11)

In a rather Conradian stroke, the speaker travels deep into the self until meeting its alien kernel to find that "we" are indeed the animal of dark, uncontrollable desires—"the crouched beast," which might be modeled on the Leviathan in the book of Revelation and Yeats's "rough beast" in "The Second Coming" (187). Such a revelation on the truth of desire is unavailable to those who stay complacently at home: "The other sons asleep / With their wives in complacent dreams / Wait in emptiness and do not know / That it is emptiness, that they are waiting" (*FF* 162) because it comes only as the reward to the displaced explorer who "became / The eyes of sleep that chased receding fires / Through the bodiless exile of a dream" (*FF* 11). Instead of repeating the Shakespearian lament that we are such stuff as dreams are made on, Merwin has radicalized the nonsensical, hysterical, and dreamlike devotion of the self to what remains unknown and heterogeneous.

Although chasing the "receding fires" leaves a subject burnt out, a subject of debris and ashes—"the still / Smoke eternal in the mind" (*FF* 5)—Merwin's speaker in the 1950s has remained implausibly undaunted since the first cleavage became an irrevocable fact. In a post-Romantic stroke, Merwin's speaker, sick as he often is in these early poems, attempts to give full leash to his desire for the unknown, wading through the weariness of both body and mind toward a supposedly brave new world. At the end of "Anabasis (II)," the speaker declares triumphantly that "in fear of the swift bird that shouts and sees / In these tides and dark entrails the curled / Augurs of unreasonable seas / We seek a new dimension for the world" (*FF* 11). No one can accomplish these journeys without seriously scathing himself, since these anabases embody the terrible, posthumous death-drive that insists on the impossibility of its own satisfaction. Nausea and ecstasy surely follow those who venture to explore and confront the alien world.

WELCOME TO THE SEA OF THE REAL

Merwin's early poetry, as Charles Molesworth and a number of other critics have noticed, clearly follows "the structures of quest-romance" (145) that postulate the transcendence of truth and subjectivity. Escaping the restrictive socio-symbolic order through both land journeys and sea voyages, Merwin's early work seeks to evoke a series of phantoms with a mixture of joy and terror, yearning and avoidance. The sea, as the reservoir of uncanny simulacra and *déjà vu*—"it harbors monsters in its depth," as exclaimed by Cheri Davis (64)—opens up dimensions of the unknown which disrupt the continuum of normally perceived time and space. Commenting on the sea poems of Merwin, Brunner points out that "the poems center on moments when we are confronted with extraordinary situations, when disorientation is the norm" (*Poetry* 54). The "extraordinary situations" Brunner wonders at are in fact both outward realities and the poet's own projection. The things and beasts Merwin evokes carry such eccentric allusions that any univocal interpretation would seem reductive. Merging familiarity and otherworldliness, vulnerability and violence, detour and exigency, Merwin in his traveling poems has created a horribly fantastic situation in which the inhuman Thing will repeatedly capture the subject's desire. As said by Cheri Davis, again, "Navigating deep into the psyche, Merwin finds a place full of horror" (66).

The new dimension for the world Merwin so eagerly pursued in the 1950s did not turn out to be an illusion as the prodigal son had discovered but had its edifying effect: it taught the "unreasonable" danger of radical otherness, by which Merwin seemed at once chilled and fascinated. Water, the most tender element on earth, is at the same time the most perilous, for beneath the calm surface of the sea lurks the most unexpected disaster. Some of Merwin's early sea poems only cast a glimpse at "so fearsome a destroyer" (*FF* 222), while others treat the subject with almost photographic meticulousness. For instance, in "Two Paintings by Alfred Wallis, I. Voyage to Labrador," Merwin imagines the invisible danger in crossing Labrador: "there dog-hunched will the high / Street of hugging bergs have come / To lean huge and hidden as women" (*FF* 210).[5] Such light-hearted comicalness and false familiarity will soon disappear, and "then we will be white, all white, as clothes sheening, / Stiff as teeth, white as the sticks / And eyes of the blind." Like in a horror film, instead of presenting a close-up of the monster, the deadly iceberg, Merwin portrays its effects on the passengers/viewers, whose white faces indicate that they just had a very close call. This nightmarish encounter only lasted for a short time, and when the morning came, the passengers, "mindless / And uncaring as Jesus, will find nothing / In that same place but an empty sea / Colorless, see, as a glass of water" (*FF* 210). The homonym of *sea/see* invites the human gaze to penetrate the surface of the sea and its treacherous reflectivity as the recurrent sibilant *s* makes audible the seething undercurrents. The dreaminess of the scene, however, suggests that the iceberg may have been a collective optical illusion, a displaced and condensed (two main mechanisms of Freudian dreamwork) "representative" of the passengers' desire for the new dimension of the world.

The Greek name for this missed encounter is *tuché,* as we learn from Lacan: "We have translated [*tuché*] as the encounter with the real. The real is beyond the automaton, the return, the coming-back, the insistence of the signs, by which we see ourselves governed by the pleasure principle. The real is that which always lies behind the automaton" (*Seminar XI* 53–54). Humans are governed by the repetitive use of symbols and signs, which facilitates our communication but at the same time turns us into agents who do not question the automatic exchange of meaning based on the inherent arbitrariness of signs and symbols. The "chance work," however, interrupts this automatic exchange of signs and redeems us from symbolic repetitions, conferring certain subjectivity on us—"this real brings with it the subject" (54).

What enthralls Merwin then comes close to this *tuché,* the irruption of the Real in the boundless sea that causes the subject to be other than its symbolic determination. It is in the unreal sea that the Real preponderates over reality and acquires its positive embodiment. In another poem, "The Iceberg," Merwin presents a frontal portrait of the deadly Thing and his spectacular enthrallment:

It is not its air but our own awe
That freezes us. Hardest of all to believe
That so fearsome a destroyer can be

Dead, with those lights moving in it,
With the sea all around it charged
With its influence. (*FF* 222)

Unlike the Labrador poem, the iceberg here does not even appear falsely homely but totally inanimate, deprived of anthropomorphism. The astounding enjambment of *be/Dead* creates a strong psychological suspension together with a prolonged amazement. The "fearsome" "destroyer" is not without its moment of sublimation as the "lights moving in it" also make present a certain mysterious and unknowable entity. Merwin's iceberg seems to disrupt as well as organize the apparent reality of the sea, "charging" the sea with its constitutive "influence." It evokes the nonhuman "vibrant matter" that, according to Jane Bennett, acts as "quasi agents or forces with trajectories, propensities, or tendencies of their own" (viii), for matter, far from being dead, possesses a kind of non-animistic "thing-power" (2). The iceberg here, like a hyperobject, can "emit zones" that surround the viewers and unconsciously affect their actions and choices (Morton, *Hyperobjects* 143).

In Merwin's poem, the Thing, however, rather emerges from the domain of psyche. Merwin's speaker failed to notice the abyss in the seemingly homogeneous sea until the moment: "It seems that only now / We realize the depth of the waters, the / Abyss over which we float among such / Clouds" (*FF* 222). The allegory of the poem becomes clearer when it reveals the terrible abyss in the heart of our falsely secure reality. Lacan would say that, most of the time, the abyss of subjectivity is covered from our view to make reality function smoothly; only occasionally do we get a glimpse of the Real. In Merwin's narration, we are simultaneously terrified and magnetized by such an alien and sublime (un-representable) occurrence: "And still not understanding / The coldness of most elegance, even / With so vast and heartless a splendor / Before us, stare, caught in the magnetism / Of great silence . . ." (*FF* 222). In another prose poem, "The Songs of the Icebergs" in *The Miner's Pale Children* (1970), Merwin tells of the uncanny splendor of those destructive (non)entities viewed in a distance: "They have taken the form of illuminations rising from within, toward the surfaces of the leprous cliffs, like the northern lights themselves still searching for them, or like arms and faces drowned in slow rivers, appearing and then sinking again, to reappear farther along" (*BF* 101). Entering what T. S. Eliot calls "death's other kingdom" (80), the poet seems to be spellbound by such inhuman "elegance," such "heartless" "splendor" emanating from the Thing. Echoing Odysseus, who likewise "had coursed a strange ocean" ("Cape Dread," *FF* 232), the speaker claims the iceberg to be "the terror / That cannot be charted," the event that comes to meet the subject as *tuché*, the encounter.

Merwin's nautical poems might be modeled on Herman Melville's *Moby-Dick*, a work that probes into humans' fatal encounter with the Thing incarnated in the Sperm Whale.[6] If Merwin treats the terror of the sea (icebergs, sea monsters) with ominous nonchalance, that's probably because Melville has prototypically delayed Ahab's deadly encounter with the Thing until the last pages of the novel. *Moby-Dick* has a tremendous amount of indeterminate anxiety and is a proto-postmodern text full of simultaneous deferral of and yearning for meaning (for instance, the chapter on Whiteness). The numerous digressions and expositions in *Moby-Dick* would greatly appeal to Merwin's sensibility of nonconfrontation. Usually, Merwin would start a narrative on nautical experience with light-hearted understatements, but soon a vague feeling of anxiety surfaces to disturb the reader. Lacking Melville's audacity, however, Merwin's speaker, when faced with destruction, takes no direct actions due to the stultification of the senses before the Monstrous. Since Merwin's forte is more of phenomenological *epoché* than mighty opposition, he would infinitely prolong a poetic involvement without a proper denouement.

In "The *Portland* Going Out," Merwin chronicles the sinking of a ship with the silent intimation that some unknown disaster may have touched all of us—passengers on the ship of "fate." "Going out" carries the antithetical meanings of "going out of home (to explore the new world)" and "going down," "coming to an end," so the title has already exposed the inherent instability of the structure of the poem. As is customarily seen in Merwin's sea poems, things start smoothly, as the speaker and his friends are on another ship, watching with much glee the launching ceremony of the *Portland*: "Passing so close over our stern that we / Caught the red glow of her port light for / A moment on our faces" (*FF* 229). The intimacy and liveliness conveyed by "the red glow" on "our faces" will soon stand in appalling contrast with the coming destruction. The poem goes on to record the change of weather in a distant, journalistic tone: "Only / When she was gone did we notice / That it was starting to snow," and at the climax of the narrative we do not have a panic-stricken Titanic but a Merwinesque adumbration of disaster—distant, nonchalant, third-personal. As every encounter with the Real is a missed one, so Merwin's *tuché*, via the sinking of the *Portland*, produces not so much a direct blow as retroactive concussions and ruminations. After the event, the speaker realized that disaster was "a gulf / Beyond reckoning," an abyss that opens repeatedly yet unexpectedly—"It begins where we are" (*FF* 230). This gaping gulf, as Cheri Davis locates it perfectly, "is lodged within ourselves" and "emanates out from us, precluding all other intimacy" (66).

The poem is more than the aestheticization of destruction but an elevation of an object to the status of the Thing.[7] Since subjectivity is established on the ground of such *tuché*, one would risk one's life for a glimpse of that "inhuman" beauty: "Foresails and clouds hiding / Such threat and beauty as we may never see" (*FF* 210). In "Cape Dread," fear and exhilaration intermix when the poet encounters *l'homme fatal* in the sea: "we sighted / The shape of what we knew we would not pass" (*FF* 232). Unlike the unfortunate crew on the *Portland*, our eagle-eyed poet made out the shape quickly: "You cannot mistake it: the dun headland / Like a dreaming Dutchman, dough-faced, staring / Seaward to the side we did not penetrate." After describing the treacherous waters around what he called "Cape Delight" or "Dutchman's Point," the speaker savored the cove he found there: "In / The south corner of the cove there is / An inlet flowing with sweet water, / And there are fruits in abundance, small / But delectable, at least at that season" (*FF* 233). Edenic, the cove symbolizes the far reaches of human reality and the final object of the sea journey.

Most of Merwin's sea poems are ambiguous in that they cast a veil over invisible dangers yet at the same time try to tear that veil, to probe into the infinite abyss of the sea. Sometimes, Merwin would even go down to the ocean floor, assuming the tone of the mythically drowned sailors to tell their story. In "The Bones of Palinurus Pray to the North Star," Merwin adopts an Eliotic combination of mythology and religiosity:

> Console us. The wind chooses among us.
> Our whiteness is a night wake disordered.
> Lone candor, be constant over
> Us desolate who gleam no direction. (*FF* 45)

In Roman mythology, Palinurus was the helmsman of Aeneas's fleet. It is told in Virgil's *Aeneid* that the god Neptune (through the agency of Somnus) had enchanted Palinurus into sleep to let him fall overboard into "the limpid waters" (5.1135). Palinurus somehow got onshore but was later killed by the barbarians, and his body was left to the sea waves. Embodying the Eliotic posthumous yearning, Merwin's poem evokes the timelessness of the Real vis-à-vis the temporality of desire. Palinurus still feels discontented and grievous ("Console us") after death, his bones crying for a certain order or direction from the North Star, which echoes book 6 of *Aeneid* where in the underworld Palinurus would beg Aeneas for a proper burial on earth (6.475–89). "The wind choos[ing] among us" suggests that man's desire, tangled with gods' plans, is basically metonymic, like the wind seizing and choosing its objects. Palinurus fell into the sea out of the wind/will/whim of Neptune, who decided that one mortal must be sacrificed to save many.[8] The bones are the remnants, the ashes, of gods' desires, and possessed by a libidinal drive to obtain consistency, Palinurus's bones linger in the limbo between life and death and become what Žižek terms the "organs without body" (*Organs* 30), the scattered, blind life-force that demands for eternity.

The drowned sailors in Merwin's poems find little peace in death but keep feeling, cognizing, and even philosophizing. In "The Eyes of the Drowned Watch Keels Going Over," the dead would "shift and turn over slightly" as if sunbathing under the sea; their scopic drive is hardly less salient: "Looking / Upward through the leaves that turned over and back / like hands, through the birds, the fathomless light, / Upward" (*FF* 216). Shooting through various obstacles ("leaves," "birds"), the gaze of the dead persistently follows the sunlight "upward" like the eyes of the living; moreover, the dead begin to reconsider the purpose of following the stars, for they find the keels that they watch actually "follow nothing." Gradually the dead realize that "our eyes fastened upon stars" simply because "we traced / in their remote courses not their own fates but ours" (*FF* 216). In this way, Merwin reveals that our spiritual quest for eternity is largely a human presupposition, a psychic movement producing its own goal—what the New Critics term the "pathetic fallacy." The persistent drive to see the stars is reversed into making oneself recognized and thus guided by the stars ("be constant over / Us"). Giving voice to the dead, the poem exposes the rationale behind all myths: it is actually the human drive that is pulling the string of fate. The undead not only lie deep down the sea but exist in the realm of subjectivity, taking the form of a powerful, insatiable propulsion for the self-reflexive gaze, as Merwin also laments that the dead are unable to die: "The darkened dead have no peace, / World-without-end shifting; / All, all are there, and no resting" (*FF* 217).

The survivors who have made it to the land do not fare better; a sailor on shore at best resembles a fish out of water. Accustomed to the hallucinatory instability of the sea, sailors find it difficult to readapt to the stable, worldly reality. Their perception of the world is irreversibly changed because they have lived on the sea for too long. Reentering the human world, they can only stumble and stagger. In "Sailor Ashore," Merwin tells what happens when the sailor goes onshore: "What unsteady ways the solid earth has / After all. The lamps are dead on their feet / Blinking and swaying above the wet cobbles" (*FF* 228). Like a drunkard, the sailors have lost their sense certainty, mistaking illusion for reality: "The sleeping houses / Reel and almost fall but never wake; / And the echo of feet goes round and round / Like a buffeted gull," fully registering Einsteinian relativity: "If you / Put your foot down the spot moves: the waters are / Under the earth." As if in Alfred Hitchcock's film *Rebecca,* the sea has become a returning ghost, a specter that haunts the sailor's senses: "Gull shriek, boozy guffaw, woman / Laughing—turn your back on each in turn / And you hear the waters' laughter."

In this reading, Merwin's sailors have become obsessional neurotics whose libido is fixated on the water image, on its instability and lack of signification. At the end of the poem, Merwin commands the sailor to "get back to the bare-faced original / Bitch-sea. Which is what they gave you legs for" (*FF* 228). The grim humor here subverts the common preference for equilibrium in an organism by presenting the sailor's pathological attachment to alternative/displaced reality. Merwin's oxymoronic phrasing points out the ambiguous charm of the sea—it is the origin of meaning ("original") due to its utter lack of meaning ("bare-faced"). For the poet, seas and rivers both reveal and cover the void of subjectivity; in a folkloric voice Merwin would sing: "for so long / It will be the seethe and drag of the river / That I will hear longer than any mortal song" (*FF* 190). More than a feeling of nostalgia for the transient object, it is rather an outburst of the retroactive effects of the first decision of home leaving. Seas and rivers have become the enigmatic objects stuck in the throat of the enunciating subject: the poet and his sailors can neither swallow it (subjectivize it) nor spit it out (reject it or fully articulate it). This is perhaps why the speaker anathematizes it as the "Bitch-sea," the sticky object that one has to enjoy in such *Angst.*

ALL THE UNCOVENANTED TERROR OF BECOMING

Merwin's impassioned sea journey is largely a mental excursion full of imaginary projections from the human psyche. The icebergs, capes, shipwreck, and sailors dead and alive are not so much mythological as pathological: they repeatedly evoke scenes of destruction with a mixed feeling of horror and exhilaration, anxiety and release. From very early on, Merwin has indulged himself in the interplay of psychic and physical realities to explore a radical otherness in selfsameness, a nonhumanness in humanity, a death in the very center of life. It seems hard for Merwin to get rid of this "fierce devotion" (Merwin's term for Richard Blackmur) to *tuché*, in which the poetic language burns "intensely, unremittingly, and fiercely," to use his comment on the poetry of John Berryman (*SD* 45).

Apart from the sea, the legendary sea monsters and creatures provide another fantasy frame for Merwin to stage his poetic cathexes, his encounter with the unknown. In *Green with Beasts* (1956), Merwin paints several "sublime" animals in a highly intensified poetic language. Critics are quick to point out that almost all of these animal poems are linked with the sea. For example, Brunner has noted that "the sea is a presence to which the [creature] poems compulsively return," because both the sea and the creature "escape his understanding," and "even as [the creature] sets a limit to our knowledge, it compels us to imagine its infinity" (*Poetry* 43, 44). Brunner traces Merwin's "Physiologus" back to the twelfth-century tabulations of biblical animals, characterizing them as "objects of endless speculation that can never be resolved into simplifying categories" (*Poetry* 39).[9] What preoccupies Merwin then is the mystery of signification because the sublime/monstrous animals simultaneously absorb and subvert the descriptive power of words, functioning as the extimate object of humans' epistemological, metaphysical desire.

In "Proteus," the earliest poem manifestly dealing with a sea monster in *The Dancing Bears* (1954), Merwin dramatizes man's struggle with his own radical otherness embodied in the beast-god who can assume various shapes as he wishes. Such a struggle is not only comical: by dispersing man's blindness to his own absurd existence, it also endows him with a kind of tragic courage to face up the fundamental *Spaltung* in his earthly existence. The poem starts as the outcome of an Odyssean quest: "By the splashed cave I found him" (*FF* 110). The legendary sea monster does not appear to terrify the speaker at all: "His face flicked with a wisp / Of senile beard, a frail somnolent old man." This deceptively amiable portrait only sets up the stage for the later drama of metamorphosis. Dallying with the fateful encounter, the speaker gratifies himself temporarily in hearsays or what Brunner calls "extravagant digressions" and "lavish allusions" (*Poetry* 46):

I had heard in seven wise cities
Of the last shape of his wisdom: when he,
Giver of winds, father as some said
Of the triple nightmare, from the mouth of a man
Would loose the much-whistled wind of prophecy. (*FF* 110)

Wind is synonymous with desire for its insubstantiality and mobility. In the Homeric tradition, Odysseus's return was delayed because Poseidon had simply changed the wind, that is, changed his will, his desire. Like the amorphous water, wind stands between something and nothing; coming from a void, a crack, an opening, wind can yet be extremely propelling. Lacan points out that "The question of *das Ding* is still attached to whatever is open, lacking, or gaping at the center of our desire" (*Seminar VII* 84). Merwin in his own context also traces out the etiology of desire: "The nothing into which a man leans forward / Is mother of all restiveness, drawing / The body prone to falling into no / Repose at last but the repose of falling" (*FF* 110).

The real battle begins when the pilgrim-speaker "seized" Proteus— the Other as the posited locus of knowledge—"by sleeping throat and heel" and remained deaf to the beast-god's "pleadings," "arguments," and "threats," forcing him to divulge the prophecy. At this moment, the wonderful Ovidian metamorphosis occurred:

When he leapt in a bull's rage
By horn and tail I held him; I became
A mad bull's shadow, and would not leave him;
As a battling ram he rose in my hands;
My arms were locked horns that would not leave his horns;
I was the cleft stick and the claws of birds
When he was a serpent between my fingers. (*FF* 111)

While suggesting the temptation scene in Eden and the sacrifice story of Isaac, Merwin here mainly aims to blur the boundary between self-sameness and otherness, protagonist and antagonist, to intimate that this struggle is largely self-reflexive—all the surreal transformations happen in the domain of human psyche. The ego seemed to prevail upon its double when the speaker "felt the beast's sinews / Fail, the beast's bristles fall smooth / Again to the skin of a man," and not surprisingly, the speaker came to find that "the head he turned toward me wore a face of mine" (*FF* 111).

These lines dramatize Merwin's vehement desire to access the alterity of the Other: both imaginary and real.[10] Proteus is at once Merwin's ideal ego—man of sinews, visions, changeability (since then, Merwin's style has changed so much that Harold Bloom has to call him "the Protean Merwin" [11])—and his own non-understandable yet commanding otherness. Here Merwin would agree with Lacan that "The ego is this master the subject finds in an other, whose function of mastery he establishes in his own heart" (*Seminar III* 93). The mastering ego has to constantly battle the surging otherness in the id. At the end of the struggle, Merwin's narrator was disillusioned, enlightened, accepting that "Here was no wisdom but my own silence / Echoed as from a mirror; no marine / Oracular stare but my own eyes / Blinded and drowned in their reflections" (*FF* 111–12). Hearing his own voice saying, "You prevail always, but, deathly, I am with you / Always," the narrator does acquire a certain truth of desire by the end of this pantomime: "I am he, by grace of no wisdom, / Who to no end battles the foolish shapes / Of his own death by the insatiate sea" (*FF* 112). Pushing one's desire for truths to a repetitively nonsensical self-struggle marks the poet's resolution to work through the problem of self-alienation by recognizing it as constitutive of his own subjectivity.[11]

If in "Proteus" Merwin battles with his own mirror image, in another epic poem, "Leviathan," he would encounter the ghostly object of desire and transmit his otherwise narcissistic cathexes onto the object. Manifestly, the apocalyptic sea monster from the book of Revelation inspires much of Merwin's imagery, but he has added more savory details to invest the monster with an aura of psychic reality. As in the iceberg poems, the sea here unmistakably figures as the vast reservoir of id in which the core of the Real hides and from which it occasionally emerges.

This beast is truly sublime in the Kantian sense in that its dynamism and dimension surpass human imagination, holding the viewers in fear and trembling, exposing their helplessness before raw, dangerous nature. In order to introduce this gigantic beast that overwhelms any adjectival approximation of words, Merwin employs a dizzying syntax that permits the gradual laying out of subordinating clauses and adverbials. The heavy, wavelike enjambments contribute to the unusual proportion of the subject, as the describer's imagination is trying hard to catch up with the movement of such a Leviathan, Merwin's version of Moby-Dick:

> This is the black sea-brute bulling through wave-wrack,
> Ancient as ocean's shifting hills, who in sea-toils
> Traveling, who furrowing the salt acres
> Heavily, his wake hoary behind him. . . . (*FF* 141)

Through alliterations of the explosive *b* in the first line of the quotation, the monster seems to jump out of the sea, "bursting the bounds of the poetic form" (Andersen 280), during which the dynamism of raw life-energy is conveyed by the successive motion of *bulling, shifting,* and *traveling.* The metaphor of plowing ("who furrow[s] the salt acres / Heavily") intimates that the whale is existentially at home in its environment; it has its own life-world, which radically differs from man's but shares the same characteristic of being an *Umwelt.* With much authenticity and majesty, the sea monster marches undaunted: "ravening the rank flood, wave-marshaling, / Overmastering the dark sea-marches, finds home / And harvest" (*FF* 141).

In this fantastical scene, the poetic signifiers are saturated with jouissance, as an autonomous aestheticism prevails over historicity. As Mark Christhilf notes, Merwin's animals "exist in human's preconscious depths and are prior to historical life and the domesticating consciousness in which humans conduct their lives" (57). Evoking the prehistoric creature in its horrifying dynamism, Merwin would get even closer, presenting us a frontal snapshot of the Real: "The hulk of him is like hills heaving, / Dark, yet as crags of drift-ice, crowns cracking in thunder, / Like land's self by night black-looming, surf churning and trailing / Along his shores' rushing, shoal-water boding / About the dark of his jaws" (*FF* 141). The present participles here, as in the famous opening in Eliot's *Waste Land* ("April is the cruelest month, breeding / . . . mixing / . . . stirring / . . . covering / . . . feeding"), create not only a sense of rhythm and motion but also a deferral of ultimate confrontation with "the dark of his jaws," the abyss of the Real. The movement of signifiers via multiple similes reveals Merwin's, as well as any poet's (Melville included), inability to accurately render the Thing through the verbal form, and it is in this domain of impossibility that poets toil and compete. The excessive use of similes does not testify to Merwin's poetic eloquence; rather, it lays bare a certain linguistic disorder in contiguity. It seems that Merwin was stunned by the presence of this ultraphenomenon and could not find the right word for it, doing what Lacan says about a delusional subject who "employs enormous, extraordinarily articulate bla-bla-bla" and "can never get to the heart of what he has to communicate" (*Seminar III* 220). Anyone who stumbles upon this Leviathan "would find gates of no gardens, / But the hill of dark underfoot diving, / Closing overhead, the cold deep, and drowning" (*FF* 141). Merwin is again engaged in a self-defeating enterprise to name "the nameable beyond the name, the unnameable nameable" (Derrida, *On the Name* 58). Facing the phantasmal, infinite (non)entity, what can the poet do but plunge into these vertiginous as well as orgasmic alliterations of "wave-marshaling," "hills heaving," "crowns cracking," "black-looming," and "hill of dark . . . diving . . . Closing . . . drowning"? Merwin's naming procedure thus happily founders and flounders.

This confrontation with the Real involves what Gilles Deleuze and Felix Guattari formulate as the "anomalous": "The anomalous is neither an individual nor a species; it has only affects, it has neither familiar or subjectified feelings, nor specific or significant characteristics. Human tenderness is as foreign to it as human classifications. Lovecraft applies the term 'Outsider' to this thing or entity, the Thing, which arrives and passes at the edge, which is linear yet multiple, 'teething, seething, swelling, foaming, spreading like an infectious disease, this nameless horror'"

(*Thousand* 244–45). Deleuze and Guattari read Moby-Dick as the anomalous "borderline" that represents the outer limit of a given pack or band, claiming that, in order to penetrate into the multiplicity of the whales, Ahab has to strike this "white wall," this borderline that is Moby-Dick. Fascinated by this mythical, multiplicity-defining beast, Ahab could be said to have "an irresistible becoming-whale, but one that bypasses the pack or the school, operating directly through a monstrous alliance with the Unique, the Leviathan, Moby-Dick." In other words, Ahab has made "a pact with a demon" (243).

It seems that Merwin has made a similar pact with the demon, if more tenderly. For Merwin, the beast is the first creation of God: "the curling serpent," "the shadow under the earth," "a lost angel" (*FF* 141). It beholds the empty, unpopulated world: "With one eye he watches / Dark of night sinking last, with one eye dayrise / As at first over foaming pastures" (*FF* 142). Before long, we will have the whole story of paradise lost and original sin, but at this moment we only witness a world that is still in the process of becoming. As Brunner points out, "The leviathan is only a beginning, a prototype. He is not crude, only incomplete. . . . The ocean too remains incomplete, the mark of 'the hand not yet contented / Of the Creator,' still in the process of being shaped" (*Poetry* 44–45). Language, signification, and subjectification have not entered this primordial world and have not alienated the Leviathan from its *Umwelt*. The beast is not only a Jungian archetype, as Brunner suggests, but also the Lacanian Thing, or the Deleuzean simulacrum that "implies huge dimensions, depths, and distances that the observer cannot master" ("Simulacrum" 258). Unlike Adam and his descendants, the beast lives without what Deleuze calls the "structure-Other," without the differentiation between consciousness and object. Swelling perpetually in the undifferentiated Real, the Leviathan is directly identified with its environment. Merwin's similes and metaphors ("ocean's shifting hills," "crags of drift-ice," "surf churning and trailing / Along his shores' rushing") all register a merging of the beast with the ocean. Unlike the Leviathan in the book of Revelation, the beast here can hardly be described as "evil," since the dichotomy of good and evil is not formed yet; it is monstrous without being evil, "await[ing] as emblem of all possibilities, the conditions of the world that wait for man" (Benston 190).

In fact, Merwin admits that he has never seen a sea monster. In a memoir about George Kirstein, the former publisher of the *Nation*, Merwin recollects his experiences with the sea and the conception of the sea monster: "It was a subject that had occupied my imagination since childhood. . . . But my actual experience of the sea, apart from a couple of Atlantic crossings, was limited almost entirely to some sailing in summer with friends almost as inept as I was, on an old Dutch fishing boat off the south coast of England" (*EE* 3). When George, who was passionate about sea voyages himself, wrote to Merwin inquiring after his poem on the sea monster, Merwin admitted, "I need hardly say that I had never beheld a sea monster, and my piece was a complete fiction" (*EE* 4). In retrospection, Merwin attributes the conception of the monster to possible optical illusions due to "cold rains and fogs" and "the complicated tides and currents" (*EE* 3–4). These situations, as Merwin explains, "were not extensive but they were, and they remained, immediate, and they came to focus years of reading and daydreaming about the sea into the writing of the poems that occasioned George's letter," so the fantasy of the sea monster serves not so much to excite sensation as to blur "the distinction between the waking world and the world of sleep" (*EE* 4). From Freud and Lacan we have learned that it is in dreams that the unconscious and the Real could be released, so Merwin's sailing experience provides him a good chance to stage imaginary yet *real* meetings with what is other than the sociohistorically determined self and reality—a rendezvous with the "elusive semblance" (Žižek, *Ticklish* 197).

The terror of becoming the Other, becoming the sea monster that symbolizes the object of desire, culminates in "Sea Monster." The poem is more about the hallucinatory aftermath of the encounter than the encounter itself, which only makes it more haunting. Calling into question the boundary between facticity and fantasy, Merwin's mise-en-scène of the inner fantasy reverses the usual relationship between subject and object and thus summons up the whole philosophical problematic of perception. The poem, again, begins with the bright day, the shining sea, and all seem felicitous, but then "after / The noon watch, it was, that it slid / Into our sight: a darkness under / The surface, between us and the land, twisting / Like a snake swimming or a line of birds / In the air. Then breached, big as a church, / Right there beside us" (*FF* 231). These lines do not endeavor to encapsulate or represent the phantom but largely work through similes to create an ominous, amorphous, and unnamable presence. The proximity of danger ("Right there beside us") spellbinds the beholders, echoing "The *Portland* Going Out" and "The Shipwreck," in which destruction wears a deceptively homely mask. The strange thing, however, is that "None of us will / Agree what it was we saw then, but / None of us showed the least surprise, and truly / I felt none" (*FF* 231). Merwin may have familiarized himself with the sea monster through "years of reading and daydreaming," yet the lack of surprise nevertheless invites a deeper psychological explanation.

In effect, this nonsurprise betrays the internal exteriority of psychic fantasy: the sea monster is not merely a psychic projection but an incarnation of the nonhuman core or object-cause of desire, and that is perhaps why Merwin deprives the monster of all human or animal features, rendering it an empty husk of the Lacanian Thing or Deleuzean simulacrum, a pure appearance: "I would say its eyes / Were like the sea when the thick snow falls / Onto it with a whisper and slides heaving / On the gray water " (*FF* 231). The beast's eyes open up an abyss of meaninglessness that silently absorbs the natural process, the "snow." More uncannily, the beast "looked at us / For a long time, as though it knew us, but / Did not harm us that time, sinking at last, / The waters closing like a rush of breath." It hardly matters whether Merwin has invented the whole epiphanic scene or not; the crucial point is that the poet portrays the beast as looking at us, the humans. This reversed gaze immediately reduces the onlookers to humiliation: "We were all ashamed at what we had seen, / Said it was only a sea-trick or / A dream we had all had together." They felt ashamed because their object of desire had been externalized and substantiated. Under normal situations, the object is repressed into the unconscious, while at that moment it emerged to the surface of consciousness, confronting the subject with its monstrosity.

Also, the viewers feel ashamed because their secret jouissance has been exposed before each other, and it is this exposure from the reflexive gaze that constitutes their jouissance proper. Jouissance comes from being watched by the third eye, the impersonal gaze, the gaze that belongs more to the object than to the subject (Lacan, *Seminar XI* 83).

This kind of impersonal gaze has been one of the topoi in Merwin's early "Physiologus." Urged by a curiosity to understand nonhuman existence, Merwin would probe the creature's consciousness through its very eyes, expanding the domain of poetry into the gray zone—the zone between the Symbolic and the Real, desire and drive, signification and asignification. For instance, in "Dog," Merwin reports that the dog's "glazed eyes / Fixed heavily ahead stare beyond you / Noticing nothing; he does not see you" (*FF* 148). This, however, does not mean that the dog sees nothing. Merwin continues: "But wrong: / Look again: it is through you / That he looks, and the danger of his eyes / Is that in them you are not there." Animals have this nearly "psychotic" vision that instantly annihilates human pride: "You are not there." In a mixture of superstition and humor, Merwin reminds us that there might be eyes that can look through us and our painstakingly constructed civilization of signs, meanings, and intentions, reducing us to "that punctiform object, that point of vanishing being" (Lacan, *Seminar XI* 83). The dog's eyes are Cerberus's eyes, piercing us with infinitely melancholic jouissance: "For he guards all that is gone" (*FF* 148). The dog's gaze exposes the hubris of human intelligence as we are invited to question the validity of the habitual sense of the self as the observer and object as the observed. These two poles are deliberately reversed in this disquieting play of gazes.

Standing for what escapes symbolization, Merwin's animals all share certain characteristics of the Real, and in this way the poet has conjured a whole spectral world by defamiliarizing and enigmatizing the creatures that seem too common in daily life to arouse amazement. Edward Brunner considers one of the themes in Merwin's "Physiologus" to be "a virtue to proceed without fear of hesitation into unpredictable areas—areas inherently unstable or on the margins of the comprehensible" (*Poetry* 48). Such an unpredictable effort would lead to tragic outcomes in the coming epic "Two Horses," in which Merwin fantasizes about the glory emanating from the two mythical horses. Waking up in an artificially idyllic garden consisting of "grove," "bees," "fountain," "gold light," and "olives," the narrator found "wild horses tethered improbably / To the withes of a young quince" (*FF* 145). Similar to the description of the Leviathan, rhetorical maneuvers are lavished to bring out a sense of motion and stasis: "Their flexed tails like flags float," "their brows down like bulls," "the broken arches / Of their necks in the dim air are silent / As the doorways of ruins." In this *ekphrasis*, the archetypal horses have been sublimated into the stand-ins of the object of desire: "Dawn would be eastward / Over the dark neck, a red mane tossed high / Like flame," and, echoing the steeds in the Homeric tradition, the beasts dragged a long trail of war and destruction: "All dust was of their making; and passion / Under their hooves puffed into flight like a sparrow / And died down when they departed."

The moral of the poem soon becomes clear: the coming and going of the two horses (agents of war) inspire artistic creations but also cause irremediable damages to the world. The dialectic of desire and disaster is set in motion by the intrusion of this agency of fate, this inexorable Other, when "the blood of beasts herald morning" (*FF* 146). After evoking wars, ruins, and vicissitude of dynasties in a Shelleyan vein ("chariots are broken," "wailing at sundown," "mourning for kings," "Weeping of widows," "columns have fallen like shadows," "fires drifting in darkness like the tails / Of jackals flaring"),[12] Merwin brings the scene to a halt by spreading out before us a vast mythical space that avoids temporality and historicity:

> Beyond the terraces the misted sea
> Swirls endless, hooves of the gray wind forever
> Thundering, churning the ragged spume-dusk
> High that there be no horizons nor stars, and there
> Are white islands riding, ghost-guarded, twisted waves flashing,
> Porpoises plunging like the necks of horses. (*FF* 146)

Only by the end of the poem do we catch the full import of the "two horses": they are pre-creaturely animals, as the "porpoises" here also recall an earlier poem "Proteus," in which Merwin classifies both porpoises and horses as Proteus's "daughters" (*FF* 110). If Ted Hughes has written about the quiet dignity and stoic endurance of the animal in his well-known poem "The Horses," Merwin goes further in mystification by transposing the animal into a Deleuzean simulacrum and placing it in the "anomalous" zone ("the misted sea") that resembles chaos prior to the Genesis. Like the Leviathan, the fiery horses "become exotic sea creatures, uncontained and uncontainable" (Davis 55), incarnating the demonic id that resists symbolization and socialization.

"Two Horses" embodies the full Merwinian paradigm of the minimal and elemental (gold, flame, passion, summer, sea, rain, wave, whiteness, silence, departure), and this chiaroscurism has remained largely unchanged throughout his entire career. The contrapuntal employment of fire and water epitomizes Merwin's *ars poetica* as a tender subversion—to withdraw from the sociopolitical system toward amorphous nature, and to invoke destruction, not in its manifest horror and cruelty, but in its theatrical anamorphosis: destruction viewed from the tender side. What concerns Merwin then is not just animality in humans but how this asignifying rawness operates unconsciously. Unlike Shelley, who is emphatic and univocal, Merwin transposes violence and destruction to what Freud called "the other scene," and this is perhaps where he parts from Shelleyan Romanticism, although Shelley has been a major influence on him. Merwin's displacement renders the poem more indeterminate, for we could always read the epilogue in a "spectral" way: it is neither presence nor absence; thematically, it is neither inside nor outside the poem. Merwin might have used this epilogue to signify the closure of human history, conjuring the non-representability of the horses qua death-drive, and just as Alice Benston perceives the situation to be: "destruction accompanies creation, which seems to be Merwin's point" (192).

The question of the animals' participation in human desire and signification culminates in "White Goat, White Ram," the last long poem in Merwin's "Physiologus." In this single poem Merwin deals with the entire theo-philosophical problematic of representation: how animals become the objects of desire, how they submit to signification while ultimately escaping it. The poem differs from "Two Horses" in that Merwin here employs a meditative instead of a descriptive mode—the speaker is incessantly reasoning with himself. The tone of the poem is lighthearted at first but soon turns serious and finally becomes pious, paralleling the three stages of phenomenon, essence, and transcendence of the text. H. L. Hix's comment that, "as he had done with the leviathan, Merwin uses the goat and the ram as points of reference for understanding ourselves," only catches part of the story (*Understanding* 27), because Merwin also fathoms the nonhuman creatures themselves instead of merely "using" them "as points of reference for understanding ourselves." Cheri Davis's analysis seems more justified. Davis claims that the goat "has spiritual powers beyond human scope or comprehension," though she admits that the animals are "language-blind," lacking "mental constructs" and "cognitive memory" (44). As we will see, the interception of transcendence by immanence, of infinity by finitude, of "beyond" by "below," is the textual axis around which "White Goat, White Ram" endlessly turns.

Desiring a certain spirituality that carries throughout his entire work, Merwin resorts to Christianity and scatters divine signs here and there to set up a quasi-biblical backdrop. Again, we enter a landscape that resembles more a psychic projection than normally perceived reality: "The gaiety of three winds is a game of green / Shining, of gray-and-gold play in the holly bush / Among the rocks on the hillside, and if ever / The earth was shaken, say a moment ago / Or whenever it came to be, only the leaves and the spread / Sea still betray it, trembling" (*FF* 150). Merwin then introduces the goat as "stand[ing] at the side / Nearer the sea, not far from the brink," and "her back and belly / Slung like a camp of hammocks" and her "eyes wide apart like the two moons of Mars / At their opposing." Treated as a lesser version of the Heideggerian Dasein, Merwin's goat finds herself thrown into the world, unable to account for her own existence. Like the dog with its empty eyes abhorred by the speaker, the goat here is deprived of any orientation toward *the* meaning in this flood of meanings: "So broadly is she blind / Who has no names to see with: over her shoulder / She sees not summer, not the idea of summer, / But green meanings, shadows, the gold light of now."

Not without a twist of irony, Merwin laments that the goat and the ram have been mercilessly used by us humans as signifiers for our own desire (as sacrifices). We unjustly equate the animals' whiteness with a loss of memory and a radical innocence that could have been exploited by our own "gracelessness," recalling the biblical story of Abraham's sacrifice of "the thicket-snared ram" instead of his son Isaac to propitiate God. As if to counter any possible abuse of animals under the name of religion, Merwin reflects that these beasts need not be gentle "for us to use them / To signify gentleness, for us to lift them as a sign / Invoking gentleness" (*FF* 151). We humans only need metonymies for the articulation of *our* desire, and that is why we need the animals:

> . . . conjuring by their shapes
> The shape of our desire, which without them would remain
> Without a form and nameless. (*FF* 151)

Human desire is nameless because ontologically it is no-thing, merely a *Spaltung*, an abyss between need and demand, "a pure action of the signifier" (Lacan, *Écrits* 253). It has no shape, for it is in the constant process of becoming another one—of transformation, transmutation, and transgression, bringing what Merwin calls "the uncovenanted terror of becoming" (*FF* 152). Sacrifice is directly related to the desire of this posited big Other, since the purpose of sacrifice, as Žižek surmises, is to "conceal the Other's lack, inconsistency, 'inexistence,' that transpires in this desire" (*Enjoy* 64). In a mixed tone of satire and lament, Merwin's speaker peers into the abyss of desire, that is, the split between need and demand, exclaiming that "our uses / Also are a dumbness, a mystery, / Which like a habit stretches ahead of us / And was here before us." Human desire is inexplicable in that it is at once familiar ("a habit") and alien ("a mystery"). Facing the unknown subjective becoming, as Merwin foretells, we are prone to use the beasts to "designate what was before us, since we cannot / See it in itself." Therefore, the beasts conveniently function as stand-ins of our desire for divine intention in that the animals follow "their own preference": their desire is not alienated by language, signification, subjectification, and *thus is freer*. Merwin further insists on the infinite alterity of the beasts by claiming that they choose "routes through no convenience / And world of ours, but through their own sense / And mystery." Very soon the poet uncovers the cause of man's desire as the unbridgeable gap between signifier and signified as reflected in the difference between animals-in-themselves and animals-for-us:

> ... yet the mystery they stand in
> Is still as far from what they signify
> As from the mystery we stand in. (*FF* 152)

A double difference occurs: first, between animals as signs and animals in themselves; second, between us humans as socio-linguistic subjects and animals as pre-symbolic, prelingual creatures. For Merwin, these antipodes cannot be sublated into a certain humanism that exercises hegemony over the nonhuman world. Rather, Merwin acutely perceives the limit of signification faced with this "mystery" that enshrouds both humans and animals, a divine mystery. Merwin further observes, "There in the thin grass / A few feet away they browse beyond words; for a mystery / Is that for which we have not yet received / Or made the name, the terms, that may enclose / And call it." To "enclose" or call by a name implies the human endeavor to delimit the Thing, to treat it as an object and type of epistemology. This naming desire is, however, what elevates us above worldly beings or what Merwin calls the "small voice":

> And by virtue of such we stand beyond
> Earthquake and wind and burning, and all the uncovenanted
> Terror of becoming, and beyond the small voice; and on
> Another hand, as it were, a little above us
> There are the angels. (*FF* 152)

Here we may pause for the word *beyond*, as it is composed of *be* and *yond* (yonder, there) that corresponds to Heidegger's notion of Dasein (being-there). *Beyond* has several meanings, all associated with transcendence: "out of the reach or sphere," "surpass," "in addition to," and so forth. In Merwin's creature poems, this word reveals existents' yearning for the sublime and the Infinite. Rather than meaning "having nothing to do with" or "spectating indifferently," to *stand beyond* means *to surpass by having worked through*. Standing by the angels "beyond the small voice" entails the most painful, most ecstatic transformations, as readers readily recall Rilke's cry in *Duino Elegies* that "Ein jeder Engel ist schrecklich" (150).

What can humans know about angels and their desire? "We know only the whisper of an elusive sense, / Infrequent meanings and shadows, analogies / with light and the beating of wings" (*FF* 152–53). "Wait[ing] / Beyond our words," the angels are *above* and *in addition to* words, speeches, and logos, standing "beyond earthquake, whirlwind, fire" and "all the uncovenanted terror of becoming." A glimpse of the legendary war between Satan's army and the archangels, as narrated by John Milton in *Paradise Lost,* tempts us to read Merwin's *beyond* as "working through." There are indeed "whirlwind" and "fire" in paradise, and this apparent contradiction discloses the poet's desire to plunge into the unforeseeable and unshielded process of becoming *beyond* any religious discourse. Toward the end of the poem, the narrator finds himself caught in the purifying fire, desire, wind, will, and whim of God:

> . . . Listen: more than the sea's thunder
> Forgathers in the gray cliffs; the roots of our hair
> Stir like the leaves of the holly bush where now
> Not games the wind ponders but impatient
> Glories, fire: and we go stricken suddenly
> Humble, and the covering of our feet
> Offends, for the ground where we find we stand is holy. (*FF* 153)

Cary Nelson questions the authenticity of the poem; he thinks that Merwin "tries unsuccessfully to draw an organizing symbolism from

Christ's story by adapting it ironically to fit our situation" (85). Setting aside Merwin's real intention of the poem, which is unfathomable as well as largely indeterminate since New Criticism, what strikes readers most is not how Merwin "adapts" the antiquated sacrifice story from the Bible and "fits" it to "our situation," supposedly the postwar US society, but the poet's meditation on the perennial questions of perception, signification, and transformation, which brings the poem, tonally and thematically, close to Hölderlin's *Hexameters and Elegies* (1800) and Rilke's *Duino Elegies* (1923). Nelson's historicizing might have missed the inherent unrealness of Merwin's poem, and as Merwin's irony does not usually carry throughout the whole poem, he would treat the imaginary subjects rather seriously or even piously.

Merwin's bestiaries are thus more real than normally perceived reality in that they incarnate our unconscious projections. Although we use the beasts as signifiers, they ultimately elude symbolization by being *pure* symbols that erode the binary opposition of signifier/signified as we learn that "the mystery they stand in / Is still as far from what they signify" (*FF* 152). This aporia of signification could be pushed even further: "Oh, we cannot know and we are not / What we signify" (*FF* 153). As Lacanian psychoanalysis reveals, there is always some alien object (fragmenting otherness) stuck in the very heart of subjectivity; all our efforts to articulate, represent, and signify this traumatic Thing are doomed to fail. Particularly, as Merwin suggests, we cannot signify our desire for the holy without betraying that desire, and it is exactly this grand failure that constitutes the flesh and bone of Merwin's writings. At the end of an earlier poem, "Anabasis (II)," after a long, hard journey, the disembodied speaker comes to the same limit of naming and signification: "Fixed to bone only, foreign as we came / We float leeward till mind and body lose / The uncertain continent of a name" (*FF* 12).

Continuously, Merwin's speakers are losing their names, escaping a name, and thus being made anonymous, desubjectivized, working at the "dissolution of self in the chaos of sea reality," as Stephen Stepanchev comments on the above poem (110). The poet would go on to become the Nobody that Odysseus once proclaimed himself to be, not in the cunning or ironic sense, but in an excessively devotional gesture. The poet would go on to confront the void of subjectivity, the abyss of freedom, to suffer the irruption of the Real, to welcome "the Stranger who disturbs the being at home with oneself" (Levinas, *Totality* 39), and to suspend the hegemony of signification by conjuring "anomalous" simulacra—all these gestures distinguish Merwin's project of the 1950s from those of his contemporaries. Merwin's poetics is that of "not knowing," of ecstatic *tuché* with the infinitely holy Thing; a poetics of primordial loss and (re)finding, of conjuring and confronting anonymous holiness.

This fascination with psychic processes and incessant becoming imbues Merwin's early poetry with a liberating potential, which becomes more pronounced in later anti–Vietnam War poems in *The Moving Target* (1963) and *The Lice* (1967). Incessantly undermining the bedrock of ideology—the subjection to sameness—Merwin, from his early stages on, has compelled us to imagine the beyond-of-the-signified that keeps sliding away from our perceptual apparatus. Contemporary life, marked by the quantifiable and daily shadowed by the terrible (nuclear warheads, natural and manmade disasters), may begin to investigate the irrationality of its own cultural logic. Merwin locates this "terror of becoming" not in any preconceived national or global agenda, but in what is unrealized, unprotected, and outside the Law—the "uncovenanted."

2

SPIRIT IN FLAME

Merwin's Dallying with Anonymous Holiness

The dance around the holy, around what Emmanuel Levinas mysteriously calls "the holiness of the holy" (qtd. in Derrida, *Adieu* 4), has mesmerized Merwin since the early 1950s.[1] Merwin has remained concerned with the realm of the holy, even when postwar thought tends to discredit all established belief systems, including the Judeo-Christian notion of the holy, which has preoccupied him for quite a long time. In Merwin's early work, the urge to suspend the existing symbolic order in favor of a "higher reality," what Jacques Lacan formulates as the Real, finds its convenient outlet in religious and spiritual motifs. "Wild as heaven erupting into a child" ("Proteus," *FF* 11), the spiritual revelation that affords ecstasy would ever haunt Merwin and become a major form of divine contact which brings mystical jouissance at the moment of separation. Merwin's poetry evokes a kind of fleeting holiness, not only in religious but also in existential spheres, that prompts the self to follow the traces of the posited holy Other. In his obsessional pursuit of the phantasmal object, Merwin attempts to subjectivize the traces of the immeasurable object through poetic fantasies in order to become the authentic cause of his own poetic career. The spirituality of Merwin's poetry is produced by the speaker's proximity—forever diminishing yet remaining distance— to the posited sublime object rather than its direct attainment.

While commentators emphasize silence, absence, lack, void, alienation, depletion, fragmentation, asceticism, and generally, *via negativa* in Merwin's poetry in the 1960s, I tend to read Merwin's poems from that period and later as a Derridean *supplément,* a substitutive supplementation, to his earlier Christian poems. Merwin's divine comedy does not end with the intrusion of apocalyptical events (the Vietnam War, the nuclear tests) but persists in a more devious and spectral mode in his later work. Critics have noticed the continuous medievalism in Merwin's early and middle period. Victor Contoski, finding that "Necessary pilgrimages of discovery permeate his work," places Merwin among "anonymous craftsmen of the Middle Ages, artists whose vision was so fixed on the spiritual world and our journey thither" (319–20). In a more comprehensive study, Reed Daniel Wilson defines Merwin's corpus as deeply religious, elaborating how Merwin "has journeyed toward an affirmative vision founded on and grounded in an experience of the dark night."

These studies have proposed the existence of a religious consciousness, or what Reed Daniel Wilson calls the "animistic visionary root of all religions" in Merwin's poetry, but since they tend to align that consciousness with either a known spiritual tradition or a univocal devotion to nature which can be traced back to American Transcendentalism,[2] the existing criticism on Merwin may not be sufficient to fully address the poet's longtime engagement with the aftereffects of the divine contact and his uninterrupted play with the holy and its traumatic self-distancing. The poet's spiritual journey is not only a "search for a meaningful life in a world apparently devoid of meaning" (Contoski 310) based on the binary opposition of meaning/void; this journey is rather accompanied by highly cathected acts to capture and (re)find the traces of the holy Other. The spiritual aura of Merwin's work in the 1950s and onward consists of a poetic surplus that stands in contrast to the limitations of ordinary human life, especially of American life during the booming 1950s and the restless 1960s. Just as artists who "construct a place in which people can ecstatically perceive the traumatic excess around which their life turns" (Žižek, *On Belief* 96), Merwin presents various epiphanic states to enunciate the surplus object of Christian theology in order to work through that theology and its ideological corollaries. If in the 1950s Merwin was chiefly concerned with the "enigmatic" desire of the Judeo-Christian deity—if we can attribute this quality to a holy entity with the understanding of its anthropomorphism—and the death-drive of the saints, in the 1960s and afterward Merwin's speakers seemed to directly adopt the status of *objet a*—"the non-symbolizable surplus" (Žižek, *Metastases* 179).

THE UNBEARABLE HOLINESS OF BEING

Orthodox Christianity had played a structuring role in Merwin's early texts such as "Rime of the Palmers," "Dictum: For a Masque of Deluge," "Carol of Three Kings," "The Passion," "Saint Sebastian," "The Annunciation," "White Goat, White Ram," but in 1960, when *The Drunk in the Furnace* was published, Merwin rejected Protestantism for its primness and narrow-mindedness, calling Martin Luther "that old slider, the Prince of Falsehood," who "took the pulpit," "mocking me with a scholar's prim tone" ("Luther," *FF* 240). Consequently, he would identify with his drunken grandfather the boat pilot rather than with his Protestant grandmother, who believed in "the strait gate and the needle's eye" (*FF* 270). In his later work, Merwin seldom wrote about Christianity at length as he did in the 1950s. It seems that Merwin grew more cautious about religious intentions, rituals, and sacrifices, maintaining a distance from them. In 1967, stunned by US military actions in Vietnam, Merwin declared the total lack of divinity in humans, refusing any gnostic spark: "The gods are what has failed to become of us / Now it is over we do not speak // Now the moment has gone it is dark / What is man that he should be infinite" (*SF* 100). Had the "receding fires" ("Anabasis [II]," *FF* 11) Merwin chased in the early 1950s died when the real, mass-destructive fire broke out in Vietnam? Was the gesture of closure the only choice left for a poet when the atrocity of history had so repeatedly intruded upon his imagination that the idea of the holy itself was reduced to nothing but a failure of divinity to account for the limited state of human beings? After the war, man's resemblance to God, upheld in the Judeo-Christian tradition, seemed to have disappeared due to the common failure of both men and God, or the failure of the holy.

In his seminal work *Das Heilige* (1917), which was translated as *The Idea of the Holy*, Rudolf Otto wrote that, different from the good, the holy or holiness "contains a quite specific element or 'moment,' which sets it apart from 'the Rational,'" because it "remains inexpressible—an ἄρρητον or *ineffable*—in the sense that it completely eludes apprehension in terms of concepts" (5). Alien to the order of the good and the useful, the holy initiates what Otto coined as the "numinous" experience—creature-feelings and mystical tremor, for example, which cannot be "taught" but have to be "awakened" (7). Otto also placed religious experience in the category of the "wholly other" (26). This designation, together with the formulation of the numinous, has exercised a tremendous influence on contemporary theological, philosophical, and psychoanalytical discourses on the radical status of the other.

Merwin in his poetic praxis similarly espouses such a notion of the holy beyond conceptual realization, but unlike Otto, who analyzed the holy within a theistic framework, Merwin does not locate holiness in any established religion with its respective Holy Scriptures—be it Judaism, Christianity, or Zen Buddhism, the last of which he studied in the 1970s. Merwin's stance seems more equivocal and elusive. Instead of associating the holy with an orthodox belief that involves rituals, practices, norms, prohibitions, and sometimes even schisms, Merwin, like any post-Romantic poet, understands it as manifested in the essential freedom of human spirit embodied in the poetic process. For Merwin, holiness does not interpellate a person into a religious subject but secretly incubates an umbilical connection with the numinous inside the person.[3] In "Notes for a Preface" (1966), Merwin puts forward his rather "Judaic" view on poetry: "The encouragement of poetry itself is a labor and a privilege like that of living. It requires, I imagine, among other startlingly simple things, a love of poetry, and possibly a recurring despair of finding it again, an indelible awareness of its parentage with that biblical waif, ill at ease in time, the spirit. No one has any claims on it, no one deserves it, no one knows where it goes" (*RM* 295).

Like the Prodigal Son, the biblical waif is the one who is not at home, out of home, unhomely (*unheimisch*) and uncanny (*unheimlich*), whereas the spirit, as the biblical waif, may refer to the elemental wind, fire, passion, desire, specter that animates and inhabits a poem as a chain of words. The waif incarnates the spirit and is driven forward by it. Merwin suggests that to find poetry again means to release historically conditioned subjectivity into an alienation that alienates the very cause of its own genesis, which further leads to the paradoxical position of being an heir without any property, for the biblical waif, as Merwin says, is the dispossessed yet the *inviolable* one. When Merwin states that "No one has any claims" on the spirit, he is asserting its essential freedom to wander wherever it wants, a freedom born of inner necessity and outward struggle against "man-made circumstances" (*RM* 295).[4] Seen from a postmodern perspective, what Merwin regards as the spiritual may correspond to a phantasmal, indestructible surplus over mechanic, material life.

The unforeseeable terror of becoming God's chosen is rehearsed in such rapturous and symptomatic poems as "The Passion" in *The Dancing Bears* (1954), and "Saint Sebastian" and "The Annunciation" in *Green with Beasts* (1956). These poems palpably convey a sense of pain combined with elation, as if Merwin, with an unusual capacity for empathy, took up the role of divine suffering himself. These poems also seize upon what Merwin calls "presence": "Presence is inescapable and at the same time it's something that we cannot express, we cannot hold, and yet cannot escape. And that's why one of the main forms in which presence comes to us is through suffering, and sometimes through moments of great joy, too" (Irwin 48). We are caught in a strange situation: the present can only come to us in the form of either euphoria or anguish, as Merwin's perception of presence normalizes psychic traumata as constitutive of the poetic process. The poets are those who maintain a constant vigilance before the flux of phenomena and a compulsive proximity toward the traumatic present.

As if to practice John Berryman's dictum that "great presence / that permitted everything and transmuted it / in poetry was passion" (*FH*

156), Merwin's "The Passion" centers on the double meaning of *passion* as divine suffering and human desire. These two levels are so libidinally interwoven that readers cannot tell whether Merwin was narrating the Crucifixion of Jesus or lamenting the two lovers who were persecuted by the public. For Edward Brunner, "The Passion" simply "compares the public exposure of a love affair to the Crucifixion" (*Poetry* 33). The poem, however, is not so much about the consecration of a secular love affair as about the explosion of the inner split of Christ himself between divinity and mortality. Shifting between the first-person singular *I* and a collective *we,* the narrator's role ranges from Merwin himself to Jesus, Christian martyrs (St. Peter or St. Paul) and the two thieves who, according to the Gospels, were nailed up together with Christ. To push the textual indeterminacy to an extreme, the whole speech addressed by the speaker to the unspecified *you* can be read as an anguished internal dialogue between Jesus's mortality and his divinity.

Critics, Cary Nelson for example, who treat Merwin's religious poems as ironic, seem to neglect the elegiac tone in them (85). Consider this stanza:

> We heard the nails scream
> In the wood as they were drawn
> Out from the last time,
> And felt their pain; the cry
> You swore was old affection
> And smiled upon the sound
> Not woodenly, but I turned
> My wooden face away. (*FF* 84)

The pathos, terror, and jouissance of the situation derive from the fact that *you,* the all-powerful deity, "swore" my death-cry as an "old affection" and "smiled upon" the sound of the nails that were driven into my flesh. Here the "wooden" face indicates that the divine suffering was so excruciating even for Jesus himself that his flesh could hardly endure it.

Apparently, Jesus here is presented as a hysteric torn between bodily pain and spiritual faith in a God who inflicted this pain as his divine side reassures his weaker side that all this drama of death has to be lived through: "The earth shook; and, although / You said it was not real, / The dark was ours . . . / Doubt not, love, though the first / Death is original" (*FF* 84). It is only through this "original," gratuitous, and nonsensical sacrifice—a sacrifice eluding symbolic exchange of words and intentions—that the "logic of sin and punishment" would be "suspend[ed]," as Žižek suggests, and that a new ethical order as Christian love could be established (*Did Somebody Say Totalitarianism* 49). What attracts Merwin, however, is not Christian theology per se but how this theology is inscribed on human body, or to apply the words of Levinas, how "the Infinite passes the finite," leaving a "holy" subject hystericized, decentered, and eventually devastated: "This being torn up from oneself in the core of one's unity, this absolute noncoinciding, this diachrony of the instant, signifies in the form of one-penetrated-by-the-other. The pain, this underside of skin, is a nudity more naked than all destitution" (*Otherwise* 49).

Confronting the desire of the God-Other, Merwin's disoriented speaker in the poem seems to oscillate between, or rather combine, Levinasian obsession and Lacanian fantasy: "Che vuoi?" ("What do you want from me?"). Is all this suffering staged for the sole purpose of fulfilling what is prophesied in the Scripture? Will this pain, "this underside of skin," be healed by divine love when this tragicomedy of holy suffering is over? Merwin offers a rather ambiguous ending:

They led us away
To this place we were to harrow
And rise from, the third day,
And how so scripture be truthful,
Yet this pain we pass through,
Though shared, consumes us by
Dividing infinitely,
Is at all times eternal. (*FF* 85)

Instead of obtaining mystic unity with the Christian God, the speaker finally realizes that the holy oneness is unattainable. The speaker is enabled to approach the transcendental holiness through human sacrifice, only to find himself caught again in an endless separation from that holiness. For Levinas as for Merwin, the holy encounter has already presupposed separation, or put more directly, the encounter *is* the separation: "In order that the desire beyond being not be an absorption, the desirable (or God) must remain separated within desire: near, yet different—which is, moreover, the very meaning of the word 'holy'" (Levinas, *God* 223).

Merwin's spirit and saints answer the interpellation of God while remaining helplessly distant from Him, and the war between one's corporeality and spirituality produces a voice that is internally split. In "Saint Sebastian" for example, we witness the speaker's inability to integrate/contain his traumatic desire for God; as Merwin uses the first-person narrative to present a varied version of the Passion, the scene would come more acutely alive. St. Sebastian died a martyr: he was tied to a post and shot with arrows. In "St. Sebastian" painted by Giovanni Antonio Bazzi (1477–1549), the saint is shown tied to a withered tree, three arrows shooting through his neck, rib, and leg, his head turning upward with a terrible agony on his face, and above him an angel visibly hovers and shines. Merwin might have had this picture in mind when he wrote the poem. What strikes readers first is a painful admittance that welcomes death as the absolute unknown Other, as the final moment of ecstasy, what Heidegger in *Being and Time* famously formulates as "the possibility of the absolute impossibility of Dasein" (294). The poem begins:

> So many times I have felt them come, Lord,
> The arrows (a coward dies often), so many times,
> And worse, oh worse often than this. Neither breeze nor bird
> Stirring the hazed peace through which the day climbs. (*FF* 176)

The repeated conjunctions of sibilant *s* with long vowels (*ai, i:, ǝ:* in *arrows, worse, stirring, peace, times, climes*) set up a certain Latinate heaviness characteristic of sacred occasions, as if the impending death were all but solemnly silent with each breath prolonged and then fading away.[5] The speaker here, watchful of the "hazed peace through which the day climbs," epitomizes what Levinas says about awakening and insomnia as "an exigency or demand," "a more within the less," "a piercing or a fission" in the subject (*God* 209–10). In this seemingly peaceful opening, Merwin introduces the violence of the holy Other done to the self, a recurrent topos in Christian spiritual writings as can be found in the works of St. John of the Cross and St. Teresa of Avila. Discourses, poetic or prosaic, on holy afflictions (wounds) abound in church history; Merwin, however, seems to play with the idea of it without truly committing himself, for the poetic mask always invites a double reading.

Merwin reports that, like Jesus in "The Passion," who observed that "virgins darkly / Coming with their lamps untrimmed" (*FF* 84), St. Sebastian in his own moment of death keenly observed what was happening around him. He heard "few sounds that come / Falling" and doubted whether "the noise of angels, // The beat and whirring between Thy kingdoms" could possibly "Be even by such cropped feathers raised." Here Merwin intimates that St. Sebastian in his dying moment might have mistaken the sound of the flying birds for "the noise of angels." The saint's final fear is surely not death but the possibility that God might have abandoned him in death to death with nonaction, recalling Jesus's agonized death cry: "Eli, Eli, lama sabachthani? that is to say, My God, my God, why hast thou forsaken me?" (Matthew 27.46). What if the noise of angels is nothing but the sound effect of the birds in the air? This could be one of the final questions flashing through St. Sebastian's mind. The speaker was further hystericized when he stunningly found that he was unable to "fly from Thee," "for it is / Thy kingdom where . . . I stand in pain" (*FF* 176). The anticipated passage from the secular where "the archers move" to the holy kingdom, in its Christian context, appears not liberating but restrictively ominous. The mystical jouissance is engendered exactly in the final cry that initiates the believer into the holy— there seems no other choice—through the crack of wounds: "entered with pain as always, / Thy kingdom that on these erring shafts comes."

The tone of the poem is far from univocal, since Merwin frequently engages his speakers in an unironic, or sympathetic, religious narrative in which the subject goes through various symptoms before the enigmatic demand of the Judeo-Christian God. The most epic treatment of this divine affliction is found in "The Annunciation," a long poem dealing with Gabriel's annunciation to Mary about the birth of Jesus. Like "Saint Sebastian," the poem records the fantastic inner process of divine penetration. H. L. Hix has observed that the poem "appears to focus not on the annunciation but on the immaculate conception, the event in which the Holy Spirit causes Mary to conceive a child," attributing Mary's mental confusion to her failure of language and weakness of memory (*Understanding* 30). Consider the following lines:

> . . . And I thought, Lord, Lord, and thought
> How if I had not gone out on the light
> And been hidden away on the vanished light
> So that myself I was empty and nothing
> I would surely have died, because the thing
> That the darkness was, and the wings and the shaking,
> That there was no word for it, was a thing that in myself
> I could not have borne and lived. (*FF* 166)

As in "Saint Sebastian," we witness a hystericized subject before the desire of the God-Other when Mary asked: "what am I / That He should be mindful of ?" (*FF* 169–70). What is this recurrent thing that Mary saw? Is it the Lacanian Thing caught in the throat of the believing subject, the Thing as the void-kernel of subjectivity ("myself I was empty and nothing") placed by the Christian God in her own body? It is impossible for Mary, a mortal woman, to bear—that is, to conceive and to endure—Christ the divine Thing in her body without some kind of miraculous intervention. Mary tries to articulate this intervention, but her speech at best resembles the discourse of a psychotic subject for her verbal hallucinations and confusions of syntax, preposition, and conjunction. Merwin's transformation of this failure of language into the triumph of poetry is worth considering, for poetry (*parole*) may proceed, or succeed, where language (*langue*) blunders.

The linguistic dysfunction resulting from cognitive dissonance is surely a sign of panic in this dazzling play of light and darkness in which the Thing, the embodied Word, emerges. To apply Jean-Luc Marion's notion of "saturated phenomenon": Virgin Mary here has suffered from "an excess of intuition and thus from an excess of givenness" as her "intuition is no longer exposed within the concept, but saturates it and renders it overexposed—invisible not by lack but by excess of light" (33). Yet Mary's breathless reiteration of "the thing . . . / was a thing" exceeds the exceeding iconic bedazzlement theorized by Marion; rather, it comes closer to a fear that can only be found in nightmares or horror films. In a Dantean stroke, Mary's cry that "there was no word for it" thus names the Christ-Thing as the sublime: "there was suddenly / A great burning under the darkness, a fire / Like fighting up into the wings' lash and the beating / Blackness, and flames like the tearing of teeth, / With noise like rocks rending . . ." (*FF* 166–67). Such an ultraphenomenon has penetrated Mary's perception-conscious apparatus and left memory traces which she tries in vain to integrate. Randall Stiffler's comment on Mary that "her memory cannot grasp nor her language reproduce the breadth, depth, and intensity that her experience of the body of God possessed" conveniently summarizes the situation (qtd. in Hix, *Understanding* 32).

The most intriguing thing in "The Annunciation," however, may not be the failure of language and weakness of human memory but the paradoxical notion of encounter as separation. Mary's meeting with the holy is already a separation, a deferred action, since she could not locate the vital break from pre-creational chaos (*apeiron*) to origin (*arche*), from "there was no word for it" (*FF* 166) to "If I could only remember / The word" (*FF* 171). For Mary, the "word," God's logos, is that ghostly Thing that has disappeared before it can appear, or, the logos appears exactly by fading away. It never appears as such. Merwin's Mary becomes a melancholic subject whose libido is excessively fixated on the loss of the Word, for "the subject possesses [the lost object] in the very mode of loss" (Žižek, *Plague* 195). Hence Mary's endless sense of guilt and self-recrimination: "Only / If I could remember, if I could only remember / The way that word was, and the sound of it. Because / There is that in me still that draws all that I am / Backward, as weeds are drawn down when the water / Flows away; and if I could only shape / And hear again that word and the way of it" (*FF* 170–71).

What is the way of the Word? Did Mary ever grasp it in a certain, univocal fashion? Contrary to standard Christian theology, which regards the "word" as the Logos or Christ himself, Merwin's Mary understood it as a plenitude, an undivided One: "It was a word for / The way the light and the things in the light / Were looking into the darkness, and the darkness / And the things of the darkness were looking into the light / In the fullness" (*FF* 167). Although she believed that she had grasped the "word": "I knew it, and held it and knew / The way of it," she soon conceded that "Or almost, / Or believed I knew it, believed, like an echo" (*FF* 168). Mary's contact with the divine word is based on an infinite withdrawal of the "word" which is forever to come ("the coming of it," "when it comes"), and this coming and going, this trace of the holy, would haunt her till the end of the poem, and as James McCorkle said perceptively, "The poem is itself a recounting or remembering—thus a supplementation—of the loss of the vision, rather than a re-creation of the vision" (*Still* 135). The ultimate pathos of the poem comes from the fact that after the divine visitation Mary lost her former self and was caught in the predicament of having to articulate that which would constitute her new identify as Mother of Christ, a "terrible" gift indeed. In a compulsive repetition, she laments her infinite (non)separation from the divine thing (Christ, word, logos, revelation) that was once part of her own soul and breath:

> If I could only remember
> The word, if I could make it with my breath
> It would be with me forever as it was
> Then in the beginning ... if I could remember
> And make the word with my breath. (*FF* 171)

DISTANCE IS WHERE WE WERE

The Christian poems in the 1950s, as Merwin's first stage, laid down a matrix of poetic cathexes that Merwin would employ later in non-Christian modes. The "passion of signifiers" around the holy Other produces a spiritual discourse that does not consist in one's mystical union with this Other, as some critics have conceived. For instance, Anthony Libby concludes his long essay on Merwin's 1960s poems: "In Merwin's world, human union with animals and gods can come only through an acceptance of otherness so complete that it obliterates the doomed human self, now unable to hear the messages that might save it" ("W. S. Merwin" 40). Libby's observation of the "complete" "otherness" is accurate, but the "human union with animals and gods" seems too simple a formula to explain away Merwin's encounter with the holy. Instead of a wishful union, what happens to Merwin and his speakers comes closer to an anticipated or missed encounter as witnessed by his representations of St. Sebastian and Virgin Mary.

This provides a new paradigm in locating Merwin's continuity; although entering a new phase of writing in the early 1970s, Merwin would frequently return to the earlier Christian motifs, with a less recognizable form but an equally conspicuous signature. Those critics who see personal pessimism and cultural dissolution in *The Moving Target* (1963), *The Lice* (1967), and *The Carrier of Ladders* (1970) as definitive are reluctant to acknowledge Merwin's longtime transferential relationship with the deified Other.[6] This reluctance, unsurprisingly, reveals that critics in the 1970s were not ready to credit Merwin's dallying with an uncanny God in place of urgent national and political agendas. But if we have really probed into Merwin's noncommittal gesture, we could see what occupied Merwin in the late 1960s and early 1970s was not merely the merging of historical closure with an inner emptiness, but his continuing exploration of what he elsewhere calls "the other side of despair," the exterior to the fallen socio-symbolic order. The undespairing side manifests itself in the indefatigable demand for a more fragmented, therefore more truthful, self who keeps its integrity by staying with uncanny wilderness.

One of the opening poems in *The Moving Target*, "Lemuel's Blessing," focuses on the relationship between spirit and wilderness, subject and object, the Same and the Other; again, Merwin inhabits the conscious-ness of a biblical figure, conflating author and persona. The poem her-alds the dramatic turn of the biblical Lemuel into the Lacanian object and his experience of becoming "one-penetrated-by-the-other," or being taken as hostage, as it were, by this extimate Other (Levinas, *Otherwise* 49). Cheri Davis points out that "Merwin creates a Lemuel who *is* the wolf who begs his Spirit to give him purity and strength in his inde-pendence and solitary exile" (52). H. L. Hix likewise notices that "the identification with the wolf becomes so thorough that the subject and object are hard to distinguish" ("This Simple Test" 69). The confusion of identity is already implied in the epigraph Merwin quotes from the English poet Christopher Smart (1722–1771): "Let Lemuel bless with the wolf, which is a dog without a master, but the Lord hears his cries and feeds him in the desert" (*SF* 12). Readers do not know for certain whether the pronoun "which" refers to Lemuel or the wolf; we can read it either way: the wolf is a dog without a master, or, Lemuel is a dog without a master. Both readings suit Merwin's purpose of portraying a dislocated subject who has abandoned the symbolic community by forming a nonreciprocal relationship with the wolf-spirit qua the het-erogeneous Stranger. As Paul Carroll says aptly, what Lemuel prays for "is to become free of the human community, its traditional values, and its definition of who or what he is or should be" (146).

The poem begins with a Hölderlinian apostrophe: "You that know the way, / Spirit, / I bless your ears which are like cypresses on a mountain / With their roots in wisdom. Let me approach" (*SF* 12). This opening makes explicit Merwin's preference for the psalmist tone throughout his writing career. Unlike other postmodern poets who adopt irony as the governing principle (John Ashbery, Frank O'Hara, Ginsberg), Merwin sticks to a tone that joins elegists with psalmists, which may sound familiar or even outmoded to modern ears. Yet the poetizing of spiritual matters (saints, angels, Godhead) does require a pietistic procedure to stage the enthrallment of the finite by the infinite. Before the wild wolf-spirit, Lemuel willingly surrenders all his egoity; he was desubjectivized on the Symbolic level—rid of his social ties—while resubjectivized on the Real level, that is, tied to a Thing he could not quite understand. The nominative address ("You that know the way, / Spirit") places the Other into the Same, establishing the "exceptional" notion of infinity with "its ideatum surpass[ing] its idea" (Levinas, *Totality* 49). This mysterious *you*, as Bin Ramke remarks, is "assumed to have insight or answers unavailable to the poet" (135). From Lemuel's pleading for proximity ("Let me approach") we can extrapolate that the spirit as the desirable still remains remote, just as Lemuel's desire is directed "toward an absolute, unanticipatable alterity, as one goes forth unto death" (Levinas, *Totality* 34).

Lemuel's unconditional devotion to the wolf-spirit reverses the normal relationship between subject and object: "For without you / I am nothing but a dog lost and hungry, / Ill-natured, untrustworthy, useless" (*SF* 12). The deprecation of the self before the Other originates from the superegoic function of the divine as creating a primordial sense of guilt, which is also seen in Mary's lament over the lost "word." Like St. Sebastian's ecstatic cry of "Thy kingdom . . . comes," Lemuel anticipates that which is not exactly anticipatable: to be led by the spirit into the wilderness in order to escape his community: "Deliver me // From the ruth of the lair, which clings to me in the morning, / Painful when I move, like a trap" (*SF* 13). "Ruth" is an archaic word for "grief," yet Merwin may have chosen it out of its similar sound to "ruse," "trick." Lemuel's long litany provides an intriguing case of Merwin's medievalism that denounces worldly symbolic exchange as vanity or trick: "From the ruth of kindness, with its licked hands; I have sniffed baited fingers and followed / Toward necessities which were not my own: it would make me / An habitué of back steps, faithful custodian of fat sheep; // From the ruth of prepared comforts, with its / Habitual dishes sporting my name and its collars and leashes of vanity." Lemuel therefore becomes a saint who adamantly refuses false necessities in order to realize a higher, capitalized Necessity: "May I bow to Necessity not / To her hirelings" (*SF* 97).

Reading the poem along with other biblical psalms, Paul Carroll finds that "here the Psalm is used to petition a spirit who seems to embody characteristics which are anti-communal" (145). Actually, Lemuel has gone much further to transform himself into a Christian counterpart of Antigone who, in a psychoanalytical interpretation, might have equated "her particular/determinate decision with the Other's (Thing's) injunction/call" (Žižek, *Did Somebody Say Totalitarianism* 163). Seduced by the spirit of the infinite Other, Lemuel becomes the death-drive that endures triumphantly, ignoring all worldly hindrances: "Let my nails pour out a torrent of aces like grain from a threshing machine; / Let fatigue, weather, habitation, the old bones, finally, / Be nothing to me, / Let all lights but yours be nothing to me. / Let the memory of tongues not unnerve me so that I stumble or quake" (*SF* 13–14). With such iron fortitude, Lemuel equates himself with the *spirit*, the nonsymbolizable excess over material life that takes care of its well-being, "a pure impersonal Willing . . . that wills nothing" (Žižek, *Abyss* 15).

Since "Lemuel's Blessing," Merwin has preferred a merciless and even antihuman evocation of sainthood, fostering what Paul Carroll characterizes as "lonely austerity" (148). Through a psychological identification with the holy, Merwin's saints are those who have replaced desire (spiritual yearning) *for* the holy with their own drive (repetitive gestures) *as* holy. Such a Merwinesque reversal is best seen in "The Saint of the Uplands," which supplements "Saint Sebastian" by continuing what was left unsaid about entering "Thy kingdom." Customarily, Merwin himself dwells in the consciousness of the saint, exploding the inner nonidentity of the holiness of the holy: "Their prayers still swarm on me like lost bees. / I have no sweetness. I am dust / Twice over" (*SF* 20). The repetition of sibilant sound coupled with long vowels, like a long strain of sighs, introduces an elegiac tone, and the decreasing length of each line adds finality to the declaration of a burnt-out holy subject: "dust / Twice over," because the saint, unlike ordinary people, assumes the lack not only of humanity but also of divinity. It may seem paradoxical that the saint, as the poem tells us, does not possess divine knowledge (a higher value) but disavows it. This is exactly where my reading differs from that of J. Scott Bryson, who sublates the saint's "humility of ignorance" into an "opportunity for true understanding" (105). Rather, the poem uncovers the irreducible inscrutability at the core of any religion, Christianity included. To exasperate the case, the following lines exhibit a kind of non-Christian holiness that associates Christian sainthood with a simulacrum, an appearance that refuses or is unable to offer gnosis or salvation:

> In the high barrens
> The light loved us.
> Their faces were hard crusts like their farms
> And the eyes empty, where vision
> Might not come otherwise
> Than as water.
> They were born to stones; I gave them
> Nothing but what was theirs.
> I taught them to gather the dew of their nights
> Into mirrors. I hung them
> Between heavens. (*SF* 20)

These lines are unusual for their exhibition of the saint's problematical, surreal denial of a higher vision concerning spiritual redemption. This is not the only place where readers are left with a non-operative deity, and it is easy to conclude that in the 1960s Merwin's deities were alien to mankind: "irreducibly alien" (Libby, "Merwin's Planet" 37), or empty: "the nothing behind everything" (Bowers 252), or simply nonexistent: "Merwin is a symbolist emptied of God" (Gross 105). These comments might have overlooked the uncanny, shimmering, and transparent *something* in Merwin's God, gods, and saints. In this poem, the saint was both alien and intimate, a mirror reflecting the believers' own images:

"I gave them / Nothing but what was theirs." In a Socratic manner, the saint of the uplands confessed his own lack (parodying the Genesis) and mocked the believers' blind desire for revelation:

> I took a single twig from the tree of my ignorance
> And divined the living streams under
> Their very houses. I showed them
> The same tree growing in their dooryards.
> You have ignorance of your own, I said.
> They have ignorance of their own. (*SF* 20)

Presupposing a sort of enigmatic holiness, the believers in the poem confer their asymmetrical trust in the saint, who exposes his own emptiness as foundational of religious discourse: "I taught them nothing. / Everywhere / The eyes are returning under the stone. And over / My dry bones they build their churches, like wells."

"The Saint of the Uplands" deviates from traditional Christian poetry if we take that to mean carols, hymns, and psalms, and more generally, poetry that centers on God's supreme powers of redemption and damnation (George Herbert, John Donne, T. S. Eliot). Merwin's poem is not simply a recasting of biblical themes but an ironic—bordering on "heretical"—treatment of Christian sainthood that overshoots the canonical denotations of the holy as shown in the Old and New Testament. The poem stretches readers' expectation toward a more primitivistic, anonymous, and fragmentary holiness, laying bare the inner contradiction in sainthood. Like the elements of water and light, divinities are phantasmagorical entities showing no concern for humans. In a poem titled "Divinities," Merwin writes: "The air itself is their memory / A domain they cannot inhabit / But from which they are never absent // *What are you* they say *that simply exist* / And the heavens and the earth bow to them / Looking up from their choices / Perishing" (*SF* 116). Instead of denying the existence of gods, Merwin exposes gods' own inanities and the false necessities imposed by them, and this redefinition of divinity perhaps constitutes Merwin's "critical move" typical of his generation—disillusioned Americans in a postwar, postindustrial era.

The exploration of the divine simulacra is relentlessly launched in a later poem, "Words from a Totem Animal," where Merwin abandons the Christian narrative and lives in the voice of a pagan totem. Similar to Robert Bly, who claims to feel the "nomad bands" under his own skin (*Selected* 94), Merwin would inhabit the soul of a nomadic animal, entering, as it were, the sacred spirit to see what happens there and report it to readers. Consistent with his Christian poems, Merwin would make the divine Thing talk about itself: "Distance / is where we were" (*SF* 141), echoing an earlier line that "remoteness is its own secret" ("The Wilderness," *FF* 156). Fleeing from the socio-symbolic order into the undefined wilderness seems to establish an extimate aura through which the poetic subject is speciously immortalized: "When you think of the distances / you recall / that we are immortal" (*SF* 230). The immortal totem goes on to confess "its own secret," its own *Spaltung*: "I would rather the wind came from outside . . . / ghost of mine passing / through me" (*SF* 141). The "wind" inside the totem animal, like Rilke's "der Wind voller Weltraum" (150), maddens even divinity itself for the vast, wild, and excessive emptiness, as Hix puts it aptly, "this wholly disembodied voice speaks from nowhere, to no one, and a propos of nothing" ("This Simple Test" 73). To explore the inwardness of poetry is a shared concern among American deep-imagists such as Robert Bly, James Wright, and Charles Simic, who endeavor to do what Bly urges as "journey into dark place," "leap to spirit," and "solitary wildness" (*American Poetry* 48). But Merwin's strategy here is even more radical in that it debunks the unicity not only of the lyric subject but also of the deified object, which are one in "Words from a Totem Animal." Merwin has pushed Bly's program of an unconscious poetics toward the great purge of authorial control, dallying with the alien spirit to create an undead, uncontainable state in which we—readers situated exactly in *nowhere*—only hear "the repetition / like that of a word in the ear of death / teaching itself / itself" (*SF* 141).

Although exclaiming the totem as the "god of beginnings / immortal," Merwin insists on a heterogeneity that resists any anthropocentric categorization: "Caught again and held again / again I am not a blessing / they bring me / names / that would fit anything" (*SF* 142). In these lines Merwin criticizes man's presumptuous act of reducing animals to a "name," a holy signifier which substitutes and erases its own being.[7] In fact, Merwin has been very cautious about the double use of naming, as he said in a 1984 interview with David L. Elliott: "[Naming] sets up a concept between you and what you are looking at. The cat doesn't know it's a cat until you teach it that it is a cat" (*CW* 107). The naming process, as Derrida would say, is indeed a violent imprint of human signification on innocent nature. What Merwin strives at here is crossing the manmade border of *les mots* to get into the heart of *les choses:* "there is an evocation of the thing that is there before there's a name, before there's a concept of it" (*CW* 107). This would involve the paradoxical procedure of having to enunciate the phantasmal Thing in words, as Merwin did in "The Annunciation," before it is subsumed under a fixed identity and to expose its constant flux without resorting to any fixed concept. Looking back at Merwin's "wild" imagination in the early 1960s, Richard Howard finds that "the generally unpunctuated poems look as though they had been exploded, not written down, the images arranged so that the lines never enclose but instead *expose* them" (436). Through evoking and exposing the desire of/for the holy, Merwin's images send readers on a strange, vacuum-driven, minimalistic journey few US poets have embarked upon: "My eyes are waiting for me / in the dusk / they are still closed / they have been waiting a long time / and I am feeling my way toward them" (*SF* 142). Embodying the lack in the chain of signification, the totem is caught in the eternal flux of becoming, entering a domain where "there are no stars / there is no grief / I will never arrive / I stumble when I remember how it was / with one foot / one foot still in a name." Such an exposure is not readily available in a postindustrial world where the *spirit* is daily threatened by machines or uncannily produced by them, nor is it a representation of the wilderness that one may simply escape into. It offers a picture of *the uninhabitable,* the otherwise unseen interval between mortality and immortality as laid down in theology and philosophy.

CLIMBING THE HOLY MOUNTAIN

Throughout his poetical career, Merwin longs for the redeeming spirit that can elevate one above a life that is all too human, although the nature of that spirit remains unknown and unclear. As in many extant spiritual writings, the ascension takes the form of mountain climbing. The approach to the infinite seems to necessitate a distance from the maddening crowd, so the mountain felicitously serves as a spiritual elevator for its auratic proximity to posited divinity. In fact, Merwin's 1960s poems are conspicuously marked by the climbing gesture: "The heavy limbs climb into the moonlight bearing feathers"; "Climbing northward / At dusk when the horizon rose like a hand I would turn aside"; "I have climbed a long way / there are my shoes"; "and once more it climbs / trying to cast again" (*SF* 108, 114, 188, 254). "Climbing northward," Merwin would "once more celebrate our distance from men" (*SF* 114). Merwin's endeavor, however, is directed at diluting the Judeo-Christian connotation of the mountain image while maintaining its rapport with spiritual quest. Even in the most manifestly Christian poems we find a landscape quite different from what Dante or Eliot, in his late work, have portrayed. Instead of preaching Christian values, Merwin explores the speaker's consciousness when it is confronted with the divine. The poet associates the ascent of mountains not only with spiritual advancement of *Homo sapiens* but also with an eager attempt to explore the division between mortality and divinity, temporality and eternity.

The mountain was a mysterious subject as early as *Green with Beasts* (1956), which contains a long discursive poem, "The Mountain," recording the searing power of the divine on high. The mountain, like Sinai, the site of the Judeo-Christian God, remains inaccessible to mortals, except for those like Moses, enwrapped in a shining aura. "Only on rarest occasions, when the blue air, / Though clear, is not too blinding / . . . can one trace the rising / Slopes high enough to call them contours" (*FF* 172). Allegorizing the mountain in the vein of Dante, Merwin conjectures that "the slope, to be so elusive / And yet so inescapable, must be nothing / But ourselves." If the "elusive" yet "inescapable" presence of the holy corresponds to an uncontainable longing in the human psyche, then the mountain as the site of the infinite would help to release that desire for its intimate strangeness: "its / Strangeness composed of our own intimacy / With a part of it" and "our necessary / Ignorance of its limits." The sublimity of the mountain escapes common observation, so instead of portraying the mountain from a tourist's point of view, Merwin approaches it with a folklorist's curiosity and awe: "No one, / From whatever distance, has ever so much as seen / The summit, or even anywhere near it." He further compares the mountain to "Mecca / For fanatics and madmen" and calls any attempt to approach it "a kind of holy maelstrom," "a mode of ritual / And profane suicide." Manifestly echoing an earlier poem, "White Goat, White Ram," while foretelling "Words from a Totem Animal," Merwin's holy mountain is again full of "ceaseless wind / With a noise like thunder and the beating of wings" (*FF* 173), a familiar representation of divinity in the Christian tradition.

There are those who try to approach the inapproachable, and as Merwin reports in fear and trembling, "Very few / Who set out at all seriously have / Come back." The poem invests the mountain with what Walter Benjamin calls the "divine violence," which strikes "without vanity, without threat, and does not stop short of annihilation" (*Reflections* 297). The blinding force on top of the mountain, if not totally annihilating the climbers, at least maims them for their lifetime: "For of those / Who attained any distance and returned, most / Were deafened, some permanently; some were blind, / And these also often incurably; all / Without exception were dazzled, as by a great light" (*FF* 174). The symptoms resulting from the *tuché* (encounter) with the holy mountain are consummated in the dysfunction of the signifying chain, as the farthest climbers, when they came back, "completely lost the use of our language" and only "babbled incoherently / Of silence bursting beyond that clamor." The climbers suffered from an infinite vision that could not be contained by their forms of life and speech.

Like a gigantic magnet, the mountain draws the psychic energy of the climbers and pilgrims, standing as the (hyper)object of man's metaphysical desire. Levinas asks: "Does not the desiring one derive from the desirable a satisfaction in desiring, as if he had already seized the desirable?" (*God* 222). Similarly, the desirable, the holy mountain, the Promised Land, still remains distant, which only makes the spirit torture itself in its incessant pursuit. In the prose poem "Hunger Mountain" in *Houses and Travelers* (1977), Merwin shows the possibility of redemption after a long, hard pilgrimage, yet with such indeterminacy that we may divest it of any Christian intention and read it as a manifesto of one's metaphysical desire—"a bursting of the Same, whom the Other disturbs or tears out of his repose" (Levinas, *God* 195):

> Who has been to the top of Hunger Mountain and seen what can be seen from there, and returned? The view of The Promised Land. Most who have come to tell went only part way. Many have died part way. And even they have seen things that no one else ever saw, things they could not describe, too hard for the words, and then too hard for them, the witnesses. But certain ones who never forget and who never sleep gave us their words to eat. They buried their words in us and went away, leaving us hungry, part way. (*BF* 263)

The paragraph above is full of allusions to the Bible: the historical Exodus of the Israelites, their wandering in the wilderness, and Joshua and Caleb, who, together with ten other men, "spy out" Canaan the Promised Land from the top of a mountain, and the virgins in the New Testament who "slumbered and slept" while waiting for the resurrection of Christ (Numbers 13.16; Matthew 25.5). In this paragraph Merwin reveals the presencing absence of the mysterious "things" and their inexplicable hold on the travelers' psyches. In its exigent desire for the Land, provoked by what Derrida calls "the irruption of a speech or a promise," the *spirit* shatters the repose of the self, "leaving us hungry, part way," undermining the divine speech that made the very promise. If, as Derrida says elsewhere, "language, the word—in a way, the life of the word—is in essence spectral" (*Sovereignties* 103), then we may regard Merwin's account as a description of how desire is exactly maintained on the level of the revealing "words." Merwin's climbers are always on the way toward the holy without ever arriving, and it is this immeasurable mirage of the holy that affords jouissance and directs the projection of the poetic self, which persists by eating words left by the "witnesses."

Amy Newman says of Merwin's poetry that "His is not a poetry of rhetoric, but of spirit" (127), but we know how much suffering without knowledge, as organized through speech, could inhere in this kind of spiritual recording. If in the 1950s Merwin was still an apprentice of spiritual writing, honing his talent on carols, hymns, and psalms, in the late 1960s the time was ripe to launch a less ornamental, yet more authentic, even bare-knuckled spiritual discourse. The desire to transcend the mundane permeates Merwin's most "pessimistic" book in the 1960s, *The Lice*, as a defense mechanism against historical impasse. Reading *The Lice*, William Rueckert finds, as a few other critics also have, that "it is one of Merwin's attempts to understand the other, nonhuman world—not to find reasons to explain it away, but to understand it and himself in relation to it" (61). We may note that Merwin's relation with "the other, nonhuman world" is also a diachronic non-relation simply because for him hope comes from a radical heterogeneity. In the preface to the 1960s poems Merwin writes: "Wild aspiration and vertiginous despair existed not alternately but at once, and at times we may have clung to visionary hopes . . . because we felt it would be not only mean-spirited but fatal to abandon them" (*SF* 1–2). The "wild aspiration" and "visionary hopes" presuppose an omnipotent Other who is capable of redeeming the believers from their specific historical conditions. Read together with earlier Christian poems, *The Lice* is not so much a book of desperation as of anticipation. Although different from the sea poems of the 1950s in detail and treatment, Merwin's pilgrimage poems in the 1960s largely continue the search for the sublime object—the mysterious aura outlined but not contained by language and speech.

"December Night," a poem about climbing, typifies Merwin's approach to the non-Christian holy in the 1960s and in his later period. Presently he drops biblical figures, experimenting with a sort of anonymous holiness. The poem begins with what he elsewhere calls "a description of darkness" (*SF* 99): "The cold slope is standing in darkness / But the south of the trees is dry to the touch" (108). The landscape stands in a time devoid of human meanings and intentions, a dark, strange domain: "The heavy limbs climb into the moonlight bearing feathers / I came to watch these / White plants older at night / The oldest / Come first to the ruins" (108). Merwin might use *feathers* to suggest the vestige of divinity, partly fulfilling the responsibility of a poet in a "destitute" time: "to attend, singing, to the trace of the fugitive gods" (Heidegger, *Poetry* 94). But in Merwin's stanza the situation is more equivocal for the oxymoronic coupling of "heavy limbs" with "feathers"; Merwin seems to emphasize the interrelation between mortality and divinity, which both Rilke and Heidegger have thought of as constitutive of humanity, while at the same time Merwin intimates that such a relation may be intrinsically ironic and even violent. Though the climbing gesture recalls Dante's ascent in *Purgatory,* it still remains undefined for its mergence into the anonymous moonlight.

The speaker came to the slope to watch the old trees that were struggling through the hard winter. The "ruins" may hint at historical closure, but they might as well indicate the cycle of nature that begins a new life on the debris of the "oldest" ones. The next stanza continues in its otherworldliness, rendering the speaker *I* a mere spectator in the nightly mountain-view:

> And I hear magpies kept awake by the moon
> The water flows through its
> Own fingers without end. (*SF* 108)

Merwin's pilgrimage, although conducted in the month of Christ's birth, proclaims not the birth of a personified savior but an anonymous purification in the wilderness. He ends the poem with lines that Dante would never have written: "Tonight once more / I find a single prayer and it is not for men." The lesson the speaker gleans on the desolate mountain slope substitutes cosmology for theology, as the prayer is directed toward the unknown force that operates through animate and inanimate worlds.[8] But we should not hasten to crown Merwin "a poet of animism," as some critics do (Hix, "This Simple Test" 68); Merwin's climbing spirit desires a holiness that transcends any known formulation or thematization, recalling Zen Buddhism that he has practiced since the 1970s, for Zen similarly cancels the ontological status of ego to reach a numinous whole. It is on the mountain that Merwin beholds the origin of life and death—the holy water. In another poem, "The Herds," Merwin also witnesses the hushed baptism of the dead on the mountain:

> Sleeping by the glass mountain
> I would watch the flocks of light grazing
> And the water preparing its descent
> To the first dead. (SF 114)

The mountain represents the primitive site where the dead, as American Indians, receive a natural and mystical ceremony that welcomes their return to Mother Earth. On this "magic mountain," life and death are not sociohistorical processes but natural mutations, subjected to a higher necessity than intersubjective norms. The juxtaposition of the grazing flocks and "the first dead" has diluted the intensity of personal mourning when the water descending from the high mountain prepares the dead for the netherworld.

The surreal image of the "glass mountain" strikes us as luminous and evasive, producing an auratic shimmer or what Mark Christhilf calls "the creative, celestial dimension" on the height (50). Climbing the mountain, the speaker discovers an ultra-world where historical time is foreclosed and where light and darkness, life and death, mysteriously interpenetrate. In "The Dream Again," for instance, the speaker gradually merges himself in the glory on the height:

> I take the road that bears leaves in the mountains
> I grow hard to see then I vanish entirely
> On the peaks it is summer (SF 113)

Manifestly echoing Goethe's famous lines "Über allen Gipfeln / ist Ruh" (58), this Zenic tercet visualizes the author's spiritual ascendance toward an anonymous, luminous, and overwhelming presence that felicitously obliterates the individual self, if only temporarily. The poetic aura is completed in the convergence of temporal and spatial altitudes: "On the peaks it is summer."

The title of the poem "The Dream Again" suggests the unrealness of the epiphany, just as the repeated dream makes known Merwin's uncompromised drive toward wholeness, even at the expense of completely erasing the self.[9] That the union with the anonymous presence happens in the season of summer, which is highly transient as Merwin records in his memoir *Summer Doorways* (2005), exposes the very momentariness of that union. As Edward Brunner has noted, the other unfragmented world sought by Merwin is itself an ephemeral one: "The silent world of immanent origins is viewed, if at all, as a matter of fleeting impressions, flashing glimpses, for that is the only way we can perceive its unimaginable wholeness" (*Poetry* 287).

Merwin's imagination thus rests on the present that looks so much like death, on the wild anticipation that the old self is dying, making room for a new one. In *The Lice* Merwin often combines the spatial climbing with a temporal one, standing on the threshold of both space and time: "I desire / To kneel in a doorway empty except for the song" (*SF* 111). In "How We Are Spared," the mountain image is associated with the beginning of a new time sequence: "At midsummer before dawn an orange light returns to the mountains / Like a great weight and the small birds cry out / And bear it up" (*SF* 113).[10] The birds and magpies have replaced the saints and angels in the 1950s as the anonymous messengers of the divine, bringing the speaker undecipherable news which nevertheless concerns him. Climbing the mountain of time, the poetic self is able to evolve with the constant renewal of the days, seasons, and years.

The "orange light" on the mountain, like the "receding fires" Merwin's travelers chased in the early 1950s, animates the poet's spirit and sets it in "conflagration"—to urge him toward a transcendence of imagined origins. In a discussion of Georg Trakl's poem "Grodek," Heidegger explores the motif of spirit as flaming: "The spirit is flaming. . . . Flame is glowing lumination. What flame is the *ek-stasis* which lightens and calls forth radiance. . . . The spirit chases, drives the soul to get underway to where it leads the way" (*On the Way* 179–80). Derrida explains that "Heidegger can claim to de-Christianize Trakl's *Gedicht*": Heidegger ventures to locate in Trakl's poetry "an *other* birth and an *other* essence, origin-heterogeneous . . . to all the testaments, all the promises, all the events, all the laws and assignments which are our very memory" (*Of Spirit* 108, 107). This suspension of personal history before the "origin-heterogeneous," infinite Other who has ignited the destructive flame of spirituality prepares the rapturous re-temporization of Dasein by burning away false necessities—historical closure, limitations of ideology and habit, and so forth. For Merwin, as well as for Trakl and Heidegger, the commencing and ending of years, the destruction and rebirth of time, claim the status of being "spiritual" and "revolutionary" and thus historic (Derrida, *Of Spirit* 89). Merwin's poems in the 1960s, in this reading, are conspicuously marked by a quest for what Otto, Heidegger, Levinas, Derrida, Lacan, Žižek have all thought about in their own different ways—an otherness that constantly dislodges one's sociohistorical identity by returning the subject to an origin that ceaselessly auto-affects its inscriptions.

The initiation of a new temporal-symbolic relation provides a basic pattern for Merwin to stage his searches for what is other than the historically determined being. The circle of time brings not sameness but difference; the metamorphosis of the self into the other happens within time and through time. Just as Merwin asks his French neighbor in the early 1970s: "Shall we set out for the great days / and never be the same / never" (*SF* 149), every decision to break with the personal past automatically opens a new horizon for projection, though this opening can be quite indefinite and disturbing. Merwin is in fact highly aware of, and even obsessed by, the passage of time, which can be glimpsed from the titles of poems such as "New Moon in November," "December Night," "After Solstice," "Midnight in Early Spring," "Late Night in Autumn" and so on. In "Early January" for instance, the speaker recognizes the New Year as the heterogonous stranger who has "arrived from an unknown distance / From beyond the visions of the old" (*SF* 110). The desire to supersede history ("the visions of the old") toward an unknown futurity would even take the poet himself by surprise, since "Everyone waited for it by the wrong roads . . . / A stranger to nothing / In our hiding places." Surely there is pain in suffering existential nothingness, but there is also joy in anticipating that the new beginning may bring an unexpected change. In a later poem, "End of Summer," Merwin envisions a new self which, though arising from the old one, is different from it: "High above us a chain of white buckets / full of old light going home // now even the things that we do / reach us after long journeys / and we have changed" (*SF* 229).

The vicissitude of time brings forth a correspondingly decisive change of the self illuminated by an other who carries water or wine "high above us," yet the "old light going home" evokes not an ecclesiastical holiness but a naturalistic one, and if we take "light" here as a metaphor for time, then it is time itself that has become luminous. Although disavowing an omnipotent God in the 1960s, like many of his contemporaries, Merwin does not abandon faith—he puts it in the wandering spirit that "marched and marched on the candle flame / hurrying / a painful road" (*SF* 182). Merwin's redeeming spirit, his personal messiah, is always on the way, forever to come, yet to come. This encounter-in-anticipation marks Merwin's works in the 1960s as pious without being overtly religious or animistic. In "Midnight in Early Spring" the speaker was wide awake and anticipating what was not exactly anticipatable:

> some alien blessing
> is on its way to us
> some prayer ignored for centuries
> is about to be granted to the prayerless. (*SF* 184)

The exteriority of the blessing evokes the radical contingency of salvation in the postmodern age characterized by flux of all kinds, and the question *who* is going to "grant" the blessing remains unanswered, but it does not mean that it is forever unanswerable.

CALLING FROM ABOVE: EXPERIENCES ON MT. ATHOS

Merwin's contact with the divine—Christian as well as non-Christian— is a mixture of unchangingness and fleetingness, encountering and anticipating, conviction and illusion. In the early 1970s Merwin visited the Virgin's Holy Mountain of Athos in Greece several times and recorded the journeys in a long essay, "Reflections of a Mountain," which was titled "Aspects of a Mountain" when it first appeared in 1975. The essay reveals Merwin's unusual interest in holy services and the meditative tradition of the Orthodox Church. However, Merwin's identity, as the Christian monks on the mountain perceived it, was curious: occasionally he was denied entrance into the ikonostasis because he was not an orthodox Christian, while most of the time he was received cordially for his sympathy for spiritual matters. He was fascinated by church histories, buildings, murals, frescos, icons, and legends of the saints; from the text, we learn that he was already familiar with Church history and Orthodox Christian art before his visit. The Fathers also shared with him their private stories, cooking for him, trusting him as a brother (*EE* 102).

Throughout the visit, Merwin consciously adopted the posture of an outsider: he was suspicious of those monks who proclaimed themselves the owners of spiritual truths, listening to their theological arguments without truly committing himself. In one episode, a young monk lectured him "severely on the perilous folly of [his] heretical state," for Merwin was not paying attention to the sermon but looking elsewhere to find that "The courtyard was more beautiful: the smooth pallor of the stones in the open air" (*EE* 107). He seems to derive more spiritual revelations from amorphous nature, "the open air." Merwin visited the monasteries for a glimpse of the "living" holy—the Edenic landscapes on Mt. Athos, the hospitality of the monks, and their simple and pious lives. It is with a photographer's eye that Merwin captures the flashes of the holy. He describes the landscapes on the way to Karyes, a settlement on Athos: "Sounds of horsebells, finches. The road switches back and forth, climbing, heads up a wide ravine, doubles back to a point above the sea, turns inland. Holly oak, arbutus, bay trees. Bees. Large languid butterflies in the morning stillness" (*EE* 61). In this condensed, fragmented, breathless description, the author's feet could hardly follow the swift succession of scenes, which, functioning as endless metonymies for the desirable, have only left shining traces for him to pick up. The signifiers point to a vacant center that eludes thematization, for the desirable, the real—"The gods belong to the field of the real," according to Lacan (*Seminar XI* 45)—presences in its transience. This transient center prods Merwin to climb higher and higher, literally and metaphorically, vertiginously yet indefatigably, till the first view of Karyes:

> The ascent continues as steeply as before. . . . The sun climbs but the heights grow cooler. . . . The last mists have burned off; the road winds higher and higher. Then, without warning, a sudden presence, off to the right, across a great empty space: the first view of the mountain. Once it has been seen, the sense of it remains wherever one goes on the promontory, whether or not the peak itself is visible. The road clambers on over the ridge, and the eastern sea, the Holy Sea, comes into sight through the chestnut leaves, and down through the woods the roofs of Karyes appear. . . . (*EE* 61)

The weavings of emergence and disappearance, visibility and invisibility, literality and metaphoricity, realism and dreaminess, make Merwin's travelogue a locus of spiritual discourse. Every natural, phenomenal object he encountered on the mountain—trees, flowers, bees, rocks, vines, stairs, gates, mists, waters, fountains—was charged with extra denotations, echoing *Psalms*, a book rich in divine metaphors. But Merwin is not a religious psalmist; he did not impose the Jewish or Christian God, nor would he expose his state of mind easily. Epiphany is for Merwin a hidden, anonymous, even agnostic matter. Although the openness of Merwin's text allows no univocal, theological conclusion, the inner joy of the pilgrimage cannot be mistaken: "On the way down from Koutloumousiou to the south there is a high arch over a rocky torrent . . . the hidden water whispering and splashing like mice. Rags of the cloud appeared up on the ridge and vanished over it. Bright sun on the slope to the south" (*EE* 73). It is the hidden water, the vanishing cloud, the bright sun—the living manifestations of the holy—that have spellbound Merwin in his ascent on the mountain. "I had climbed through a grove with another spring . . . the path growing even steeper and less probable, but the horsebells still rang from above me, in the cloud" (*EE* 83). With subtlety and grace, nature's alterity has been sublimated into signs of the infinite. Merwin's faith seems to lie in exterior intimacy with the holy, in the separation-in-encounter with the object of divinity that eludes Judeo-Christian thematization, though bearing a conspicuously nonconclusive mark of it. At the end of the visit, when Merwin was preparing to leave, his last glimpse of the Holy Mountain revealed a shimmering landscape embodying concealment and revelation: "The mountain itself had been hidden in cloud all morning. The rain stopped. For a moment the clouds separated and a part of the peak could be seen—then the blank clouds closed over it again. I could not tell which part it had been" (*EE* 133).

The inability to locate the infinite constitutes infinity proper, and all of Merwin's poetry can be defined as the desire to capture its traces. Like Trakl who claims, "Gott sprach eine sanfte Flamme zu seinem Herzen: / O Mensch!" (54), Merwin by poetry and prose has incessantly fanned the "sanfte Flamme" of the spirit which "drives the soul to get underway to where it leads the way," as Heidegger said. In 1977, ten years after *The Lice,* Merwin set out for another pilgrimage of the phantasmal fire:

even our names are made of fire
and we feed on night
walking I thought of a fire

turning around I caught sight of it
in an opening in the wall
in another house and another
before and after
in house after house that was mine to see
the same fire the perpetual bird. (*FH* 66)

In these obsessional pilgrimages toward the same nameless and sacred flame, Merwin stages the self's constant dislocation and projection, not in this historically determined, "known" world which is "death to accept" (*RT* 74) but in the fertile rupture between mortality and divinity. It is this eerie yet fundamental gap that directs Merwin's writings toward an ever-growing manifestation of spirituality. Merwin's open form has thus approximated the diffusing lights, the shimmering sounds, and the infinitely compelling messages from the fantastic (hyper)object that resists categorization. The proposition of a trace-leaving holiness as what the self cannot bring into discursive knowledge is especially meaningful in today's highly administered and systemized world where the exterior is daily encroached upon by technocracy. Instead of offering a dry "secular theology," as concluded by Byers (*What I Cannot Say* 114), Merwin offers a rather precarious deployment of desire: to desire an infinity without God or gods, an alterity without a stable Other—a desire that is problematic and vulnerable, more tenuous than humanity, yet stronger than God. Merwin's petition that "let me love what I cannot know / as the man born blind may love color / until all that he loves / fills him with color" (*SF* 288), as if echoing what Derrida, in a critique of Levinas, calls the "transcendental violence" (*Writing* 156), exposes the inadequacy of both techne and episteme in confrontation with what might be other than self, logos, God, and named essence. Such a violent, impossible realization beyond knowledge perhaps affords us a chance to obtain individual freedom by forming deeper bonds to the immanent calling for abolishing any forms of "in-the-name-of," self-legitimating theology, ideology, and religiosity.

THE INFINITE FOLDING OF THE CLIFFS

Merwin's attempt to write from the outside, from the other side of Euro-American centrism (including its monotheism, the Judeo-Christian God), has been consummated into a single 325-page poem *Folding Cliffs* (1998), which evokes Hawaiian deities/spirits that hide in the infinite folding (valleys and cliffs) of the Kauai island. The poem tells the story of a Hawaiian family's resistance to the provisional government's segregating policy regarding leprosy in the late nineteenth century. Based on *The True Story of Kaluaikoolau*, Merwin's poem mainly focuses on Pi'ilani, her husband Ko'olau, and their son Kaleimanu: the family fled into the wild valleys after Ko'olau had shot Louis Stolz, the sheriff who led the armed cleansing of the leper valley in Kalalau, also known as Battle of Kalalau (1893). Eventually, Ko'olau and Kaleimanu died of leprosy during their hiding, and Pi'ilani, stricken by grief, alone returned home. She was acquitted by the new sheriff and told her story to several sympathetic white people, including the Sheldon family, who received her warmly and took great interest in her story, which was finally recorded and published in Hawaiian by the journalist John Sheldon.

Merwin's belated poetic account of what happened in the Hawaiian mountains while a coup d'état (led by the Americans) was displacing the monarchy in Honolulu has been hailed by Ted Hughes as "a truly original masterpiece, on a very big scale," on the book cover. Such a scale, approaching Williams's *Paterson* and Olson's *Maximus Poems,* although less laden with cultural anxieties and reflections, troubles contemporary readers for some other reasons. Commentators are quick to point out Merwin's "folding" procedure: how he works to distance Pi'ilani's traumatic *story-in-itself* from a white Christian's (Sheldon's) retelling of it, and how his own version, being a poem, would essentially differ from both. John Burt, for instance, alerts us that "Merwin intends Sheldon's account to serve as a cautionary example about the ways even very sympathetic (and anti-colonialist) listeners might get Pi'ilani's story wrong," simply because her story has been mediated through a different value, perspective, and style; therefore, in order to reproduce the Real, Merwin has to resist the impulse to "imitate her style" (116). Understandably, Merwin has to get to the traumatic, ahistorical core of any colonial history in order to overflow its reclamation by language. Jeff Westover points out Pi'ilani's self-alienation in telling her story: "Merwin's readers experience Pi'ilani most intimately through her alienation from 'her' story as told by Sheldon. . . . By making readers keenly aware of the mechanics of his storytelling, Merwin offers a model of narrative ethics that respects the individual's alterity" (54). Despite much storytelling, Pi'ilani, the central figure in the poem, like Merwin's other figures who suffered loss and griefs, is still enwrapped in mystery as her "alterity" has been maintained to the very end of the poem: standing before Ko'olau's unnamed, unmarked grave, she felt "she was / a stranger like a dream that had vanished upon waking" (*FC* 293). Laurence Lieberman acutely perceives the poem's mythically alienating effects such as Pi'ilani's "special gift of time travel," her power of prophecy, and her "layer-by-layer partitioning of time consciousness" ("Apotheosis" 42). The dynamic of Merwin's poem, as Lieberman sees it, consists in the "twirling gyrations of the stanza units [that] provide special opportunities for the author to render in verse physical or mental events that would otherwise appear to leap impossibly beyond normal limits" (42).

Visually laid out on the page like zigzagging mountain trails, *The Folding Cliffs* could be read as at least three independent series of infinity enfolding upon each other: historical, geological, and mythological. Underneath its daunting scale and sublime staging, it is first of all a *labyrinth*—both textual and extratextual—where one first gets lost in Hawaiian names and places, then in a dazzlingly unpunctuated versification that attempts to hold onto a certain continuity of events, and finally in the non-localizable recurrences of rituals, ghosts, and memories, which are intermixed with, or rather interrupted by, the eruption of Nature as seen in waters, stones, caves, trees, branches, birds. Apparently, Merwin tries to connect what Deleuze in *The Fold* (1993) has conjectured about matter and soul: "a correspondence and even a communication between the two levels, between the two labyrinths, between the pleats of matter and the folds in the soul" (4), and just as such "pleats of matter," Merwin's folding cliffs would generously harbor huts, houses, voices, or the realm of soul, in their "[f]olds of winds, of waters, of fire and earth, and subterranean folds of veins of ore in a mine" (6). The folds of soul (loss, griefs, prayers, and so on) have been projected into the folds of nature, so that the two orders would be infinitely mutual-referring.

But primarily, for Merwin, as well as for Pi'ilani and Ko'olau in the poem, the Hawaiian cliffs function as movable, impenetrable screens/ walls to keep off the Other, the government forces, or anyone attempting to track down the fugitives. (There was a reward on Ko'olau's head.) The cliffs contain folds that shield the Pi'ilani family from their enemies, those foreigners who approach the Kalalau Valley not with prayers but with guns and howitzers. This weird battle (one Hawaiian family vs. a whole army) reaches a climax in the sixth section, titled "The Cliffs": now Ko'olau took an advantageous position on the cliff that "beat anything they had ever seen / they knew where he was now but they saw that he could not be / approached except by one man at a time . . . / it would be suicide to try to get him that way" (*FC* 250). Ko'olau had to shoot three approaching soldiers before giving up the ledge. High in the air, the Hawaiian mountain becomes a divine echo-chamber:

> At first they heard nothing except the echoes and echoes
>   of the rifle and then the sounds of falling and slides
> and shouts from below them and then only the cries
>   of white birds sailing circling the cliffs and then voices again
> smaller and farther down in waves like rain blowing
>   then bullets began banging into the rock over their heads. (*FC* 248)

Uncannily, the Ko'olau family, being thus elevated, cannot see the pursuing soldiers but only hear "echoes and echoes / of the rifle" and "the sounds of falling and slides" indicating the attack "from below." This is an invisible, miniature war fought in the mountain folds, where cannonballs and bullets have been deflected or buffeted by the natural screen, the rock face—pleats of matter that exhibit neither pain nor suffering.

The "white birds sailing circling the cliffs" at the same time suggest the presence of some spiraling, perhaps protective, power *from above*, counteracting the human violence from below. Birds are symbolic entities. "The eon of the birds," Merwin reminds us earlier, "seemed perpetual like the mountain / long before another side of the night gave birth to humans" (*FC* 8).

The human figures in *The Folding Cliffs* thus constantly find themselves on the other side of the cliff, elevated, separated, and shielded. Much later in the poem, when Pi'ilani was finally reunited with her mother, Kepola, she asked her how she made it home since their last meeting. Merwin then reveals the dangerous jouissance in climbing up and down the mountain, being pursued by armed soldiers: "Kala led us along the loose rock into the ferns / where there was a pig tunnel and we crawled after him," and "then we came out on the other side / of the rock wall" (*FC* 287). Miraculously, porous nature provided shortcuts to the other, safer side, but fugitives still had to climb in "a crack of the cliff," which was very frightening, and when they heard the shooting, Kepola recollected that

> . . . the soldiers were on the other side
>   of that cliff where it runs out and we even heard bullets
> but nowhere near us—And Ida said—Kala told us
>   that the soldiers could not see us but I was afraid
> that they would see us when we got higher and we would
>   not be able to move there in the rock and when I looked down
> it was a long way to fall but we kept on climbing. (*FC* 287)

These lines echo Merwin's own translation of Dante's *Purgatorio* (2000), a book saturated with woes and joys of climbing the symbolic Mount, as Merwin's choice to translate *Purgatorio* instead of *Inferno* or *Paradiso* shows his concern with earthly bonds. If Dante's is an archetype of infinite unfolding of human gullibility and suffering, Merwin's then would be that of the infinitely withdrawn dimensions of self and world, or what he elsewhere calls the "concern for the deeper reality" (*CW*

148). "[I]t was a long way to fall but we kept on climbing," in its Dantean tone, bespeaks all the existential impetus for a finite life: while the very act of "looking down" shows one's attachment to the past, "keeping on climbing" rather drives one forward to new possibilities, new horizons.

In the spaces opened up by *The Folding Cliffs*, climbing is not just a symbolic act but a daily practice for mountain dwellers. Both lepers and non-lepers climb up and down the valley, so the mountain has come to resemble an all-inclusive hyperobject. In a 1998 interview, Merwin cautions against reading too much good and evil into his poem: "What happened to the 'lepers' in Hawaii was unjust and immoral and destructive. But that doesn't mean that everybody behaved all the time out of injustice and destructiveness or that Hawaiians didn't do a lot of destructive things, too" (*CW* 142).[11] Foreclosing value judgment based on identity politics, Merwin's poem on the Hawaiian landscape offers rich variations of contingency and necessity, theism and agnosticism, virtuality and actuality. More than a record of the conflict between the natives and colonial settlers, *The Folding Cliffs* rings in one's ear as an endless ricocheting through local legends, porous materiality, and ghostly realms, which all spill over each encounter with the holy mountain.

3

FROM EROS TO NATURE

The Impossible Partner in Merwin's Love Poetry

When Merwin wrote in *A Mask for Janus* (1952) that "Mirrors we lay wherein desire / Traded, by dark, conceits of fire" (*FF* 64), he was heralding a whole spectrum of erotic desires that would make him suffer and enjoy, lament and celebrate. Following the tradition of biblical psalmists, Merwin blends holy hymns and love poetry into a single discourse, closely knitting together the sacred and the secular. Yet unlike the psalmists, who emphatically use the secular as a vehicle of the sacred, Merwin sings of secular love alone, for love is already divine. Although at the beginning of his career Merwin was preoccupied with ultraphenomenal and religious experiences, since he settled down on Maui in the mid-1970s, he has paid more and more attention to the mundane that is more than mundane. Merwin's wandering, creative spirit yearns for the distant and the infinite, yet it also "dwells" and lives in a local, present situation. The transformation from severity to sensuality in *The Compass Flower* (1977) and *Finding the Islands* (1982) witnesses Merwin's immersion in and enjoyment of what Edmund Husserl calls the life-world, the "prescientific world of experience" where everything is "given concretely, sensuously, and intuitively" (Zahavi 125, 126).

Critics are divided in their views on *The Compass Flower*. Some condemn Merwin's turn from negation to affirmation as ontologically inconsistent with his tragic vision in the 1960s (Nelson 113) or aesthetically tactless and naive (Hix, *Understanding* 91; Byers, "Present Voices" 259), while others greet the turn as salutary and ground-breaking (Davis 160). On a more fundamental level, *The Compass Flower* is not so much about affirmation as about "an assertion of presence" or "the moment of ecstatic presentness" as suggested by McCorkle (*Still* 162, 161). Is Merwin's turn to Eros in a "destitute time" a tactless, naive move? For Merwin the Janus-like poet, the turn to sensual fecundity after spiritual austerity merely offers another mode of transcendence embodied in excessive, extimate love relationships. Swerving from previous ontological and aesthetic controversies, Merwin's post-1960s work, particularly his love/ nature poetry, can be seen as a transference of libidinal attachment to the primal scene—the fleeting alterity, which in its very transience offers a redemptive moment for the male speaker, who seems "spellbound" by the female Other (woman/nature) who is supposed to possess more knowledge about love than the speaker himself. The female Other here includes the natural objects as far as they have been feminized and infinitized. The protagonist would stage his indefatigable detour of desire by seeking, finding, and refinding woman/nature. The dialectical relationship between the little female other, woman in a reciprocal, romantic relationship, and the big female Other, who embodies radical alterity, largely structures Merwin's love/nature poems.

Merwin's encounters with nature/woman raise questions about the possible modes in which man may relate to nature or be part of it. In *Staying with the Trouble* (2016), Donna Haraway explores the many modes we can get on with beings of the earth or critters. Haraway advocates "making oddkin" in what she calls Chthulucene as a response to the angst caused by the Anthropocene and the Capitalocene (4). Such a "sympoiesis" of earthly beings or collaborative survival is quite visible in Merwin's nature writings, yet Merwin would rather romanticize that "odd" kinship into an asymmetrical emotional investment between self and Other, thus tilting his poetic planes from an equalitarian mapping-out of beings. Can we decenter human beings into just one actant among numerous other critters without abolishing at the same time our subjective position of enunciation? Humans have claimed an uncanny power/mastery over the earth since time immemorial, and part of that power is language, which weirdly puts us back to the double position of soothsayer and destroyer. Merwin's work will provide a fertile ground for further discussions on the poetic relations between man and critters, trees, rivers.

On the other hand, ecofeminists can quickly point out that Merwin's love poetry is caught in what Stacy Alaimo calls "the historically tenacious entanglements of 'woman' and 'nature'" (2). Timothy Morton even argues that Nature is masculine, not feminine, and desiring/loving nature, in terms of gender performativity, amounts to heteronormativity ("Queer Ecology" 279). Merwin's work can be thus critiqued on the grounds of gender studies and Queer Nature. I won't try to justify his conflation of nature and woman but will simply point out why such an entanglement for him is necessary and productive. I seek to answer the question: How is the nature of love positively correlated to one's love for nature? Merwin's message seems to be that, the more we "love" nature (attuned to its unnamable desires), the better we can love or know how to love each other. Since the mid-1970s, Merwin's work has been increasingly characterized by a problematic combination of nature with Eros and the subsequent eroticization of flora. For Merwin, nature is basically feminine for its magical, sensual, fluid, and non-phallic qualities, and man's encounter with nature is unpredictable as it can be beautiful, sublime, and dangerous (detrimental to the self) if carried to certain psychic extremes. Merwin's fantasy of pan-eroticism in these sensual encounters with woman and nature can be reckoned as a strategy—an extension of his earlier efforts—to fend off the void left by his renunciation of the socio-symbolic order in his quest for the holy in the 1960s.

DESTRUCTION AND CREATION: THE PARADOX OF LOVE

The early stage of Merwin's love poetry follows the tradition of the troubadours in the Middle Ages for its conventional portrait of woman as both goddess and *femme fatale*. In *The Dancing Bears* (1954), Merwin allegorizes the incessant hindrance, torment, and enigma of love in such poems as "The Lady with the Heron," "When I Came from Colchis," "Fable," "East of the Sun and West of the Moon," "December: Of Aphrodite," and "Canso." These poems are more meditative than erotic, more imaginative than realistic as love still remains an abstract notion for the poet to explore. In some poems, the male speaker seems to derive a pleasure-in-torment from the failure to be united with the female Other, while in others he preaches unreservedly a religion of love, celebrating love in an impossibly elevated language. Knowing well the risks of sexual desire, Merwin strives to sublimate desire into love through an idealization of his partner.

The cruel tension between love and sex constitutes the motif of the highly symbolic and phantasmal poem "Fable." It recounts the story of two lovers who decided to make "one heart" between them (*FF* 80), but when the night came, the object of desire emerged as an invisible beast, teasing them and reducing the lovemaking into a comic scene. The lovers only heard a "noise as of a breathing beast / Swung between them; when they kissed, / All about them it raged and played / But nothing could they see"; they "sank upon knee" for having recognized "What had failed them from their creation." Toward the end of the poem, the two lovers were humiliated by the revelation and had to accept the constitutive lack in their subjectivity, as the harmonious oneness in the sexual relationship proves to be an illusion, as if in response to Lacan, who famously claims that "there is always the One and the Other, the One and the *a* [*objet a*], and the Other cannot in any way be taken as a One" (*Seminar XX* 49).

Lacan has remarked that "there's no such thing as a sexual relationship" because the male subject relates to his partner through partial objects instead of the whole person (*Seminar XX* 12, 80). The fusion of two subjects in a love relation is at best a fantasy, if not a purposeful deception, to screen off the fundamental antagonism of the two sexes. In Merwin's poem, the illusory oneness torments the two lovers beyond measure. The voyeur-poet reports that next morning, when the lovers watched each other, they "saw within the other's eyes . . . / Where they all tenderness had set, / Burning upon the day, a great / Bull-shouldered beast with horns of brass / Who cried in fury, // Who lunged between them like all pain . . . / In mortal rage, till brass and beast / Gored nothing but the ground at last, / And empty, where a heart had been, / Love's body lay" (*FF* 81). If Robert Lowell has spoken of the woes of marriage, then Merwin has spoken of the woes of sexual love, even more relentlessly.[1] By alluding to the apocalyptic beast, Merwin expresses his reserve about sexual desire: frustration, monstrosity, and even destruction are waiting upon it.

To grasp the imaginary treasure in the other—*objet a,* the object of desire as formulated by Lacan—lovers could torment each other till death, turning love into a hunting game. Since desire is inherently linked to lack/loss, the sexual act may become a crude, even desperate, strategy to cover up one's lack. The pleasure of the flesh worries Merwin, for it embodies death-drive, the blind, autonomous repetition that brings excessive jouissance. In the poem "Song," Merwin laments: "In married dark these fevers learn / Alternate loss; the bodies, worn / Indefinite, attend together / Night's pleasure and the press of weather" (*FF* 64). The poet, however, is not a Platonist who prefers mind to body; instead, as Dinitia Smith says, "Merwin is a curious mixture of sensuality and reserve" (*CW* 132). Far from condemning man's carnal desire, Merwin fully recognizes its ambiguity, its mixture of tenderness and violence, attraction and repulsion, necessity and crudity.

Biographically, these poems mark the failure of Merwin's first two marriages. Raised up in a priest's family and sexually repressed in his youth, Merwin was eager to have a girlfriend at Princeton, and as he recollects, Princeton did not admit female students until the late 1940s, so for him "The idea of having a woman partner living in one's own room was a tantalizing notion" (*SD* 47). Urged by both desire and vanity, Merwin in his early twenties asked Dorothy Jeanne Ferry, a teaching assistant he met at Princeton, for marriage after knowing her for only a few months. In "a rush of impatience," young Merwin plunged into his first marriage and fully tasted its pleasure and bitterness soon after. After the young couple moved to London in the early 1950s, Merwin came to know and fell in love with Dido Milroy, a well-known English playwright who was fifteen years older than him. Merwin married Dido right after he broke up with Dorothy. The second marriage, however, was not entirely successful, though it was more dramatic and lasted longer than the first one. Unlike Dorothy, who stood utterly out of Merwin's literary world, Dido, according to Dinitia Smith, played the "devouring" mother figure who "wanted to inhabit Merwin's very existence" (*CW* 134). Dido arranged for Merwin's career in London, introduced him to literary circles, and helped him get translation jobs with the BBC. As Moira Hodgson, a one-time girlfriend of Merwin, says, Dido "had a very powerful personality" and was "a bit like the mother who says, 'Let my son bring his girlfriends home'" (*CW* 135). If Dorothy Ferry failed to share Merwin's literary interest, Dido Milroy had an overwhelming presence in it. What attracted Merwin in Dido was perhaps her combination of maternal tenderness and dominance, an image of the (m) Other who "introduces the phantom of Omnipotence" despite her own unperceived lack (Lacan, *Écrits* 299).

Like Ted Hughes, Robert Graves, and Gary Snyder, who have been exploring the mythical nature of Eros, Merwin intimates from the very beginning that the female Other, as the *infinite* object of man's desire, can be both redemptive and destructive, and the irony of Eros is that it is always under the shadow of Thanatos.[2] In his second book, *The Dancing Bears*, dedicated to Dido Milroy, Merwin idealizes the female figure as the goddess of love who stands high above human interests, emanating an infinite aura. The paradox is that, when the goddess of love descends, strife, not peace, prevails on earth. Love, as Merwin sees it, is both creative and destructive—it enchants humans exactly because of its double face. Following the Greco-Roman mythology, Merwin portrays Aphrodite and her agent, Helen, as the prototypical femme fatale. Behind Helen always lurks Dido, the queen of Carthage, whose curse on Aeneas had presaged the three Punic Wars as recounted by Virgil. In "December: Of Aphrodite," Merwin recasts the legend of Helen/Dido in a dramatic monologue, with the poet himself inhabiting the consciousness of the heroine, telling the story from her perspective. The poem can be taken as an apology for love, and the tone of the poem calms down so that readers are induced to forgive the terrible wreckage a powerful beauty can bring to the world. Merwin's Helen acquits herself of guilt imputed to her by historians, claiming that she only acted in the name of love:

> Whatever the books may say, or the plausible
> Chroniclers intimate: that I was mad,
> That an unsettling wind that season
> Fretted my sign and fetched up violence . . . do not
> Believe them. In her name I acted. (*FF* 115)

Helen goes on to argue for the innocence of love/Eros: love itself is innocent; it is humans who kill in the name of love, although she confesses that

> . . . I in my five senses
> Cut throats of friends, burned the white harvest, waged
> Seven months' havoc even among
> Her temples; but because she waited always
> There in the elegant shell, asking for sweetness.

The terrible contrast between throat-cutting and divine sweetness indicates that the violence of love transcends the normal boundary between good and evil. The notion of love, as Žižek puts it, might belong to "the domain of pure violence" (*Violence* 205), which categorization Merwin has exploited by understatements and paradoxes in the poem.

Hatred, strife, and retribution are all inherent in love, as the Other enters into such a diachronic relationship with the self that the result can be detrimental, even disastrous. Merwin revisits this karma of love— love entwined with retribution—in "The Judgment of Paris" in *The Carrier of Ladders* (1970). As a mortal, Paris has to select the fairest woman among "the three / naked feminine deathless" (*SF* 146). The first two candidates tempt him with wisdom, power, pride, and glory, while the goddess of love, the last one, promises him a woman, but together with an ironic prophecy of doom: "*Take / her / you will lose her anyway*" (*SF* 148). Merwin recounts with a telepathic view that when Paris

reached out to the voice
as though he could take the speaker
herself...
then a mason working above the gates of Troy
in the sunlight thought he felt the stone
shiver. (*SF* 148)

The goddess of love, as the object-cause of man's desire, as can be in-
ferred from mythological and philosophical discourses on love, must
remain partly invisible, "slipping away," as Levinas says of the beloved
(*Ethics* 67). The goddess, being divine, maintains her invisibility and
infinity before the mortals, so Paris and we, the readers, witnesses of his
ill fate, can only infer the event from the aftereffects of the confrontation
with the divine. But strangely, what Paris really wants in the poem is
not Helen but "the speaker" herself, and Helen seems to be reduced to
a stand-in of love, not love per se. Even so, Paris's love for Helen could
not pacify her alterity—her destructive otherness. The poem ends with
a tragically beautiful scene:

and Helen stepped from the palace to gather
as she would do every day in that season
from the grove the yellow ray flowers tall
as herself
whose roots are said to dispel pain.

This ending intends not only irony but also lament. For Paris, Helen
is *infinite* in that she arouses in his heart an uncontainable ideal of love
detrimental to his own symbolic world, the city of Troy. Her innocence
and goodness (gathering pain-dispelling flowers) only enhance her ideal
image and the final irony. The momentum of this last stanza derives
from a Merwinesque understatement—a dreamlike, auratic, and indeterminate description that resists any univocal interpretation and value
judgment. It rather leaves the question of love unsettled.

The powerful alterity of love not only annuls but also creates. The genius of love is that it brings forth a new temporal-symbolic relation by obliterating the old one, and it can maintain this renewal constantly. Love smites, soothes, and heals. The speaker in "December: Of Aphrodite," after enumerating irrecoverable damages, beholds a renewed world nevertheless: "where I stand / In the hazed gold of her eyes, the world is green" (*FF* 116). As the speaker knows the pains of desire so well, he plunges into a praise of love, fervently expecting love to frame "the single metaphor of coherence / In the dying riot of random generation" (*FF* 118). Merwin aims at breaking the vicious circle of desire through an encounter with the beloved so as to replace lack/loss with plenitude, if tentatively, as he attempts to conjure up a sort of completeness from the figure of Dido, who he believes has opened up a new dimension of existence for him. In three long poems titled "Canso," a song style used by the troubadours, Merwin praises the goddess of love passionately, deliriously, almost religiously. Following the troubadour tradition and its modernist revival in Ezra Pound, Merwin appeals to the notion of love and its redemptive power for both the self and the dying world:

> ... yet you
> Beyond words believed me to be a gentle
> Season, and I, as from sleep returning,
> Was thence the sign and green wind of spring. (*FF* 117)

Apparently, love's fantasy has concealed the fundamental division between the lover and the beloved, as the impersonal season of spring, though promising renewal, in its abstraction actually has canceled all particular human characteristics. Echoing the book of Psalms, the poet compares love to a living breath, "the infusion of the real / Upon this dust," and credits love with an event that supposedly redeems a person from his fallen state: "I walked incredible / As death, a gaunt preposterous ghost, until / Your creed included me among the living."

Merwin has thus produced a poetic discourse on love that recognizes pros and cons, benefits and risks. Eros is worthy of praise despite the destruction it can bring; by sublimating sexual drives, love elevates humans to a spirituality that reanimates the dead sensibility. The female figure, as imagined by the poet, is more faithful and more spiritual than the male—she brings out the better part of a man:

> It is by your faith that I believe, I am.
> Therein is genesis, as though a man,
> In love with existence, should bring to belief
> A divinity, an imagination
> . . . as though a man could make
> A mirror out of his own divinity,
> Wherein he might believe himself, and be. (*FF* 119–20)

Eros here is closely related with the genesis, maternity, and conception of *la vita nuova,* as Dante once emphatically expressed.[3] Love as a sacred belief produces something out of nothing:

> . . . Believing is
> Conception, is without artifice the making
> Perpetually new, is that first holy
> Aura and ordinance of creation.

In this fantasy of love, the male speaker willingly believes in the omnipotence and the oneness of the (m)Other, as he continues to confess

> That I, perfected in your love, may be,
> Against all dissolution sovereign,
> Endlessly your litany and mirror,
> About your neck the amulet and song.

Merwin has thus sublimated the female figure into an infinite goddess who mutely but effectively organizes his psychic energies, his object-libido, toward poetical creation. In an experience similar to mysticism, the speaker obtains what Lacan in *Seminar XX* famously terms the Other jouissance, "a jouissance beyond the phallus," which, as Lacan surmises, lies very close to a religious experience (74).

As already implied in many of Merwin's poems on human desire, what drives this kind of verse forward is exactly the quasi-mystical jouissance that goes beyond the phallic function of the social order. "The Other jouissance involves a form of sublimation through love that provides full satisfaction of the drives. The Other jouissance is a jouissance of love," as Bruce Fink summarizes (120). In the last "Canso," out of mere fantasy Merwin constructs an image of Dido, not as a being-toward-death, but as an immortal, life-giving sea-nymph: "She is clear amber and the heaven's face / Seen under simple waters . . . / Under the fish flying and the laugher of her dolphins, / First cold, final echoes, and the salt dead, she is marine" (*FF* 131). In her mythic creativity, the goddess builds a womb-like Eden where all evils are excluded, and lovers may simply walk there as some primitive Adam and Eve: "Here is the gate of psalms, swordless, and the angel's country / For which we became as children . . . / here will not the dark / Worm come with his sliding season, though the leaves fall / Nor the snake in the small hours / Molest the young doves and thrushes with the snare of his hands . . ." (*FF* 133–34). As a place of origin, this garden of love offers a world outside all sociohistorical process. Unlike the grievous tone of "Fable" and the apologetic discourse of "December: Of Aphrodite," the third "Canso" happily purges love of crudity and violence:

Now, now I enter the first garden and the promised moon,
The silver of her thighs and shoulders; oh, here where the sheaves
And shadows sway to her breath, in the caroling darkness
We embrace at last, and the night and morning are together. (*FF* 134)

It is at this moment that the sea-nymph becomes a full-bodied desiring woman. As the imagined goddess has answered the call of love, she also confers subjectivity to the male speaker by giving him the "answer of the Real" when "*eromenos* (the loved one) changes into *erastes* (the loving one)" (Žižek, *Metastases* 103), thus temporarily fulfilling the reciprocity of love by the dramatic turn of words. The erotic finally joins hands with the spiritual in the poet's fantasy. In Merwin's love poems of the 1950s this stanza seems the most felicitous compared with other anxiety-ridden pieces, although readers may find this redemption too tenuous to hold for very long.

"WHILE WE MADE LOVE THE ROSE OPENED"

The combination of sensuality and spirituality, eroticism and natural symbolism, characterizes most of Merwin's love poems since the 1970s. In the preface to his translation of Pablo Neruda's *Twenty Love Poems and a Song of Despair* (1969), Merwin expresses his indebtedness to Neruda: "This volume was one of the first to open my eyes and sensibility to the possibility of poetry. . . . Not only did these poems deeply resonate with me, but they galvanized me, finally, into starting to write myself. They stirred me body and soul" (xvi). Merwin admires Neruda's "connect[ing] the erotic with telluric forces and the organic cycles of nature" (ix), identifying Neruda's love poetry as a "combination of the sensory and the natural, the subjective and the eternal, the instinctual and the commonly transcendent" (x). Besides the oral, limpid tradition of the troubadours, Neruda influences Merwin yet on another level: the sensuous experience and the exuberant energy of being in the life-world. Like Neruda, Merwin celebrates the female form, linking the corporeal with the "telluric forces" of mountains, islands, trees, flowers, rivers, and birds. The female body becomes the locus not only of phallic jouissance but also of Other jouissance through its infinite revelations and withdrawals. The relationship between the self and the female Other in Merwin's poetry consists of what Levinas terms "a movement unto the invisible" through touching, caressing, and lovemaking (*Totality* 258). In the late 1970s, Merwin's partner was no longer a femme fatale as in the 1950s but a "commonly transcendent" woman who, though deeply immersed in the life-world, still maintained her mysterious alterity.

The sensual power in Merwin erupts in *The Compass Flower* (1977) and *Finding the Islands* (1982). In the 1950s, his love poetry was dominated by mythologies and abstractions; in the 1960s, haunted by historical closure caused by the Vietnam War and ecological extinction, Merwin seldom wrote about erotic experiences. "The Judgment of Paris" in *The Carrier of Ladders* (1970), looked at retrospectively, is focused more on the doom of love than on its experience. It was in the late 1970s that the influence of Neruda began to prevail, as Merwin tried to get rid of the emotional "anemia" said by Helen Vendler in relation to his 1960s poems, and to write more directly on sensual experience (233). Daringly and systematically, Merwin fuses corporeal sensuality with transcendental elements to create a poetic discourse on love that is at once surreal and lucid, raw and refined, earthly and otherworldly.

The female body enthralls Merwin for its structural similarity to unexplored nature and its heterogeneity to the postindustrial world. Jane Frazier likewise observed: "Like Thoreau, what Merwin strives for in many of his nature poems is contact with a lost, original world, free from the ontologically insular and physically threatening forces of the industrialization and technology" (16). Merwin not only contacts this original world but also grafts natural elements onto the female body to *make* such a world. The following stanza exemplifies such an astounding metamorphosis in a feminist utopia:

> You were shaking and an air full of leaves
> flowed out of the dark falls of your hair
> down over the rapids of your knees
> until I touched you and you grew quiet
> and raised to me
> your hands and your eyes and showed me
> twice my face burning in amber. (*FH* 36)

Echoing Neruda's "The great roots of night / grow suddenly from your soul" (5), Merwin here entangles his partner's body in a cluster of plants and water. The magic of this kind of erotic poetry is that it takes readers to an open, primal space saturated with feminine jouissance. By caressing and engaging the parts of the body other than genitals (hair, knees, hands, eyes), lovers obtain pleasure more refined than sexual inter-course. The male speaker reached orgasm when the female partner, as a *quiet* mirror, reflected *twice* his "face burning in amber." Femininity exposes the true state of a man's desire by setting this desire on fire and then observing it from a certain distance like Nature; the woman disen-gages herself in this erotic play by engaging the man. Touch and caress, as imagined by Levinas, already presuppose separation, as the beloved is "at once graspable but intact in her nudity" (*Totality* 258). In Merwin's heterosexual poems, the female partner is still invisible, enshrouded in darkness, and the man, though taking the initiative of touching and ca-ressing, appears deliriously passive, and in that matter "obsessive" too, as again we learn from Levinas: "Obsession . . . is inscribed in conscious-ness as something foreign, a disequilibrium, a delirium" (*Otherwise* 101).

In the naked female body Merwin sees an exuberant life form that quite enjoys itself, and this feminine autoeroticism both disquiets and fascinates the male speaker. Hence the play of gaze that entangles the male, the female, and nature:

What I thought I knew falls aside a thought at a time
until I see you naked
in your eyes the bronze ferns older than seeing
unfurling above the dark springs. (*FH* 39)

The woman's nakedness undoes the speaker's self-assured knowl-edge ("what I thought I knew") by substituting it with a kind of non-knowledge symbolized by the luxuriant plant. Indifferent to the speaker's gaze, the primeval "bronze ferns" unfold themselves like flowers over dark springs—a dynamic imagery of feminine jouissance. Merwin thus endows the beloved with a Nerudean "telluric force," fusing the erotic relations with a mysterious liaison with nature.

What is problematic and thus unsettling about Merwin's fusing procedure lies in its excessiveness, as if nature were no longer content complementing the love object but had to substitute for it. Nature and the female Other no longer stand, in Merwin's discourse, as metaphors for each other but strangely form an Ovidian hybridity of half-woman/ half-nature. In a similar poem, "Islands," the rich variety of nature is laid out on the female body to maximize the enjoyment the lover-speaker can get from this fusing fantasy:

Wherever I look you are islands
a constellation of flowers breathing on the sea
deep-forested islands mountainous and fragrant
fires on a bright ocean
at the root one fire. (FH 45)

The female body is presented as diverse partial objects (island, flower, forest, fire) around which the poetic imagination cathects its associative energy. The poet, however, does not merely use the woman's body as a means to satisfy his erotic desire. The Lacanian object causes desire and sustains it through nonsatisfaction; the object is *infinite* for its resistance to be caught in any intersubjective negotiations. Žižek describes the *objet a* in Levinasian rhetoric: "the nearer you get to it, the more it eludes your grasp" (*Fragile* 24). In the poem, the male speaker disseminates signs and symbols drawn from nature without truly encapsulating this Other or nature—his words only ignite more desire/fire.

The island, a vivid image of exteriority, recurs in many forms in Merwin's love poetry. Islands are on the outskirts of civilization; geographically remote, they become the much-projected guardian place of man's spiritual freedom. Merwin had lived on the island of Majorca in the early 1950s before settling down on Maui in the late 1970s, where he has lived for more than forty years. Many of his love poems since then have been written on the island as he conveniently combines the island imagery with the description of the female body: both are a mixture of intimacy and exoticness. This kind of "deep-forested" body commits Merwin's creativity to an uncontainable yearning:

all my life I have wanted to touch your ankle
running down to its shore
I beach myself on you
I listen
I see you among still leaves
regard of rock pool
by sun and moon and stars. (*FH* 45–46)

Rather than create a romantic setting for love, Merwin compares the beloved to the setting per se: she is both the exotic background and the heroine in the act of love. Merwin thus puts Eros into a play of infinite differentiation by introducing the "telluric force" to amplify Eros on a cosmic scale.

Although the poet lavishes passionate signifiers on the lover's body, the woman still maintains her "ex-sistence";[4] moreover, she embodies what is other than the human: the nonhuman, natural world. Hence "island waterfalls and their echoes / are your voice your shoulders the whole of you standing / and you turn to me as though your feet were in mist" (*FH* 46). Rooted in mist and mystery, the woman turns and beckons the man to follow her into a hermetic garden of love. The woman and her body, like the distant call from the mountain, is what summons without summoning and appears without appearing. She is out there, silently beckoning, always on the way, always to come: "The shadow of my moving foot / feels your direction / you come toward me / bringing the gold through the rust / you step to me through the city of amber" (*FH* 41). Even when the speaker seems to capture her body she would retain her rapport with nature, and unlike the cold, inaccessible goddess in Merwin's earlier poems, the female partner now seems to enjoy erotic love although she is partly above this game.

Merwin may have borrowed the fusing practice from Neruda, but there are biographical reasons as well. In 1968 Merwin separated from Dido Milroy, and in 1975 he met Dana Naone, a Hawaiian poet and Buddhist who lived with Merwin for several years after he moved to

Hawaii. She shared with Merwin a similar interest in Buddhism and inspired much of the fusion of Eros, nature, and spiritualism in his love poetry. If Dorothy Ferry initiated Merwin into love's first ecstasy and frustration, Dido Milroy opened Merwin's eyes to love's creativity and violence, and then Dana Naone helped shape Merwin's love poetry toward a simplicity based on an Eastern view of nature as epiphany. Sexual love is no longer complementary to spiritual love but remains originary on its own account. The book title *The Compass Flower* makes it clear: woman, by virtue of her affinity with nature, offers a compass, a spiritual guidance, to man.

This pattern permeates the love poems in *Finding the Islands* (1982) and *The Rain in the Trees* (1988) where Merwin continues to explore the positive correlation between erotic love and nature. In "To Dana with the Gift of a Calendar," the first love poem in *Finding the Islands,* Merwin describes love in a minimalistic style: succinct, crystal, epiphanic, a mixture of Japanese haiku, Neruda, and troubadour poetry:

> In the winter in the first month of every
> year of my life I was
> looking for you. (*FI* 41)

In less than twenty words Merwin opens up a vast world that comprises the season, the lovers, and an absence haunting everything. Merwin's encounter with woman/nature is still to come, caught in a temporal cycle already. This tercet illustrates, however, Merwin's concern with poetic finality. In the foreword to *Asian Figures* (1973), Merwin emphasizes the merit of poetry as "an urge to finality of utterance," "to be irreducible and unchangeable," and "to be self-contained, to be whole" (*RM* 285). He pursues this urge of brevity throughout *Finding the Islands,* adopting the tercet to establish vital connections between subject, object of love, and the outer world. Merwin's attempt at wholeness, however, does not contradict his desire for infinity. Though the poetic form is complete and finite, it cannot contain all significations of the Other functioning as the addressee: "you avoid the words / about you / like a mountain goat," or, "If I were to talk of you / how would anyone know / what the words meant" (*FI* 57, 66). Essentially, human language is unable to comprehend and circumscribe this *you*—not necessarily Dana Naone, Merwin's lover at the time—but any sublimated Other whom the poet has to "look for," not in order to find but to sustain the pure act of looking.

Irreducible exteriority invariably enters the erotic relationship. Merwin's is not one of those Renaissance pastorals like Christopher Marlowe's "The Passionate Shepherd to His Love," in which nature is reduced to the role of a handmaid in the love scene. In *Finding the Islands*, Merwin relies on the revelatory power of nature, not only to sublimate the sexual drive but also to diffuse and expand eroticism, blurring the boundary between love and spiritual ecstasy. The love scene can be very raw yet full of spiritual illuminations:

we go up to a cold high lake
and make love
before dark. (*FI* 42)

The coldness of the lake and the burning of human desire form such a sharp contrast that the Romantic projection of human feelings into nature is largely suspended; instead, here we have Nature as the uncanny Other nonchalantly watching the lovemaking. Echoing the "dark springs," the slant rhyme of *lake*/*dark* implies the allurement of death, the dissolution of self in face of mysteriously Deep Nature, or Deep Time that "warps our sense of indebtedness to earth forces and creatures past, present, and future" (Ginn et al. 214). This tercet impresses readers for its precise, Zen-like combination of reality and semblance, Eros and death, time and timelessness, the boundaries of which are never clearly cut. In another poem, "February in the Valley," nature again enters the scene of lovemaking in a highly ambiguous way:

It is winter still
but this morning while
we made love the rose opened. (*FI* 65)

Instead of comparing his beloved to a rose, Merwin synchronizes the act of lovemaking with the opening of the rose. Does love cause the rose to open? Or is it a pure coincidence? Merwin only juxtaposes the two acts to suggest some uncanny relation between nature and erotic love. The other tercet continues to explore this link in a dreamlike setting:

> as we enter
> the tender rapids
> you look up and tell me you dreamed this.

Ecofeminists may read Merwin's poem as a feminist utopia, where "there is no hierarchy, among humans or between humans and animals, where people care for one another and for nature, where the earth and the forest retain their mystery, power and wholeness" (Plumwood 7). The uncanny power of Merwin's poem, however, reaches beyond this utopian vision that equates woman with nature. If Romantics feel empathy with nature all the time, Merwin treats nature as the unfathomable third agent binding/haunting the lovers. Here nature works as a fantastic screen to conceal as well as reveal the distance between the finite and the Infinite, lover and beloved. Merwin's is not such a case of empathy as *even nature feels our love,* but rather a deep endearment with nature: *because we both love nature, we can love each other.* In other words, Merwin seems to be making love to Mother Nature when he makes love to a woman.

This logic sounds strange, but it characterizes most of Merwin's love poems. With Merwin, the Nerudean telluric or earthly force serves to expand Eros to the extent that Nature is saturated with Eros: "the soft rain / for seven years I have felt your skin / and the light of your fingers"; "I saw the mountains / where we were going / where you would be"; "The same sunlight on the wet / banana leaves by the window / and on your wet skin" (*FI* 42, 56, 61). If Neruda starts a love poem with a direct declaration of love, Merwin begins his with a description of nature (rain, mountain, sunlight) to attenuate the erotic intent so as to make it a part of heaven and earth. Merwin lets Eros participate in the symphony of the infinite cosmos, not vice versa.

THE LADY SITTING IN WHITE

Cheri Davis notices that in Merwin's love poems "nature is experienced as it enhances the beauty of the beloved; it creates a dynamic environment for their love, while she is the inspired and inspiring center of the poem" (122), yet this "center" could be absent in a poem, and sometimes the beloved is more on the margin than at the center. If the ideal of love is infinitely dynamic as Nature, then all separation might be justified and made into love poetry with good reason. The essence of erotic love consists in the finite being's contact with infinity, which is paradoxically a noncontact (which is not sophistry, a mere turn of words): "In contact itself the touching and the touched separate, as though the touched moved off, was always already other, did not have anything common with me" (Levinas, *Otherwise* 86). A short poem in the early 1960s makes explicit that, in the dynamics of love, the Other keeps the self in silent bondage or even holds it hostage:

Your absence has gone through me
Like thread through a needle.
Everything I do is stitched with its color. ("Separation," *SF* 15)

Robert Scholes finds this imagery "irrational": "Our spatial-visual sense tells us that a person cannot be visualized as a kind of needle going around stitching things with a thread the color of absence" (75). Exploiting the aporia of representation, this surreal image actually evokes a sense of internalized loss analogous to melancholia in which "the subject possesses [the lost object] in the very mode of loss" (Žižek, *Plague* 195). The "thread" indicates the recognizable trace left by the beloved, who has passed through the self ("needle") both tenderly (thread and needle are intimate companions) and violently (stitching causes pain). Connected with absence, love itself forbids words, so the poet can only speak of the paraphernalia or the aftereffects of love and its colorless "color." In "St. Valentine's Eve," Merwin writes with similar wistfulness: "hearing you in the house / I think of the ways / you put yourself around me," and "I remember you talking / to me a long time in whispers / our early nights our late mornings" (*FI* 70, 71). The site hollowed out by the absence of the beloved is consequently filled up by acts of hearing, imagining, and remembering—all betray the momentariness of the love object.

Merwin broke up with Dana Naone at nearly the same time he published *Finding the Islands* in 1982. Read retrospectively, those short, intimate poems bear witness to the climax, as well as the end, of a love affair that started with *The Compass Flower* seven years earlier. In 1983, Merwin married Paula Schwartz, an editor of children's books. Merwin first met Paula in 1970 and was immediately attracted; in 1982, Merwin finally obtained a divorce from Dido Milroy, so when he met Paula again at a dinner party the old affection was stirred up. They married in a Buddhist ceremony. As Merwin enters old age, the love poems for his third wife in *The Rain in the Trees* (1988) are not ostensibly sensuous; they rather strike us as a man's late spiritual yearning for love—a man who, to quote John Keats, has fears that he may cease to be. The last phase of Merwin's love poems seems to combine the goddess image of Dido Milroy with the sensual-naturalistic tendency in poems about Dana Naone. Writing more simply and wistfully than ever, Merwin exhibits the virtuosity of a master reaping his final mellowness.

"Late Spring," the first poem in *The Rain in the Trees,* envisions a goddess whom the poet fantasizes to be lost yet found again. Merwin uses a vertiginous syntax to accumulate his anticipation toward his third and last *femme éternelle:* "Coming into the high room again after years / after oceans and shadows of hills and the sounds of lies / after losses and feet on stairs" (*RT* 3). The predominant iambics and the conspicuous sibilant rhyme of *s* bring out the weariness of a pilgrim who has traveled far and wide in quest of love. The poem proceeds:

after looking and mistakes and forgetting
turning there thinking to find
no one except those I knew

finally I saw you
sitting in white
already waiting.

The lady sitting in white is both Nature (late spring) impersonated as the title suggests and an easily recognizable reproduction of Dante's Beatrice, who also famously wears white in paradise.[5] Is she waiting for the poet to greet and take her? Merwin writes elsewhere that "all the time I love / most your own longing / drawing me" (*FI* 60). After so many detours of desire (looking, forgetting, turning, thinking, waiting), is Merwin finally able to obtain what he desires and thus be satisfied? Besides purity, whiteness connotes paleness, blankness, erasure. "The *way* of the tender consists in an extreme fragility, a vulnerability. It manifests itself at the limit of being and non-being, as a soft warmth where being dissipates into radiance" (Levinas, *Totality* 256). In Merwin's discourse, love is seen as a faith in the invisible, the nonbeing, a pure anticipation for exteriority shown toward the other person who remains shielded from the view: "you of whom I had heard / with my own ears since the beginning / for whom more than once / I had opened the door / believing you were not far" (*RT* 3). To open the door repetitively for the Other, whom one has heard of "since the beginning," bespeaks all the fantasies in a romantic relationship. Merwin suggests that it is the proximity rather than self-assured understanding of the beloved that arouses this uncontainable longing.

Merwin's portrait of the distant female figure follows the tradition of courtly love which flourished in twelfth-century France. During his Princeton days, Merwin had developed a strong interest in Provençal troubadour poetry, so after graduation, partly influenced by Ezra Pound, he decided to go to southern France to study the poetry of Bernart de Ventadorn and chronicled the whole event in *The Mays of Ventadorn* (2002).[6] In this book Merwin highly appreciates Bernart's love poems, in which separation, loss, and lamentation are expressed in a limpid, artless diction. While he admires the "musical transparency" (*MV* 135) of Bernart's poems, Merwin is mainly attracted to the distance between self and Other in troubadour poetry: "The recurring burden of Bernart's song is distance . . . distance between the lover and the beloved . . . and *amor de lonh* (far away love) became essential to the tradition of the troubadours. Distance is a measure of absence. Even in Guilhem's love poem with its candid sensuality, the beloved is out of reach, too far to hear him, there is no message from her, he remembers another time when they were together" (*MV* 124). In a rather Levinasian formulation, the desired one, as for both Merwin and troubadour practitioners, Pound's "Cino" included,[7] is incessantly slipping away, for the norm of love poetry resides not in union but in separation. There is the measure of distance between desire and the desired; "no way to obtain what you desire" (*MV* 125), as Merwin quotes from Ibn Hazm's treatise on love, *The Dove's Neck-Ring*. All troubadour poetry can be reckoned as a passionate movement of signifiers to approach the enigmatic woman: "Courtly love has remained enigmatic" (Lacan, *Seminar XX* 86), partly because the love object has been divested of any identifiable particularities and thus becomes an object-in-itself.

In *The Rain in the Trees*, Merwin often associates woman with the cycle of seasons and years, identifying her with the origin of temporality. In "The Sound of the Light," Merwin chants a haunting litany of time and age:

> it is the year in which you are sitting there as you are
> in the morning speaking to me and I hear
> you through the burning day and I touch you
> to be sure and there is time there is still time. (*RT* 32)

The contact (touching, hearing) engenders a projection of the self, an instance of ecstasy that throws the speaker into the expectation of becoming, although he realizes that there is not much time left for that becoming. Echoing "Late Spring," *you* here remain indefinite: Merwin seems to refer to both the natural light as the title suggests and the beloved person, Paula Schwartz, his third wife, to whom the book is dedicated. The poet's desire for the Other is literally "blind," in that he does not describe her particularities, nor can he see her (the transparent light). In the poem, all communications are unilateral as the poet only receives silent signals from the woman/light and has to interpret them by his own efforts.

If Lacan's claim is true—femininity is subjectivity proper because "Woman has a relation to the signifier of that Other, insofar as, qua Other, it can but remain forever Other" (*Seminar XX* 81)—then it becomes understandable why Merwin anticipates his female partner and empathizes that "togetherness" so fervently. Through an imaginary union with the woman, Merwin could obtain a kind of fortitude to transcend the rigid social order organized by phallic power so as to access the Other jouissance—an ecstatic enjoyment beyond social recognition and authorization. The goddess of love creates out of raw nature an Edenic site where being-toward-death is replaced by being-toward-infinity. Dasein is no longer conceived as burdened by care and death in an existentialistic framework but as an existent that enjoys life by living on the raw elements of nature. In "Anniversary on the Island," Merwin celebrates the isolated, independent life brought about by love alone:

> day after day we wake to the island
> the light rises through the drops on the leaves
> and we remember like birds where we are
> night after night we touch the dark island
> that once we set out for. (*RT* 34)

The proximity of the beloved is supposed to bring ecstatic immersion and personal freedom to the self. As "we touch the dark island," a new configuration between human and nature is also formed via a communication different in species (as birds "touching" the island).

Unlike his earlier poems on islands, in *The Rain in the Trees* Merwin does not so much worship the natural landscape as being like the female body as attending to how time constantly renews itself in this fantastic space inhabited by lovers alone. In "Noah's Raven," a poem in the apocalyptical 1960s, the raven regretted having returned to the old, cor-rupt world.[8] After Merwin finally settled down on Maui with Paula, the couple lived like two survivors after the biblical flood, "remember[ing] like birds where we are" (RT 34). They are the ravens that, enjoying themselves in the new world, have forgotten to return to the old one. The poetic spirit is thus sustained and strengthened by this non-phallic, nonreproductive, autoerotic enjoyment:

> and lie still at last with the island in our arms
> hearing the leaves and the breathing shore
> there are no years any more
> only the one mountain
> and on all sides the sea that brought us. (RT 34)

In this secluded garden of love created *ex nihilo*, human libido is liber-ated from the "performance principle" of the capitalistic society and undergoes a "non-repressive sublimation" (170) as pointed out by Her-bert Marcuse in *Eros and Civilization* (1955), a book that prophesied the liberation of Eros in Europe and the United States in the 1960s. In Merwin's case, historical time is canceled out by sensuous moments as the poet attempts to diffuse Eros to the fullest degree, envisioning, fan-tasizing a newly found world where social prohibitions are foreclosed. Anyone familiar with psychoanalysis might know that foreclosure trig-gers psychosis, so foreclosure is in fact a more violent act than repres-sion.[9] Merwin's love poems thus are more "violent" than, for example, Allen Ginsberg's *Howl* (1956), for Merwin does not directly criticize the technocratic, postindustrial US society—he seems to live with it (if not outside it) by virtue of Eros and its fantasies.

Merwin's obsessions with the receding female figure and feminine jouissance are partly influenced by his relationship with his mother, from whom he felt helplessly alienated throughout his adult life, as he reminisces in an essay "La Pia": "But beyond the day by day aspect of her existence, which she made over to us consciously, proudly, without fail—though not without moments of resentment—there was always a trackless, twilit, secret country open to no one" (*UO* 218). Echoing Freud's remark that feminine sexuality is a dark continent and Lacan's that woman has a kind of jouissance all to herself, Merwin's sad admission sheds light on the entanglement of love, desire, enjoyment, and knowledge in his love poetry. Theoretically, it is because the m(Other) as the first love object remains inaccessible ("secret") that Merwin has to invoke her traces repeatedly in poetry. The "trackless, twilit, secret country" provides a poetic illumination on the dark zone of feminine jouissance.[10]

Merwin's mother here, and elsewhere too, represents a locus of knowledge, which, like a door left ajar, only admits a glimpse from the outside. Merwin's love poems thus can be read as a series of transferential attempts to retouch his mother's "twilit country," to overcome alienation. After his father's death in the late 1970s, Merwin tried to talk more candidly with his mother, only to find that "we can mention almost nothing of our own intimate lives, hers or mine. . . . I have grown up in the habit of being so reticent with her, that it cannot be easy now to find what we want to say to each other" (*UO* 204). But very soon Merwin would admit that the desire for knowledge was only his: "When I think of what I want to ask her now, I realize, not for the first time, that the wish to hear, the hankering for information, are almost wholly mine" (220). Whenever Merwin writes on love/nature, there's always the silent mother figure who keeps withdrawing, beckoning. In a typical late poem on erotic love, Merwin's speaker is again engaged in "touching the apricots in your skin / or tasting in your mouth the sun in the apricots" (*RT* 4) while indicating that this ravishing taste of apricots, as Merwin tells in a family poem "Apparitions," conjures up the ghost of his mother:

I wait for the smell   of parsley and almonds
   that I never imagined   otherwise than as hers. (*FH* 115)

What can be more intimate, extimate, tantalizing, agonizing, and haunting for a child than the mother's smell? This reading is not to reassert the Oedipal structure and exclude the possibility that in nonnuclear families many children may have two mothers, two fathers, or no mother at all; rather, it aims to bring to light how poetic jouissance for Merwin is already jouissance *without* knowledge. The scents of parsley, apricots, and almonds here function as the lure (the residue) of the female Other who endlessly enchants a poet's creative act. Merwin cannot track the "secret country" of nature, mother, and lover because what he has is only this fragile trace, this endless, fantastic memory/anticipation, a waiting for the (m)Other—the lady "sitting in white."

"THE MOMENT OF GREEN": MERWIN'S EROTICIZATION OF FLORA

Merwin's shift to the sensual, erotic mode coincides with his increasing interest in nature after the mid-1970s; he fantasizes about both nature and women, confusing them intentionally until one cannot be differentiated from the other. The rivers, plants, lakes, birds, and foxes all bear traces of the memory of love and enter into Merwin's poetry as channels of libidinal cathexes. It is true that Merwin is zealous about ecology, but his invocations of nature seem so compulsory that they border on hallucinatory symptoms haunting a clearly defined "nature poetry." He caresses trees and plants as if caressing a woman; he aches for rivers and lakes as if they were his living lovers. For Merwin, nature in its luxuriance has become that which entices yet constantly bursts from his grasp. In this sense Merwin's fascination with nature is *sexual,* if we include in the category of sex any repeatedly failed action to obtain the desired object (Žižek, *Plague* 71–72). Here, Merwin has anticipated Queer Ecology that sees natural spaces as basically gendered or sexualized; Merwin's sensual mode, however, promises to offer a non-phallic, non-masculine, extimate way of encountering nature.

In the early 1970s, Merwin dallied with the eroticization of flora in a luxurious, if not lustful, manner. Contrasting with the painful tone of most poems from that same period, "Marietta," a narrative in *The Miner's Pale Children* (1970), brings to light the other side of Merwin: warm, delightful, vulgarly sensuous. It manifests Merwin's unquenchable longing for the natural world, where both his own and Other's desire are put on stage. The narrator journeys through a mysterious lane that "draws near to the edge of the lake" (*BF* 53). Even before meeting the hostess, the narrator has already felt the assault of desire: he has felt his "stomach contract at the nearness of the lake" (53). Marietta, like Virgin Mary, is a mysterious figure who has both "the heavy but graceful figure" of a woman and a face "like a girl's" (54). She embodies the spirit that calls the poet to enjoy the natural elements:

> Then if it's an even day she leads you . . . into the woods. . . . leads you out into the little clearing by the backwater. . . . the woods are lush and green. The path goes on to the right through more woods, around the edge of the water, where it's almost dark. And in front of you there are more trees, looking as though they grew out of a black stretch of the water itself, which is connected with the lake and the light only by a narrow inlet. (54)

The luxuriant plants beside the water again allude to the vast reservoir of id—unbridled sexual energy and fantasies. Under the guidance of Marietta, the narrator comes through the dark forest and finally meets his Beatrice—Flora, "a girl in a white dress."

The narrative entices readers with its raw, mythic flavor, as Flora perfectly combines sensuous charm with natural intelligence like Mother Nature herself (Spinoza would say nature has both substance and thought, body and mind). Flora seduces the speaker by apparently not seducing him at all: "You can see the undersides of her thighs as she sits looking around. . . . She leans forward with her elbows on her knees and you can look down inside the opening of the front of her dress into the dark cleft between her breasts" (*BF* 55). The irony is that the other's eyes also gaze at the voyeur; Flora returns the gaze like a mirror: "She sees that you're looking" and "she keeps looking at you." Flora attracts the male gaze by her apparent nonsurprise and nonaction ("smiles," "doesn't move at all," "doesn't seem to notice," "goes on smiling"). Since her indefinite desire still baffles the speaker, the man, not the woman, is always the loser in this Merwinesque play of gazes. He fumbles and fidgets before a more knowledgeable female partner: "you hear a beating in your throat. . . . your mouth is dry and corners [of eyes] are stiff." The passive initiative of Flora impels readers to regard her as nature writ small, as she opens herself richly, unpretentiously, and unconsciously: "She undoes the button herself."

The contrast between Flora's virtuosity in the affair of love and the male narrator's utter inexperience is spread out in a breathless and nakedly sensual paragraph. Flora finally teaches the lesson of love to the man who is already riddled with desire—as W. B. Yeats, learning of Maud Gonne's marriage with John MacBride, was "riddled with light" (125). Flora reveals to the eager amour her mysteries one by one:

> And then you undo a button at her waist and slide your hand in where it's warm and feels as though it were shining. You know your hand is cold, and you're shivering harder. You kiss again, and start to undo each other's clothes while you're kissing, and only stop when you have to, so that she can slip out of her dress and her bra while you watch, taking off your shirt and your shoes and pants. You look at her, and then, looking straight at you, she slowly pulls off her underpants and you pull off yours, with your throat almost closed up, and you let your eyes rest on the mound of brown hair and then lie down beside her and from there on start to act as though you knew what to do with everything. And she knows. (BF 56)

Presupposing the woman to possess more knowledge on love ("she knows"), Merwin's speaker follows her silent instructions like a good student until he obtains certain subjectivity ("act as though you knew what to do with everything").

This poetic narrative reveals the inherent sexual fantasies in Merwin's much-celebrated nature writings after the mid-1970s. The "oneness" Merwin achieves through his encounters with woman/nature seems to be a fantasy constructed to integrate/subjectivize the traces—the silent teachings and significations—of infinite nature. At the end of "Marietta," Merwin tells us that Flora lives upstairs, reading books most of the time, while "Your chest thumps as you walk across to the door and look up the stairs" (*BF* 57). The act of looking up, the stairs that vaguely recall the Jacob's Ladder that reaches to heaven,[11] and the "thumping chest"— all suggest Flora to be enwrapped in mystery, despite her erotic games with the male narrator, who remains, to borrow from Roland Barthes's discourse on love, "the sole witness of [his own] lunacy" (*Lover's Discourse* 23).

"Marietta" foretells a series of nature poems that witness Merwin's engagement with the regional plants in Hawaii from the late 1970s to the present. In the rain forests, Merwin rediscovers the feminine who resists any nomenclature as Flora does. (Although the narrator names the girl "Flora," he never fully penetrates the enigma behind the name.) The unnamable aspect of nature compels the poet to adopt a self-defeating posture concerning language and signification. Ecologically, we lose the names because the forest is not there to name: "While Keats wrote they were cutting down the sandalwood forests" (*RT* 66). Biological extinction ushers in linguistic extinction, as Aaron Moe reminds us; after all the trees were cut down, "everything was explained in another language" (*RT* 66). Merwin conceives of the trees as belonging to a Deep Past whose knowledge is even denied to his parents. "Neither my father nor my mother knew / the names of the trees" (6). Constituting an unknown dimension or phase of existence, the archaic green obsesses Merwin in its inexplicable calling (like that of Marietta) that disrupts and traumatizes the poet's quotidian life.

"The Moment of Green," one of the several long narrative poems in *Travels* (1993), dramatizes a rather fatal call from the green. The title serves as an apt epithet for Merwin's late work, fully revealing his phenomenal effort to relive in poetry the momentary, traumatic encounter with nature. The protagonist here is Gregorio Gregorievich Bondar (1881–1959), a botanist from Poltava, Russia. In Merwin's account, Bondar, fascinated with natural plants, leaves Russia to study botany at European universities and then goes to Brazil to "work in plant pathology" (*T* 79). He returns to Russia in 1916 during World War I without apparent reason and is thus suspected by Russian authorities to be a spy. Bondar's obsession and eroticization of flora clearly mirror Merwin's own engagement, so when Bondar recalls the regional woods in Poltava, we are not surprised to learn that

> ... his hand grew
> pictures of her he traced the legs
> of her grasses lengthening he
> followed the lace of her veins to
> find where they opened from he drew
> the bees in her flowers and on
> her leaves the cicada one of
> her voices and the grasshopper
> part cloud part paper. ... (*T* 77)

Blending human characteristics with impersonal nature, these lines are quite consistent with Merwin's naturalistic fantasy about Dido Milroy in "Canso," Dana Naone in *Finding the Islands,* and Flora in "Marietta." The essence/center of nature is endlessly deferred on the synecdochic chain (legs, lace, veins, voice, grasses, bees, flowers, leaves, cicada, grasshopper, cloud) that conflates sexual allurements with natural representation.

Leonard Scigaj usefully calls our attention to Merwin's defamiliarization of "grew" instead of "drew," which reveals Bondar's anxiety to know nature, "that other he felt so compelled to bond with, until all distance vanishes" (209). Such an infinitesimal distance from nature-Other nevertheless is all that motivates Bondar's seemingly irrational decision to return to Russia during the war. Bondar is obsessed with what he could never decipher in the forest of his homeland: the illusory calling of unexplored nature. After he "had // circled the globe" Bondar comes back to see

> ... the molten plain flowing past
> the rim of forest and he heard

from the leaves the shimmer of sound
he recognized though he could not
begin to decipher it or
guess who it was intended for
but he heard that it was what he
had to go on listening to. (*T* 81)

This is what the botanist, risking his life, has come back for: "the shimmer of sound," neither an audible sound nor complete silence but a
ghostly shimmer—the Lacanian gaze as the love object. Borrowing from
Jean-Paul Sartre, Lacan elaborates on the gaze as "the sound of rustling
leaves, suddenly heard while out hunting" (*Seminar XI* 84). The gaze
originates not from the subject's eyes observing the Other but from an
imaginary feeling of being watched by this Other. Like a neurotic suffering from auditory hallucinations, Merwin's Bondar posits an imaginary, indecipherable gaze from the beloved flora and feels compelled to
listen to it repeatedly, desperately. This amorously cathected "shimmer"
transcends mortality and historicity, crossing over the speaker's symbolic world toward the unknown parts of nature, as he so marvels at its
indestructability: "it went on after the trees / fell after deaths after learning / after everything had been said" (*T* 82). "The Moment of Green"
thus establishes a dialectical bond between man and nature, pushing
one's love for nature to the risk of dying for it. The ecological bond here
has become a "fierce devotion" that ignores all impediments in its own
dangerous jouissance. "So he had gone home to be shot" (76), Merwin
has announced Bondar's doom at the very beginning of the poem.

Bondar is only one of the many figures seduced, tormented, and
infinitized by the flora. In "Cinchona," another historical narrative in
Travels, Merwin recounts the colonialists' mad desire for the precious
plants in Peru in the seventeenth century.[12] Here we meet another of
Merwin's botanists, the Englishman Richard Spruce, who feverishly
launches one expedition after another to Peru in order to transplant
cinchona, which has been discovered by the Europeans as a cure for
fever, to India. The irony is striking, clearly echoing "The Judgment of

Paris," in which Helen gathers flowers "whose roots are said to dispel pain" (*SF* 148). The fever-curing cinchona has become "something of value / like gold":

> sought stripped shipped
> to be sold in Spain carried by
> missionaries defended fought over
> killed for. (*T* 45)

Richard Spruce's motivation in the mission, however, is ambiguous: officially it is "for the sake of the [British] / empire," while privately it satisfies "his devotion to / unknown flora." Spurred by desire for botanical knowledge, Spruce keeps planning the excursion in spite of his "dubious health," for "he was sick again deaf / in left ear unable to walk or sit / without / great pain" (*T* 46, 48). Sick as he is, Spruce takes good care of the seedlings and cuttings, putting them on

> shaded beds to be kept watered
> by hand to root them then pack them in earth
> they knew
> and into baskets for
> the muleback journey over the mountains
> then into cases on the raft. . . . (*T* 48)

In these breathless and heavily enjambed lines, Merwin constructs a subject who, instead of being the master of the plant, has been continuously subjected to the plant. In a stroke of irony, Spruce, like Bondar, has suffered from that which he so loved.

In this dreamlike text, Merwin mercilessly exploits the aftereffects of Spruce's contact with cinchona, the unknown flora. Spellbound by "the daily taste of that powdered bark," Spruce and his team defy every hardship and danger in escorting the seedlings: in the heavy rain, they cross the "savage" river, and then

a narrow sluice between snatching
thickets the current at bends smashing them
three times
into the bank with such force
that the cabin collapsed and their pilot
once was swung by a branch
over the roaring water. . . . (*T* 48–49)

Later, Spruce and his men

grope[d] through the splintered bodies of trees
that had saved their lives and to feel the cases
of cuttings as though they were touching bones
of their own after a fall. . . . (*T* 49)

These lines recall Eve, about whom Adam once said: "This is now bone of my bones, and flesh of my flesh" (Genesis 2. 23). Like Eve, the cinchona is all that is left for Spruce—the adamant Adam who has lost his paradise at home—to hold onto in the dangerous forests of Latin America, for the cinchona is both his salvation and his doom. Like Bondar, Spruce and his team are also unable to provide a reason for their actions and sufferings. Traumatized by the flora, Spruce and Bondar obtain their subjectivity as agents of free choice and carry that choice to its tragic yet logical end.

The "undetermined fever" has driven many of Merwin's naturalists and botanists into conducting zealous researches on plants and flowers, all with unhappy results. In "The Blind Seer of Ambon," Merwin laments the fate of German botanist Georg Eberhard Rumpf (1627–1702), who is so devoted to the study of the flora of the East Indies—with "tenacity and love" as Scigaj says (205)—that he carries on the project, disregarding consecutive personal catastrophes. In the process of composing *The Ambonese Herbal*, a catalog covering more than 1,200 species of plants and 350 hand-drawn illustrations, Rumpf is first struck by blindness, then by an earthquake that takes away his wife and daughter, and lastly by a fire that destroys almost all of his illustrations. Like Cassandra, who could literally hear the future though no one believed her, after such dire losses Rumpf, "the blind seer of Ambon," is finally compensated by a divine ability of hearing:

> I take a shell in my hand
> new to itself and to me
> I feel the thinness the warmth and the cold
> I listen to the water
> which is the story welling up
> I remember the colors and their lives
> everything takes me by surprise
> it is all awake in the darkness. (*T* 4)

After so many vicissitudes, Rumpf has strangely retained that freshness ("new . . . to me," "everything takes me by surprise") of the natural life as if meeting it for the first time, and by listening to it he achieves a unique salvation from Nature. In fact, Rumpf readily accepts the imaginary calling from nature-Other, deeming it "my true calling" and admitting that his engagement with flora is hardly understood by his contemporaries: "I may have seemed somewhat strange / caring in my own time for living things / with no value that we know" (*T* 3). Unlike Richard Spruce, who adventures to grab the precious medicinal bark for the empire, Rumpf perseveres in a personal project that has no immediate use-value for the European colonialists. When Rumpf says, "I named for my wife a flower" (*T* 3), he explicitly equates flora with the beloved.

In his ecstatic description of natural life, Merwin constantly blends erotic desire with spiritual salvation. If he sees heaven in a wild flower, this heaven is populated not by angels but by charming, exuberant life-forces. In *Travels,* Merwin often throws away the poetic mask and meditates with unreserved passion on the raw forces of nature. Trees and flowers belong to an Edenic site where all is innocent—as innocent as the cinchona ignorant of the feverishly grabbing hands. In "The Palms,"

Merwin celebrates the telluric force of palm flowers and their dark, non-human vitality:

> they stand as though they had no secrets
> and one by one the flowers emerge from the sheaths
> into the air
> where the other flowers are
> it happens in silence except for the wind
> often it happens in the dark
> with the earth carrying the sound of water. (*T* 87)

A Freudian reading quickly reveals the sexual import in these lines: the opening flower symbolizes the female sexual organ while the "dark" water, mother's womb, reminds us of "the bronze ferns older than seeing / unfurling above the dark springs" (*FH* 39) and also the deep, luxuriant woods found in the previously discussed prose poem "Marietta." Merwin seems to derive unfathomable joy from such an encounter with the dark forces, marveling, as Rumpf once did, that "everything takes me by surprise / it is all awake in the darkness" (*T* 4), as if there is *something* in the flower that always eludes the poet and thus entices him. In another narrative poem, "Manini,"[13] the protagonist holds pearls between his fingers and similarly remarks: "there are the colors / once more and the veiled light I am looking for / warm in my touch again and still evading me" (*T* 8). What evades Manini evades Merwin as well.

Since settling down in Hawaii in the mid-1970s, Merwin has increasingly imagined or posited the omniscience of flora: she possesses a knowledge that evades him. In light of Lacan's theorem that the subject tends to fall in love with whomever he supposes to have more knowledge (*Seminar XI* 232), Merwin's obsession with the natural life on the island can be read as such a case of transference: the poet transfers his desire for the enigmatic (m)Other to the trees and flowers. In "Field Mushrooms," the poet's and the poem's desire circulates around the knowing yet unknowable flora:

I went on finding them
always at evening
coming to recognize a depth
in the shade of oaks and chestnuts
a quickening in the moss year after year
a suggestion of burning
signs of something already there in its own place
a texture of flesh
scarcely born
full of the knowledge of darkness. (*T* 91)

The mushrooms hide deeply among oaks and chestnuts, avoiding the light of human knowledge ("always at evening"), and can only be found by those who ardently seek them. As Aaron Moe has observed, in many of Merwin's poems the "stirrings of *poiesis* begin through listening to the elemental forces of the earth, the organic growth of plants, and bodily *poiesis* of animals" (94). Here, the "quickening" and "burning" of the mushrooms' "texture of flesh" not only symbolize the raw life-energy or the "bodily *poiesis*" of nature but also make visible Merwin's own libidinal drive: What really quickens and burns therefore is more than the mushrooms in the moss but the poet's own desire for Nature as the locus of "the knowledge of darkness." Similar to Gary Snyder, who brackets Nature phenomenologically,[14] Merwin has been evoking the phantoms of nature instead of trying to penetrate into its secret in the way of a scientist. Nature becomes this infinitely alien Thing that the subject can never categorize and subjectivize, because it is no-thing at all, only "scarcely born": "a *mesh,* a nontotalizable, open-ended concatenation of interrelations that blur and confound boundaries at practically any level" (Morton, "Queer Ecology" 275).

Merwin therefore not only recognizes the alterity of nature but exhibits a pathological fixation on that alterity which has its own dimension/phase of space-time. The liberating potential of poetry exactly comes from this touching of the unrealized alterity:

let me love what I cannot know
as the man born blind may love color
until all that he loves
fills him with color. ("To the Rain," *SF* 288)

Here Merwin's prayer to the rain presents "a love so fierce that it cannot be satisfied either with the mimetic desire of what it projects another to be or with the disinterested arrogance of presuming another merely existing to himself," so the poem's "rage is for the sameness" (Watkins 198). In a Pauline manner, Merwin urges us to love the unknown first and not to seek to understand it because understanding already connotes mastery and cognitive limitation. Also, Merwin urges us to be open for love, since love itself is nothing but this unconditional opening toward the Other—not the manipulable, exploitable other, the other as self-image, but the infinite Other that paradoxically is in the self but more than the self, *atopos,* possessing "a ceaselessly unforeseen originality" (Barthes, *Lover's Discourse* 34). By fostering the latent, emerging object in the self until it overflows one's consciousness, we may come to realize the inherent arbitrariness of signs, symbols, orders, and generally, all products of perceptual apparatus. This embracing of an unknown love/nature, tactless or blind at first sight, would commit the self in a reattachment to an alterity as to allow us to reinvest ourselves in the realm of the Real—the coming-into-existence of what endlessly haunts the natural, the social, and the logical.

4

WAKE UP IN A WORLD OF LIGHT

Memory, Grief, and Temporality in
Merwin's Later Writings

Before his passing in 2019, Merwin had come to resemble what David Biespiel, in a review of *Migration: New and Selected Poems* (2005), calls "poetry's Iron Man" (137): since *A Mask for Janus* (1952), Merwin has published nearly sixty volumes of poetry, prose, and translation, and his work has recently been canonized by the Library of America into a two-volume *Collected Poems* (2013). Yet unlike the critics who seek either to defend a poetics of absence/deconstruction in Merwin's middle period (Nelson, Altieri) or to advocate a poetics of ecology in his later work (Frazier, Scigaj, Bryson), Biespiel is mainly troubled by the lack of expressive urgency in Merwin's later output, as it can be difficult, as Biespiel says, to "peel away the enormous reputation [Merwin] has and get a handle on the work that's actually important" (137). Since the "handle" or the real key in Merwin's later poetry seems missing, Biespiel could dismiss Merwin's *Vixen* (1996), *The River Sound* (1999), and *The Pupil* (2001) as "placid and underwhelming": Merwin's vision in these books, he contends, has simply blurred and become inconsequential (141–42). Biespiel's criticism reflects a general tendency to read Merwin's later poetry in comparison with his earlier vacuum-driven style (particularly from the 1960s and 1970s) and to draw conclusions based on the quality of poetic visions and tones—how Merwinesque they are, that is, how acutely, surreally, and consistently they reveal our limitations as historical beings. Yet as self-manifesting temporality, history is only the most visible force that goes into the shaping of any individual or collective identity—the facade of time. Though the other side of existence looms large on the periphery of human perception, we fall short of its revelation and grace in that our reading of this alterity is always already historicized or marked by a historical necessity finally attributed to a certain national or global agenda.[1]

A certain thematic continuity informs Merwin's writing from the 1950s to the present: a vast incantation of unapparent realities (Nature is one of them, just as the old way of life is another) that tend to disappear from the current technocratic society. From *A Mask for Janus* (1952) to *Garden Time* (2016), Merwin has been conjuring and interrogating *the other side* of rationalized existence, searching for a more originary mode of being that resists/escapes the hegemony of totalized history—a signifying process that is all too human. Anonymity has remained the norm, and naming has remained at best a designation aware of its own limit. The urge to enunciate and evoke the diachronic origins that call into question the priority as well as the linearity of both personal and national histories imbues much of Merwin's writings after the death of his parents in the late 1970s.

After joyful, lavish invocations of nature, Merwin's later poetry now gives an acute sense of loss and grief, as his family losses joined hand with the loss of the earth: "If only you had written our language / we would have remembered how you died" (*RT* 68). Foreclosing the Name of the Father, the very foundation of law that initiates a subject into symbolic exchange and the network of signification, Merwin has come to search for a forlorn joy through incoherent memory traces. His transparent, unadorned language apprehends the final coming of what is essentially unnamable. Focusing on Merwin's later output, including his autobiographical works, *The Unframed Originals* (1982) and *Summer Doorways* (2005), I will employ psychoanalysis, as suggested by Mieke Bal's "semiotic model," in deciphering "the traces of the unconscious and the forms it takes which disturbs coherency" (87). I hope to elicit the latent urgency in Merwin's later work, which in its unassuming yet haunting form expresses something profoundly disturbing: loss, grief, the arrival of timelessness. Psychically, late Merwin exhibits a strong tendency to work through the mourning for his father's death (also, for the death of the Name-of-the-Father that supports rules and norms), which he achieves by resorting to ancestral origins that can only be accessed by an increasingly primordial memory. Merwin's early critique of paternal restriction, for example, "The Drunk in the Furnace" (1960), has been reversed into an uncontainable grief for the very lack/loss of paternal love, and ultimately, for time itself, although the constant renewal of time promises to end the grief for what is already lost in time.

"THAT PATCH OF SUNLIGHT": MERWIN'S FATHER COMPLEX

Critics clearly see the influence of a "prohibitive" father on Merwin's later writings. Examining one of Merwin's autobiographical poems from *Opening the Hand* (1983), Thomas B. Byers discerns that Merwin's father's "constant messages were restriction and control," and "even the poet's powerful ecological warnings may descend in part from his father's constant strictures against touching anything" ("Present Voices," 256). H. L. Hix compares the father-son relationship in *The Unframed Originals* to one between Adam and God: "Merwin playing the role of Adam/Eve, his father playing a strict God," reading the pattern of many of Merwin's "rebellious" poems as "the struggle between liberty and authority" (*Understanding* 114, 116). Both commentators have reduced the father's image to a stern God, a superego that prohibits and condemns. Merwin's relationship with his father, however, could be more complicated, as few critics have noticed that Merwin's father, though severe and oppressive, remains *distant* most of the time. He was "preoccupied and moody, off in his own projects and considerations," "did not normally give any thought to my company, and occasionally spoke of being much too busy for that"; summarily, "his attention to me was limited almost entirely to what I was forbidden to do" (*SD* 86, 27).

Reduced to its core, Merwin's relationship with his father is a curious mixture of both rebellion and reverence—a typical father complex. Sigmund Freud's study of the psychosis of Daniel Paul Schreber (1842–1911) offers the first detailed case of father complex that had triggered psychosis. Freud's study also brings out the interrelation between the image of sunlight and paternal function. In various delusional onsets, Schreber believes that the infinite and eternal "Rays of God" are talking to him, urging him to transform into a woman (Freud, *Three Case Histories* 95). Freud interprets Schreber's paranoia as a defense mechanism against homosexual wish-fantasies for his father (135). The sun, as Freud claims, represents a "sublimated symbol for the father," and Schreber's delusion of copulating with God can thus be interpreted as the return of his "unsatisfied homosexual affections" toward his father (130, 133). Reexamining Freud's explanation of the father complex in the Schreber case, Jacques Lacan, in *Seminar III: The Psychoses* (1955–56), proposes the foreclosure/rejection (*Verwerfung*) of the Name-of-the-Father, the phallic function, from the Symbolic as characteristic of the psychotic structure (143–57).

In her 1984 "Psychopoetics," an essay that attempts a major reevaluation of the longstanding conjunction of literature and psychoanalysis, Mieke Bal, following Shoshana Felman whom she quotes in the same article, cautions critics against using psychoanalysis as an "analogical model" because such a model only seeks to demonstrate that "a literary text displays features of the psychoanalytical process," neglecting the text's potential to modify or alter that process (83). Bal suggests that this relation be "reversed" into seeing those psychoanalytical processes, such as transference or repression, as problematic concepts instead of "staged in the text" (83). In order to gain certain "surplus knowledge" rather than confirm the psychoanalytical conclusions, critics are invited to consider how to "make explicit [the] ways the presumed subject exposes itself as existing through various psychoanalytically theorized problems" (84).

Merwin's account of his father is more than "analogical" to Schreber's complaint that his God "does not understand living men" and "was not really acquainted with living men" (Freud, *Three Case Histories* 100). It modifies the Schreber case by specifying what a functional subject—unlike Schreber, Merwin becomes neither paranoiac nor delusional out of imagined paternal oppression, though he has been deeply troubled by his relationship with his father—can do by means of poetic utterance. In Merwin's case, helpless distance from the father predominates, and it is the father's inattention or indifference rather than his oppression that truly chagrins the child. During World War II, Merwin's father was absent, serving as a chaplain in the army, and after he came back, Merwin, with the increase of age and wisdom, no longer saw him as a restrictive, punishing God but as an Other who lacked something himself, "distant, but helplessly so, without hostility, like someone adrift in himself without oars" (SD 85). Behind the paternal metaphor, or the Name-of-the-Father, a signifier "replete with cultural and religious significance" (Grigg 9) that normalizes and regulates a social being's desire, Merwin discerns the father in reality as lacking, helpless, and even impotent.

Yet to read Merwin's ambivalent biographical account of his father is very much like reading another Schreber case. Merwin's complaint about his father's neglect, "inadequacy," and "loneliness" (SD 86), as revealed by Freudian discourse, can be readily interpreted as a complaint of love, in which the poet laments his inability to help his father out. When his father, returning from the war, proposed to spend some time together to remedy alienation, Merwin admitted that he felt "hot in the face, and uncomfortable," and to make the drama of love more poignant and disappointing, "when the real time together started he seemed to have forgotten it, and to have returned to his distant and unapproachable self" (86). In the Oedipal stage, we witness not only a child's resentment and antagonism toward the father, as critics are quick to find in Merwin's family poems (Hix, Understanding 119; Byers, "Present Voices" 264), but also the exaltation of and the identification with the father. Freud's studies on psychoneuroses indicate that the male child may unconsciously treat the father as a love object: the fear of the father accompanies the child's desire to satisfy him. For instance, the Wolfman's fear of being gobbled up by the wolfs in his dream, as Freud concludes by tortuous interpretations, can be taken as "the wish for coitus with the father"

(*Three Case Histories* 231). Schreber's psychotic visions also result from his roundabout defense against the homosexual wish-fantasy for the father (139–41).

Freud's view on family romance has been critiqued on different grounds,[2] yet here I am not using it to highlight young Merwin's symptomatic desire for his father, since according to psychoanalytical researches this desire is common for both the male and the female child (Geyskens 104–11).[3] This ambiguous, ticklish desire informs and structures Merwin's later work. Merwin's love for his father takes the negative form of rebellion in childhood; in youth and adulthood, distant sympathy has replaced the discontent; while after the father's death in 1977, mourning for the father comes to the foreground, which is when the loss of the love object is acutely felt in Merwin's later poetry. As if unconsciously working through the psychoanalytical problematic of the paternal function, in many poems on his father, Merwin associates paternal authority with the declining tendency of sunlight—the image of darkness, of *Dämmerung*. The twilit space excludes normally perceived reality and becomes the field where an acute sense of grief, as Russell Grigg says of psychic reality, "returns from outside the subject, as emanating from the real" (10).

In "Sunset Water," a poem from *Opening the Hand*, the speaker laments the death of the father with a haunting imagery of twilight coupled with water. As commonly found in defense mechanisms against paternal authority, Merwin posits a vulnerable and lacking father: "How white my father looked in the water / all his life he swam doggie paddle / holding hurried breaths steering an embarrassed smile" (106). Here Merwin turns the restrictions against the restrictive and distant father himself, relegating his status to a timid child faced with infinite nature. Unconscious revenge surely exists in these lines, but there is also certain sympathy for the father—"the undercurrent of tenderness," to borrow Byers's phrase ("Present Voices" 265)—as if the speaker, standing aside, wanted to help but failed to do so. As Edward Brunner observes, "Merwin's portrait of his father eludes caricature" ("*Opening the Hand*" 282); it rather reveals his profoundly contradictory feelings toward his father.

The second stanza of the poem reactivates the ghostly presence of the father, as if the finite father, father in flesh and blood, through his own death has become an infinite one. Now the son swims in this twilight zone saturated with the absence of his father:

> long after he has gone I rock in smooth waves near the edge
>   of the sea
> at the foot of a hill   I never saw before
> or so I imagine as the sun is setting
> sharp evening birds   and voices of children
> echo each other across the water. (*FH* 106)

In a stylistic discussion of these groups of poems, Brunner invites readers to see Merwin's use of the caesura as a way to "understand the ambivalent emotions that structure the powerful family poems in *Opening the Hand*" ("*Opening the Hand*" 277). The internal caesuras in this particular stanza have indeed smoothed over the traumatic memory of the father, making the old antagonism disappear in the gently rocking rhythms. The father's image is nowhere to be found in these lines but seems *everywhere:* in sunset, evening birds, voices of children, and even in seawater. All presences convey absence, loss, and grief. The last stanza of the poem consists of a single line: "one by one the red waves out of themselves reach through me" (*FH* 106). The Real qua the lost love object is felt in this incessant impact of waves ("one by one") and the emptiness of ego (*through* me, not *past* me),[4] as immersion in water and twilight has become a way of evoking as well as healing the longtime separation between the father and the son.

Merwin's obsession with the sunlight imagery, by effectuating a reaction-formation toward the severe yet distant father, offers an exposure of what otherwise would remain a dark realm: the psychotic-like paternal imagery of grief and melancholia. By introducing the *Fort/Da* play—the first creation of meaning through symbolization of the absent referent—of the sunlight, Merwin seems to escape and simultaneously get close to the father's image in order to subjectivize the latter's severity, inattention, departure, and final death as something he could not properly subjectivize. Merwin's mourning procedure therefore modifies the classical Oedipal model of the father and the son by introducing the poetic imagery of sunlight that dissolves restriction, repression, and antagonism. In "Still Morning," a poem from *The Shadow of Sirius* (2008), Merwin resorts to a primordial memory to transcend family genealogy:

and I am a child before there are words
arms are holding me up in a shadow
voices murmur in a shadow
as I watch one patch of sunlight moving
across the green carpet
in a building
gone long ago and all the voices
silent and each word they said in that time
silent now
while I go on seeing that patch of sunlight. (*SS* 7)

In this memory flash, Merwin travels back to the prelingual period when human signification and phallic function have not yet organized the child's perceptual framework. Because the young child's ego and its operational mechanisms are still immature, its psychic apparatus remains vulnerable to external stimulations that could leave long-lasting memory traces in the unconscious (*Penguin Freud Reader* 152). This patch of sunlight, this little piece of Nature, is one of the early stimulations that the poet cannot fully integrate through retroactive, poetic signification, for children always recognize the meaning of a symbol later than its first, natural emergence. When the passage of time has silenced all the living voices, that patch of sunlight qua the alien object stays to mobilize the poet's psychic energy. The title of the poem, "Still Morning," foretells the indestructibility of memory traces from childhood or what Jerry Harp terms "the sense of childhood timelessness" (178) if we understand *still* as the continuation of a condition.

Merwin thus has something to offer to psychoanalysis in his protean and polysemous use of the sunlight image. Biographically, this ghostly presence of light is directly related to Merwin's father, who in a sense had initiated the image in the poet's unconscious, while extra-biographically, it could well be a whimsical invention of memory since "human memory is always a matter of mediation; it is never entirely direct" (Harp 179). In a 2009 interview with Bill Moyers, Merwin recollects the event of the poem as his infant baptism in his father's church in New Jersey: "I remember being held up and watching the green carpet and that patch of sunlight" (CW 175), and this is how the sunlight image acquired its first paternal and ecclesiastical meaning. Usually, children begin to have their earliest memories between the age of two and four, but these memories of childhood, recollected in later life, could be based on "the principle of selection": we select those memory fragments—what Freud terms "screen memories"—that bear relations to our fantasies from a later period (Penguin Freud Reader 543). What we remember from childhood might be insignificant in itself, such as a patch of sunlight or a person's face, but it registers significant "thoughts and impressions from a later period" (553). This is how memory revises the event—by unconsciously creating a fixation, not on the past traumatic event itself (the exact moment of the event remains irretrievable), but on its selective associations (metonymies) that are deposited in the memory. In fact, Freud surmises that early childhood memory might be altogether "inaccessible in its original form"; he even doubts that we could have any conscious memories *from* childhood: "Perhaps we have only memories *of* childhood. These show us the first years of our lives not as they were, but as they appeared to us at later periods, when the memories were aroused. At these times of arousal the memories of childhood did not *emerge*, as one is accustomed to saying, but *were formed*" (559).

Freud's formulation of the "psychoanalytical memory" (Lacan, *Seminar III* 153) reveals that Merwin's remembrance of sunlight may not be an actual occurrence but a retroactively constructed image. In his autobiographical essay "The Skyline," from *Unframed Originals*, Merwin first admits that his baptism occurred when he was only "a few weeks old" (UO 101) and then confesses that it is "unlikely that the image [sunlight on the carpet] is an actual memory, but it remains clear, and whether it comes from a dream or from suggestions or from a glimpse of the occasion itself I cannot be sure" (102). Merwin might have selected the sunlight as one of his earliest memories out of its association with the sacred occasion and its symbolization of thoughts and impressions about his father, that is, a distant father-son relationship, from a much later period.

Merwin in his late phase consciously fuses three intentions—paternal, divine, agnostic—in the description of sunlight in such a way that the signifier "sunlight" lacks a settled signified. The fantasized divinity of the father is often traversed by the son's retrospective wisdom: "During prayers I did not dare to raise my head and look at him for long, but through other parts of the service if I fixed my eyes on him I found that an aura of light came and went around. It was a trick of the eyes, and I knew it" (*UO* 109). Even if Merwin confers the divine aura on his father's head, he would make a disclaimer soon, admitting that the play of light is nothing but his own boyish prank: "I learned to make that luminous phantom grow larger, more intense, spread out like rays in water, while my father's voice rose and fell." Although the poet once regarded his father as "a mystery," "the Minister, impressive and unknowable," he would soon add that his father's magisterial role was "concocted from the whole of his life" rather than immediately perceived by the son as such (113).

Merwin's retrospective knowledge of his father's mortality and his untiring attempt to make peace with his father would make that "luminous phantom" travel back and forth in his recent poetry. This spectral presence betrays Merwin's unconscious desire for the elusive father and his simultaneous defense against it. For example, in "By the Avenue," a poem also from *The Shadow of Sirius,* Merwin remembers his father's church in New Jersey:

> . . . over there among
> the young leaves brighter than the daylight
> another light through the tall windows
> a sunbeam sloping like a staircase
> and from beyond it my father's voice

telling about a mote in an eye
that was like a mote in a sunbeam. (*SS* 8)

In these memory traces, the father figure is conjured up among a cluster of luminous, mystic images; numinous icons like "sunbeam" and "light" appear more than once, as the sloping staircase distantly recalls the biblical ladder to heaven. In the poet's vision, the father seems to be placed high above in heaven indeed, yet only by hindsight does the son realize that a mote in the eye represents no religious lesson but an optical illusion hallowing the mundane, which significantly plays down the paternal/ecclesiastic function of the sunlight by highlighting its agnostic-naturalistic aspect.

If the sunlight image accompanies Merwin's memory of his father as the Minister of God, the incarnation of the divine Other, then twilight/ night/darkness enshrouds the father as an existent conditioned by mortality. The absence of light denotes the death—both symbolic and real— of the father, just as the ghost of Hamlet's dead father comes at night to visit the guilt-stricken son. In "Waking to the Rain," Merwin suffers auditory and visual hallucinations about his dead father, who does not know that he is dead but still tries to communicate with the son:

> The night of my birthday
> I woke from a dream
> of harmony
> suddenly hearing
> an old man not my father
> I said but it was
> my father gasping
> my name as he fell
> on the stone steps outside
> just under the window
> in the rain
> I do not know
> how many times

he may have called
before I woke
I was lying
in my parents' room
in the empty house
both of them dead
that year
and the rain was falling
all around me
the only sound. (*RT* 27)

This poem exemplifies Merwin's *infinite* mourning for the dead father: the poetic self here is emptied, paralyzed, cauterized, and "torn up from oneself," as Levinas says of the searing power of the Other (*Otherwise* 75). The intrusion of the dead father, as the return of the Real, shatters the son's "dream of harmony," burning him with a sense of guilt on the night of his own birthday—an overlap of life and death. The son first refuses to acknowledge the old man to be his father, but this negation does nothing but reveal his unconscious desire to get close to the father, as the father's "gasping my name" well betrays the poet's wish-fantasy to make up for his father's neglect in the early years. The "fall" of the father first puts an irony to his own symbolic status as the Minister of God, and the father figure is further reduced to a lamentable state: "outside / just under the window / in the rain," trying to go inside but failing to reach the son. Waking up, the son feels guilty for indulging himself in egotistic sleep and failing to respond to the earnest call from the father, who in order to see the son had come all the way to a foreign land ("stone steps" hint at Merwin's stone house in rural France where he had intermittently lived for years). Written ten years after his father's death, the poem gives full release to Merwin's belated remorse and his silent, uncontainable grief.

Merwin's relationship with the paternal function is both biographically and psychoanalytically singular: it constitutes what I would call "a reverential critique": Merwin cannot help but idealize his father while at the same time he readily recognizes and accepts the discrepancy between the symbolic, restrictive father and the father in flesh and blood. He attempts to escape the former, who imposes order and law, by emphasizing the weakness he finds in the latter. The strategy is not always successful, for "the dead father became stronger than the living one had been" (Freud, *Totem* 166) in that the guilt and remorse of "kill-ing" (rejecting, foreclosing) the paternal function remain to haunt the son. In this scenario that transcends the polarity of love and hate, what Merwin truly desires is perhaps not the living father who is severe, dis-tant, "flawed and human" (McDonnell 176), but the dead yet *infinite* father—the internalized, darkly radiant father.

FORBEARS AND THE LIGHT OF ORIGIN

Merwin's increasing interest in his familial origins dates from the death of both of his parents in the late 1970s, and his various autobiographical writings, collected under the book title *Unframed Originals: Recollec-tions* (1982), can be read as a psychopoetic reaction toward this loss. Merwin seeks to overcome his father complex—ambivalent feelings toward the father—by discovering irregularity, disorderliness, and Other jouissance in his family tradition. Desiring to transcend the symbolic law of the father, Merwin relies heavily on the imago of his "libertine" grandfather. Meeting his grandfather when he was nine and immediately "entranced," to use Hix's word (*Understanding* 112), by his grandfather's luminous, Edenic garden, Merwin creates from his memory a vision of utopia where everything looks innocent and amoral: "The one I was standing in was a real garden. . . . And real things to eat grew there. . . . The sun shone straight down into the middle of the vegetable beds and held the leaves still. . . . As I looked at the vegetable beds in sunlight, with the men's voices passing over my head, I did not know how old I was" (*UO* 3–4). As the luxuriant natural scenery offers an alternative outside the rigid moralism that the father represents, this encounter with Nature will become increasingly important in Merwin's later writings. The grandfather, like a good-hearted Eve, encouraged the boy to eat tomatoes: "'Some of them's ripe,' he said. 'You can eat them right now'" (6). His grandfather, as Merwin's memoir discloses, was the first to encourage him to try new things, and the line "We seek a new dimension for the world" from the early 1950s would seem a belated echo of his grandfather's salubrious exhortation.

Mark Christhilf, a critic who valorizes the mythmaking in Merwin's poetry, dismisses the poet's autobiographical writings as basically "produced from the familiar contents of consciousness" and only touching "the surface of life" (74–75). Christhilf might be right in pointing out the questionable mystification of daily life in a "democratic nation" (74)—it is a kind of mystification without real mystery. Yet Merwin's autobiographical writings do call for a deeper reading since the author takes such pains to trace and push his family genealogy to an impossible (always anterior) origin rather than glorify the family's past by claiming its historical importance. If there were mystery in Merwin's family stories, it belongs to the mystery or magic of time itself as these stories are told through the lens of a much later period when the poet's memory has to search the past for the very event in its own construction.

In a non-mythical reading of Merwin's use of memory from the 1950s up to the 1980s, James McCorkle emphasizes memory's potential to bring the disseminated parts of history together to form a certain plentitude, to "overcome silence" (*Still* 132). Particularly, McCorkle sees Merwin's family poems of the 1980s as an attempt to "recover an atavistic poetic memory," through which the family genealogy, as "a primordial form of history," could be reconstructed by the poet himself (168, 166). Locating this "primordial" or "atavistic" memory, as McCorkle points out, is always a "conjuring of the return of apparitions" (166), so it would be beneficial to consider how memory could erase the past and rewrite it according to its law of association.

Writer and philosopher Maurice Blanchot, in a review on Marc Bernard's 1941 *Just Like Children,* attributes the power of stories of childhood to "a transfiguration of the past" (*Desperate* 47), since stories or episodes in one's early life could gain extraordinary import through narrative focalization and image production. "The slimmest anecdotes," as Blanchot says, "attract the reader as if they were the reflection of some unique and poignant truth," and this is because these moments have been associated by a later memory with "the inaccessible memory of the earliest emotions" (47). Such emotions, narrated and sometimes fabricated out of one's selective memory, together with their "glorious constellation" issuing from "a free and eager sensibility" (47), correspond to the mythical, pre-symbolic realm that occludes, and in Dr. Schreber's case forecloses, paternal laws and restrictions. Free from the requirement of a coherent plot, well-developed characters, and univocal themes, autobiography offers unique glimpses into a writer's earliest disposition and motivation by creating a telepathic connection with another self through the temporal distance between the sophisticated *now* and the innocent *then*.

In Merwin's case, this time gap is much illuminated and clouded by a mixture of authentic recollection and idealized fiction. Merwin's recollection of family anecdotes and origins shares a certain risk or unreliability found in all autobiography as a genre: later projections are interfused with earlier memory fragments to create a halo of intimate distance. It seems that these episodes refashioned out of a luminous memory could restore both the author and the reader to a more originary world, where things are said to be authentic again and, as Blanchot puts it, "natural and truthful" (*Desperate* 48). These qualities no doubt are achieved when the harsher parts of one's childhood, as Blanchot sees in Marc Bernard's narrative strategy, have been offset, glazed, and sublated by a more mature consciousness.

Critics have noticed that Merwin's grandfather is a mysterious figure in the child's imagination: the old man simply occupies an unknown zone on the outskirts of family and society (Hix, *Understanding* 109–14). What Merwin *knows* is that the grandfather once worked as a pilot on the Allegheny River—mirroring Merwin's young ideal ego as a bohemian poet—and was often drunk and absent from home, which incurred much reprobation from Merwin's Protestant grandmother and her family. General reticence, as well as a legendary aura, was fostered around him, and Merwin criticizes his father's family for its "tiny scope," its lack of interest in the family history, which "made it easier for them to drop him from consciousness" (*UO* 10). If the father resembles the ego that represses libidinal impulses, the grandfather in an earlier poem, "The Drunk in the Furnace," stands for the return of the repressed, the boisterous id: "Where he gets his spirits / It's a mystery. But the stuff keeps him musical: / Hammer-and-anviling with poker and bottle / To his jugged bellowings" (*FF* 282). In this fantastic setting, the furnace dweller leads a pre-symbolic life that largely ignores communal, intersubjective exchange. Merwin creates myths around his grandfather because he feels regrettably separated from him (they met only once and only exchanged a few words) and also because this ancestral origin eludes him: much of the grandfather's life is still clouded over despite the grandson's arduous excavation.

Merwin's ceaseless digging into the past could be read as an attempt to overcome the present mourning for his father, which he only escapes by forming an attachment to an earlier origin, an earlier father.[5] Yet ironically, the more he seeks ancestral origins, the more mythical they seem to be, until he has to give up the whole project and exclaim the total inaccessibility of the origin or any origins. In "To the Lightning" from *Present Company* (2005), Merwin compares ancestors to the transient lightning: "Now I can believe / that you never left" (*PC* 96). The trace of the distant forebear lodges within the descendant's unconscious, influencing the latter's life and destiny in an unknown way. Like the lightning, the ancestor is the one who strikes without warning, and its knowledge brings a kind of genetic predetermination that is scarcely mistaken: "ancestor // whom your children / have never remembered / not one of them / and whose illumination / they could not hope to survive" (*PC* 96). This impossible ancestral origin, as a genetic endowment, elicits a particular relationship with mystery that is only partially penetrated by science: "It is a relationship with alterity, with mystery—that is to say, with the future, with what (in a world where there is everything) is never there, with what cannot be there when everything is there" (Levinas, *Time* 88).

Merwin's contact with his grandfather resembles such a lightning: fleeting, traumatic, illuminating. Indeed, Merwin did not "survive" this illumination at the age of nine when their meeting took place, since in his entire writings there are endless retroactive outbursts of the contact manifested as the imageries of light, water, and origin. Merwin's grandfather has come to complete and substitute the role of the father as his spiritual guide. The poet fully acknowledges the unconscious influence of the ancestors: "beginning // around us all that time / unchanged as we travelled / from whom our eyes are descended / and the things we say // whenever we see you / there is a question / we do not dare to remember / and you disappear / before there are words for it // is that from you too" (*PC* 96–97). Like the lightning, ancestral origins disappear even before there are words to question them, not to mention securing any possible answers to those questions. Words, as vehicles of human signification and representation, fail to capture the *realness* of ancestors' influence, which is permanent yet transient, omnipresent but nowhere to be located.

In later poetry, Merwin constantly evokes the flaming imagery of the origin to suggest its retroactively constitutive effects on present reality. Merwin invites us to think that, unlike the spiritless and disheartening contemporaries, the forebears could be far more spirited and egoless as they existed in another space-time beyond our apprehension. "The Comet Museum" from *The Pupil* (2001) reflects upon the prehistoric nature of the celestial body: "So the feeling comes afterward / some of it may reach us only / long afterward when the moment / itself is beyond reckoning // beyond time beyond memory" (*P* 4). The comet causes a traumatic event whose effects are not attenuated but only delayed in time. The nostalgic feeling for earlier origins comes from a psyche that has been shot through by the combusting comet, whose coming and going is spectral, and in this sense the comet/ancestor has come to stand for the absent cause of the subject—although escaping our consciousness, it shapes us toward who we are.

The trace of origins seizes Merwin's imagination and drives it toward an ecstasy until that imagination collapses. The drive toward origin is surely a death-drive toward otherworldliness unbound by the paternal function. Archetypal images of animals surge from the poet's unconscious to evoke an earlier time that is diachronic with the present. In

"Ancestral Voices" from *The Vixen,* Merwin combines a totemic bird with the spirited, spontaneous grandfather image.[6] After describing a twilight scene, the poet was suddenly struck by the voice of a blackbird that "came believing in the habit / of the light." Epiphanic, the blackbird, like Shelley's soaring lark, lightens the twilit world, just as the comet burns through the night sky: "the song / of the blackbird flashed through the unlit boughs and far / out in the oaks a nightingale went on echoing" (*V* 65). These otherworldly presences have clearly transcended human history, for they "were lifted here long before the first / of our kind had come to be able to listen" (65). These birds are not only vehicles of Romantic sentiment but also represent impenetrable realities in themselves, constituting a presence indifferent to human signification: "they sang / of themselves which was what they had wakened to remember" (65).

The blackbird is only one of the many totems Merwin elevates to the status of origin to counterbalance the restrictive paternal order. The jouissance of animal origin finds its supreme realization in the title poem, "Vixen," in which Merwin lavishes high-toned, nearly hysteric praise on the noble animal. The vixen, similar to the comet and the blackbird, is certainly what the poet can neither hold nor escape. Invariably, behind the vixen lurks Merwin's grandfather, since in a related poem, "Fox Sleep," Merwin retells the Buddhist story of an old man who had been changed into a fox for "five hundred lives" and later regained his human shape (*V* 4). In "Vixen," however, the animal does not undergo a Buddhist transformation but calls for witness of its own splendor. The poem utilizes the whole spectrum of Merwinian vocabulary, from stasis to dynamism, eliciting the elemental mystery of the origin-Other:

Comet of stillness princess of what is over
  high note held without trembling without voice without sound
aura of complete darkness keeper of the kept secrets
  of the destroyed stories the escaped dreams the sentences
never caught in words warden of where the river went
  touch of its surface sibyl of the extinguished
window onto the hidden place and the other time. (*V* 69)

This Pindaric discourse turns the vixen into an infinitely auratic being as the otherness of the vixen has been sublimated into such a state that the speaker has become a pure voice for this "princess" who is apparently "without trembling without voice without sound." Far from negating the poetic self, the vixen sets the self in motion toward other dimensions/ phases of space-time; in this sense, the praising of the fox has taken on what Susan Stewart, in a discussion on the poetics of praising, terms praising's "cognitive function": "a capacious one that calls on more than either reasoning or the application of prior terms and values" (33).

Yet the vixen, the "aura of complete darkness," obviously is "never there," never captured or absorbed by the self through speech and reasoning, as if the animal has become the eroticized sublime Thing, which the poet feels so compelled to find and refind.[7] Fantasizing that the vixen was present "in the full moonlight of autumn at the hour when I was born" (V 69), the speaker entrusts his future, his want-to-be (desire), on this shimmering origin that would endlessly reproduce jouissance for refinding a more authentic self:

> . . . now when your light paws are running
>> on the breathless night on the bridge with one end I remember you
> when I have heard you the soles of my feet have made answer
>> when I have seen you I have waked and slipped from the calendars
> from the creeds of difference and the contradictions
>> that were my life and all the crumbling fabrications. (V 69)

Conjuring "the indigestible physical and psychic memory trace of other beings within oneself" (Morton, Dark Ecology 119), the messianic vixen here clearly blasts the continuum of the speaker's life, delivering him from false values, necessary lies, and dubious memories. Like the ancestral blackbird, the vixen has survived the erosion of time; though "you no longer go out like a flame at the sight of me," the speaker still acknowledges that "even now you are unharmed even now perfect" simply because this *you* come from "the other time" (V 69).

HÖLDERLIN AT THE RIVER: ANOTHER BIRTH

Merwin's desire for diachronic origins can be reckoned as a strategy to break through the symbolic order and thus to be liberated from his unpaid debts to his father. Merwin's predicament is then clear: he tries to salvage the lost connection with his father while simultaneously asking for a deliverance from this compulsive memory by resorting to an even *earlier origin* such as his grandfather. Between memory and oblivion there is a constant war, just as genesis and apocalypse, creation and destruction, are constantly opposing and transforming into each other. Biespiel captures this dialectic in Merwin: "In Merwinworld, it's always late in the season of another year. The wind is constantly remembering and the sea is forgetting, or vice versa. Language has yet to be spoken, but it's also on the verge of being lost. The birds are singing their last songs, and the light is young" (140). The polarities in Biespiel's observation point out the warring elements and tensions in Merwin's later poetry. In his later stage, Merwin rarely exhibits world-weariness or resignation as found in late Eliot, nor does he trust in a cosmopolitan wisdom as in late Pound but keeps that high Pindaric tone in the flux of time, repetitively rehearsing psychic fantasies, cleavages, deriving enjoyments from momentary meetings, separations, longings.

Merwin's "feverish" endeavor to relive the traumatic breakage from the paternal order can be glimpsed in "Hölderlin at the River," perhaps the most beautiful and elaborate poem in *The Vixen*. A full discussion of the poem helps us understand Merwin's tortuous struggle with the father complex and the intricate mechanisms Merwin's later poetry has gone through in transforming psychic realities into poetic realities:

The ice again in my sleep it was following someone
  it thought was me in the dark and I recognized its white tongue
it held me in its freezing radiance until I
  was the only tree there and I broke and carried
my limbs down through dark rocks calling to the summer

where are you where will you be how could I have missed you
gold skin the still pond shining under the eglantines
  warm peach resting in my palm at noon among flowers
all the way I was looking for you and I had nothing to say who I was
  until the last day of the world then far below I could see
the great valley as night fell the one ray withdrawing
  like the note of a horn and afterwards black wind took
all I knew but here is the foreign morning with its clouds
  sailing on water beyond the black trembling poplars
the sky breathless around its blinding fire and the white flocks
  in water meadows on the far shore are flowing past their
silent shepherds and now only once I hear the hammer
  ring on the anvil and in some place that I have not seen
a bird of ice is singing of its own country
  if any of this remains it will not be me. (*V* 29)

Readers familiar with both Hölderlin and contemporary poetry will
not mistake this piece for a pastoral: neither Merwin nor Hölderlin is a
Virgilian pastoralist. They are hymnists and elegists; they sing of what
is already gone. The river in Hölderlin's famous hymn "The Ister," as
Heidegger has explicated, connotes an ontological dislocation of the
self, a "coming to be at home" through "a passage through the foreign"
(*Hölderlin's* 49). Rivers are "remote and foreign to humans," and as origins they can induce humans' self-projection with certain metaphysical
violence. Heidegger goes on to explain, "It is precisely that which tears
onward more surely in the rivers' own path that tears human beings
out of the habitual midst of their lives, so that they may be in a center
outside themselves, that is, to be excentric" (28). Apart from *ekstasis,* the
river also connotes a returning to the origin: "the river can never forget
the source, because in flowing . . . it itself constantly is the source and
remains the locality of its own essence (138).

Like Hölderlin, Merwin is also a troubadour of the elements of light,
water, and fire, a devotional rather than a confessional poet. Merwin's

lines "I wanted to be far away like the surface / of a river" (*V* 47) could also have been written by Hölderlin. The first-person narrative, however, fuses Merwin's own psychic fantasies with Hölderlin's legendary madness about rivers. The poem begins with a dream at night: an alien Thing, "the ice," is following the dreamer. Ice, "the whiteness that we could not bear" (*FF* 227), attracts the speaker for its extreme coldness that tears the self out of its cozy inwardness. When the speaker "recognized its white tongue," the ice came to hold him "in its freezing radiance," as Merwin's Hölderlin did not survive this illumination at all but went through an Ovidian transformation, suffering the psychotic vision of broken limbs and dark journeys.

To further evoke the origin, Merwin introduces memory traces by the end of the fifth line. The speaker now wistfully apostrophizes summer, which is synonymous with the poet's youth, for both summer and youth shine gloriously yet transitorily. In the summer of 1948, Merwin first left the United States for Europe at the age of twenty-one, and that summer would serve as the prototype on which all later poems on summer are modeled. He then broke away from paternal authority, wandering around Europe as his grandfather had wandered on the Allegheny River two generations earlier. He would reap the guilt and pain of separation later; at the moment, he was full of ecstasy and expectation. In retrospect, Merwin believes he was following the calling of some unknown origin at the time, which is recorded in his *Summer Doorways* (2005), a memoir about his departure and first years in Europe. The book begins with an intimation about unknown origins: "A summer descends to us from earlier years, heir to ancestors it never knew" (*SD* 3), and the last paragraph of the book reads: "I would have the luck to discover, to glimpse, to touch for a moment, some ancient, measureless way of living, of being in the world . . . evanescent like a work of art, an entire age just before it was gone, like a summer" (216). Hölderlin's calling for summer therefore echoes Merwin's first breakage from the socio-familial life in the exploration of a more liberal, spontaneous way of living, "ancient" and "evanescent" as it may seem. For Merwin, the notion of summer exactly constitutes what Heidegger calls a "passage through the foreign" (*Hölderlin's* 49), drawing the self out of its habitual location and initiating its transmutation.

Along with summer, the poem summons other images that are heavily loaded with Merwin's childhood memories. The pond image activates the libidinal fixation on water that Merwin has had since childhood, especially in Scranton, Pennsylvania, where he first tried to sail on Fiddle Lake. According to Merwin's memoir, in the first summer in Scranton the Merwin family lived far from the city, in the woods. When Merwin's father was absent during the week, "leaving his list of prohibitions hanging in the air," Merwin would take to the lake: "I love the lake, the rowboat, the sunlit rippled sand in the shallows . . . and all that they allowed me to imagine, as I had never loved anywhere up until then, and I counted the days there, trying to keep them from slipping away" (*SD* 30). Merwin's early obsession with lakes is largely a rebellious strategy against symbolic restriction, as he confesses: "Some of my discontent and claustrophobia in those years took the form of feeling far away from water" (27). The "still pond," the "rowboat," and the "sunlit rippled sand" all convey Merwin's youthful desire for spontaneity.

This partly explains why Merwin would present Hölderlin as attached to *other* callings. Hölderlin looked "far below" and saw the "great valley" that may hint at impending yet unknown death. Merwin's Hölderlin here has witnessed the deaths of those around him: "black wind took / all I knew." The killer-wind represents both the external cosmic force that annihilates the individual and the uncontainable psychic force that strives for *the infinite* commonly seen in Romanticism. Merwin here uses the wind image to suggest what both impels humans and wears them down: a scourge of the soul like the lightning, wind violently wipes the slate clean for the reinscription of a new self.

When Merwin drives his Hölderlin toward despair, he does not forget to prepare the light of salvation. The later part of the poem reveals Merwin/Hölderlin's desire for a heterogeneous origin to compensate for the double loss. Having mourned both lost youth and family members, Hölderlin beholds the heterogeneous morning in its freshening view.

The connection between "mourning" and "morning" actually goes beyond their identical sound. First, morning puts an end to mourning by introducing a new time series, as morning offers salvation to the mourning subject mired in guilt and remorse. Second, mourning expresses grief for the bygone mornings and the inaccessible origins, parents, and ancestors. Third, morning completes and consummates mourning, as dawn consummates the vigil of night. Merwin's later work can be felicitously described as a marriage of mourning and morning: the poet incessantly laments the death of his parents and ancestors and the loss of his own youth yet at the same time ecstatically declares an alien beginning, constantly evoking the natural process as the antidote to grief.[8]

The drive toward total oblivion and final death reaches its climax via Hölderlin's infinite vision in later parts of this alexandrine-like elegy (some lines resemble the twelve-syllable, two-hemistich pattern while others do not). The "foreign morning" scenery is void of human sorrow: the sailing clouds, "the black trembling poplars," and "the sky breathless around its blinding fire," presumably the heavenly light that had struck Hölderlin and driven him mad for forty years. The shepherds here are not the passionate ones of Marlowe's pastoral but rather remain "silent." The otherworldliness of the scene is further conveyed by the distant "hammer / ring on the anvil" and the singing of "a bird of ice" in a place that the speaker could not see. The sounds of inanimate metal and the strange bird call for nothing but the dissolution of the self, which is explicitly stated in the last line: "If any of this remains it will not be me." A nature poem on the surface, "Hölderlin at the River" discloses Merwin's desire for the lost object and his drive toward what is other than self/ego, the heterogeneous origin, and "an *other* birth and an *other* essence" (Derrida, *Of Spirit* 107).

It is through such a radical alterity initiated in what Sean Joseph McDonnell calls "intrapsychic space" (159) that Merwin's portrait of Hölderlin can be best understood. Excluding the Name of the Father that constitutes a normally functional social being, Hölderlin wandered outside the socio-familial world (he lived alone in a tower for thirty-six years, during which period his mother and sister never visited him) and pursued a kind of mystic jouissance in the withdrawal of both ancient deities and the Judeo-Christian God. Has not Merwin experienced a similar other-birth, the same pleasures and pains of not only encountering the strange but also becoming the Stranger himself? Merwin's passage through the foreign—through repeated departures and journeys—sets in motion such a fundamental dislocation of the self that in later poetry he keeps asking himself what has actually happened to him, what he has really lost and kept through numerous breakages and separations.

This rite of passage and the process of rebirth have preoccupied Merwin after the 1980s when the mourning for his father began to gnaw at his spine. He attempts to ward off this compulsive memory by resorting to an origin earlier than memory, which aggravates his grief, because the possibility of such an origin is already constituted by memory. The freezing radiance and blinding fire, which cause Hölderlin's grief and are also its remedy, are both originary and mnemonic. Memory completes the rite of passage and spiritual rebirth, since all journeys, to a certain degree, are journeys of the mind. In "Memory," Merwin travels back through memory to an origin other than human:

> Climbing through a dark shower
> I came to the edge of the mountain
> I was a child
> and everything was there
> the flight of eagles the passage of warriors
> watching the valley far below
> the wind on the cliff the cold rain blowing upward
> from the rock face
> everything around me had burned
> and I was coming back
> walking on charcoal among the low green bushes
> wet to the skin and wide awake. (*RT* 58)

Drawn by some unknown force, the child came to the mountain where he saw the traces of primordial liberty ("flight of eagles") and ancient bravery ("passage of warriors"), and like Hölderlin he observed the gaping valley below. The scene echoes both the journey of Odysseus ("the wind on the cliff the cold rain") and the sacrifice story of Isaac from the Old Testament ("everything around me had burned"). Merwin, however, might not have these prototypes in mind when he wrote the poem; he might simply be recollecting a childhood journey into the wilderness. Toward the end of the poem, the child was traumatized, "wet to the skin and wide awake," unable to return to the old self. The title of the poem suggests that human memory is perhaps nothing but the inscription of the encounter with the alien Thing both inside and outside human consciousness.

The effort to recapture the traces of the other world by traveling at night through the "dark passage" (RS 15) certainly has its rewards as the poet beholds the anonymity of the world before it is illuminated by logos and order. "Wakefulness is anonymous. It is not that there is my vigilance in the night; in insomnia it is the night itself that watches" (Levinas, *Existence* 66). In the night, one directs one's desire not to any object but to the dark, objectless, anonymous space, to the ghostly "wands of the auroras," which provide a precise image for the dialectic of desire and infinity.[9] Driven by who-knows-what for the unnamed, distant otherness, Merwin's night traveler experiences the familiar alienness of the world:

> I remember waking at the rivers
> to see girders of gray sleepless bridges
> appearing from sleep out of a current
> of cold night air velvet with the secret
> coal smoke of those small hours and nobody
> on night roads the few words of toll-keepers
> old complaints of gates and cables the bark
> of bridge floors leaping up from under us
> and the swelling hiss of a surface just
> beneath us not loud but while it was there
> nothing else could be heard except as calls
> far off in some distance.... (RS 126)

The end of this poem points to some vague yet attractive otherness beckoning the traveler to continue the Hölderlinian wandering. Many of Merwin's late poems on nightly passage exemplify desire's objectless propelling; the traveler does not know what he truly wants, nor could he identify the "calls / far off in some distance," yet he follows the call without hesitation. The Prodigal Son "had to leave to be able to find" (*FF* 161), yet what the poet has found during all those years away from his home and the American continent still remains undefined, because strictly speaking, desire, being the metonymic movement of signifiers, lacks an object. When traveling in some foreign land and staying awake at midnight, Merwin himself must have felt acutely the enigma of human motivation. Christhilf understands Merwin's "world-traveler" as motivated by an urgency to "resist self-complacency" (70), yet in Merwin's later poetry this drive has been greatly accentuated by a daily necessity to deal with loss and grief and a nightly attraction into the anonymous. If there is grief in the silent sound of rain, it will be over when morning comes when the traveler is again on the road.

CROSSING THE SHADOWS: GRIEF AND MORNING

The opposition between the father as the phallic sun and the grandfather as the amorphous river, between ego and id, between the socio-symbolic life and the real or imaginary origins, finally erupts as a tension between finitude and infinity in Merwin's later writings. The side of life that has been given meaning would embrace its infinite underside, which by resisting phallocentric function provides the *real* impetus for human actions. In later poetry, Merwin plumbs the infinite depth of human existence, as the *in* of infinity could well designate the "depth of an undergoing that no capacity comprehends" (Levinas, *Collected* 163).

Evolving from a lifelong obsession with the chiaroscuro of light and darkness, Merwin's *The Shadow of Sirius* revolves around the unknown side of existence that escapes univocal meaning. M. P. Jones, for example, reads the book as "a hybrid eco-epic": "Merwin combines personal history and ancient mythology to illuminate the current ecological crisis. *The Shadow of Sirius* blends the Ancient Greek myth of Sirius, the dog star, with Merwin's own personal history of loss to create a hybrid ecological myth" (56). In addition to myth, the title also carries a philosophical lesson. Sirius is the most luminous star in the sky, twenty-five times brighter than the sun, but Merwin curiously writes about its shadow that no one on earth has ever seen. Merwin explained the title to Moyers: "We are the shadow of Sirius. There is the other side of—as we talk to each other, we see the light, and we see these faces, but we know that behind that, there's the other side, which we never know. And that—it's the dark, the unknown side that guides us, and that is part of our lives all the time. It's the mystery. That's always with us, too. And it gives the depth and dimension to the rest of it" (*CW* 162–63).

Theoretically, the shadow of Sirius is an impossibility, but as "pure metaphor, pure imagination" (*CW* 162), it symbolizes the depth of human psyche that paradoxically contains the uncontainable exterior, the unknown side that "guides us," which is better intuited than rationally explained. Rather than abolish knowledge, this dark side or dimension engenders human desire and motivation, without which we will be reduced to shadowless automatons deprived of subjectivity. In other words, this dark side is what is in us but inaccessible to us. "The infinitely exterior becomes an 'inward' voice, but a voice bearing witness to the fission of the inward secrecy" (Levinas, *Otherwise* 147). Although memory, desire, and grief are expressed through words, a large part of them still belong to the realms outside language and signification, which is also why they seize upon the poet so urgently through that "inward voice" that breaches "inward secrecy." The son's cry that "but it is the world, / Father, that I do not understand" (*FF* 109) can be supplemented by "it is myself, Father, that I do not understand." Any interrogation of the world turns out to be an interrogation of the self, not of its symbolic identity and illusionary wholeness, but of its ontological abyss (incompleteness), its irreducible strangeness that eludes the thematization of signs and language. This elision, according to Merwin, is constitutive of cognition and subjectivity: "I can't find my own face . . . because I can't see my own face" (*CW* 169).

Ever since *The Moving Target* in the early 1970s, Merwin has repeatedly resorted to the calling from the other side, although he has not quite figured out *what that calling means for him*. What corresponds to the calling is the infinite as well as infantile longing for the outside of self/ego, name, language, solidified meaning, and phallic function, for "the vast emptiness and unknown of the universe" (*CW* 164). In the late 1990s, Merwin admitted that "I thought I was getting better / about that returning childish / wish to be living somewhere else / that I knew was impossible" (*RS* 125). He is not "getting better" actually, nor does he outgrow his childhood. The first poem from *The Shadow of Sirius*, "The Nomad Flute," begins wistfully as ever: "You that sang to me once sing to me now / let me hear your long lifted note / survive with me" (*SS* 5). The speaker identifies himself with the calling of the other, which is also manifest in "Calling a Distant Animal": "Here it is once again this one note / from a string of longing // tightened suddenly from both ends / and held for plucking" (*SS* 44). Merwin compares himself to an instrument playing the music of longing, whose note can only be heard in a more ancient space-time and echoed only by "the silence it calls to," presumably the silence of extinct animals or what Aaron Moe calls "the growing absence of animals" (27). This *string of longing* sums up Merwin's stance as an Orphic bard, a nomadic singer driven by inner forces he knows little about but feels palpably. The silence to which the note addresses does not reduce the addresser's zeal, as he has recognized it not as a failure of response but as the only valid response to another even more primordial silence.[10]

Calling expresses loss and grief, two main driving forces in Merwin's later poetry. The lyric self is able to acquire certain proximity to the loss via repetitive calling when the improbable articulation of such loss activates a passionate, as well as pathological, movement of words around that silent kernel, as if all loss could be remedied by this mere saying.[11] Like the unseen shadow of Sirius, loss and grief are invisible to us, who see only the positive side of the star, not its negative, dark side, which comes very close to Timothy Morton's suggestion to think of human species as "a hyperobject that is real yet inaccessible" (*Dark Ecology* 25). Our existence on earth is always weirder than we think. Merwin, for example, tells Moyers about our strange inability to reach things: "One of the great themes that runs through poetry, all poetry, and I think is one of the reasons for poetry, one of the sources of poetry, one of the sources of language, is the feeling of loss. The feeling of losing things. Not being able to hold, keep things. That's what grief—I mean, grief is the feeling of having lost. Of having something being out of reach. Gone. Inaccessible" (*CW* 171). Unable to enunciate loss (decimation of the earth, departure of the beloved ones, including his dogs) that is on the edge of language/knowledge, a "groundless country" or an "unmapped imperium" (*PC* 34), Merwin untiringly calls upon its stand-ins. In a poem for his dead dog, Muku, which means "complete darkness" or "night without moon" in Hawaiian, Merwin denies the possibility of any positive knowledge about loss: "Now you are darker than I can believe / it is not wisdom that I have come to // with its denials and pure promises / but this absence that I cannot set down" (*SS* 45).[12]

The light of knowledge, as the word *enlightenment* indicates, sinks infinitely in this groundless country of loss, and its resultant mourning presents such a yearning that outlasts one's life, acquiring a posthumous life for its own sake:

> this endless longing that is only ours
> orbiting even in our syllables
> why do you keep calling us as you do
> from the beginning without a sound
> like a shadow. ("To Grief," *PC* 33)

This longing, being endless, does not die as one's life ends; it walks like a specter in broad daylight in its afterlife, disturbing and traumatizing the living. In "No," a poem about pure negativity, Merwin conjures the grieving voices of the dead to haunt the living:

Out at the end of the streets in the cemetery
the tombstones stared across the wheeling shadows
of tombstones while the names and dates wept on
in full daylight and behind them where the hill
sheared off two rusted tracks under a black
iron gate led up out of pure darkness
and the unbroken sound of pure darkness
that went on all the time under everything. (*SS* 21)

The poem intimates that what underlies our daily life is something we choose to ignore, because we are afraid of confronting the pure dark that supplements light/logos/order as its undesirable Other. Attending to the whimpering grief of the dead, the poet readily embraces the constitutive negativity of human existence.

Merwin explains to Moyers about his belief in the good darkness, which "is not the threatening dark, but the nourishing dark. The nourishing darkness. That there's that we all take with us" (*CW* 180). As James Wright and Robert Bly, who write in a similar vein, have recognized, "nourishing darkness" connotes a dormant pregnancy that offers vision, energy, and wildness. It's true that darkness evokes loss and grief, yet it also pacifies them. In "Curlew," Merwin appreciates darkness from the angle of a bird: "When the moon has gone I fly on alone / Into this night where I have never been // the eggshell of dark before and after / in its height I am older and younger // than all that I have come to and beheld / and carry still untouched across the cold" (*SS* 59). There is neither fear nor sadness in these lines, and grief, if implicitly felt, has been attenuated by a certain originary darkness that engenders and renews life.

Since the 1990s, Merwin has anticipated the heterogeneous morning ecstatically. As Brunner points out, the time scale has become problematic in Merwin's later poetry: "Along with physical and social boundaries that dissolve, time also becomes fluid, approaching the condition that it enjoys in nature" (*Poetry* 282). As the origin-Other, morning is a categorical imperative: morning must come at the end of hallucinatory mourning and involuntary memory. It consummates grief and therefore overcomes it. Impersonally, morning cares not for human loss, and its presence means nothing but a prehistoric birth. In a poem to his wife, Paula, Merwin declares the overcoming of all grief with the coming of a new time sequence:

the worn griefs will have eased like the early cloud
through which the morning slowly comes to itself
and the ancient defenses against the dead
will be done with and left to the dead at last. (SS 84)

The light of morning, in its timelessness, releases Merwin from the symbolic debts to his father, grandfather, and other ancestors, from whom he feels separated; the light has also bestowed a beginning that is diachronic with the past, a present that is pure decision and release.

Constantly envisioning the other side of perceived, known existence is to avow that "the foolish thing is to take that world which we have made as the real, total, absolute final world" (RM 335). The spiritual aura of Merwin's later work rests, on the one hand, on what Walter Benjamin formulates as "the unique phenomenon of a distance" (Illuminations 222), while on the other, it corresponds to a returning specter in the sense of both Levinas, "The aspiration for the return is the very breath of the Spirit" (Entre Nous 135), and Derrida, who similarly emphasizes "the returning [revenir] of a spirit" (Of Spirit 91). Merwin's compulsive journey in his later career toward the salvation of origins is not a lucky trip but a difficult pilgrimage combining self-erasing gestures and existential decisions. In his ardent desire to approach the impenetrable beginning, Merwin has come to create an authentic spiritual discourse that elevates the lost otherness to the founding necessity of personal freedom. The guarding of other origins that transcend family genealogy and identity archeology thus becomes a suitable poetic critique of any self-assured knowledge of tradition, heritage, and history, for, as Merwin's later project prophesies, something will burst out from that knowledge.

POST-SIRIUS POEMS: THE ETERNAL RETURN

Tuning in "the unbroken sound of pure darkness," a song of pure longing, Merwin's post-*Sirius* poems, collected in *The Moon Before Morning* (2015) and *Garden Time* (2016), ferry us to a virtual land of remembrance and forgetting, light and dark, where time travels faster or stands still, where shadow can stay with us without a body. We are immediately aware that we are not in the even flow of time but caught in a kind of Nietzschean notion of eternal return: past and future are two vast eternities invariably passing through the door of *now*. In the very late Merwin world, origin and end alternate so quickly that they become just one in a flash of light, the same way the biblical flood ending and beginning human civilization. "Because it is not here it is eternal / the stars we consider have long been gone" (*MB* 27), Merwin writes in "The Eternal Return." The stars have life spans far beyond human imagination, and we simply cannot say they are gone or extinct because the factor of time inevitably affects our statement about those celestial bodies. Interestingly, Merwin claims to have seen through the trick of time, and he happily surrenders poetry to its maneuvering: "I cannot recall what I was saying / while clouds melted over the morning sea." Immediate forgetting laps the little boat of memory, while nature occurs repeatedly, eternally. The poem is built on the Nietzschean motif that what returns is the Same, for example, what can happen has already happened, and we ourselves have already existed: "here is the same child without a childhood / the whole sentence present in the last word." The absence of a childhood may refer to Merwin's brother Hanson who had died before the poet was born, so they never met: Hanson "had fallen out of his empty name" (*GT* 28), but this enigmatic phrase can also mean that Merwin in his old age could not remember much of his childhood. The "last word" here, while completing the meaning of the line, serves as a reminder of Merwin's lifelong pursuit of the profound truths of the world. More of elegy than ode, Merwin's last word would testify to what keeps vanishing all the time.

Like late Leonard Cohen, Merwin in his final years constantly evokes the momentous present but could always "want it darker" or "kill the flame" in order to prepare for what is still to come. Merwin has such convictions as Cohen's:

> I do not have to see
> in order to believe
> I know that the flame tree is flowering
> when I see the petals at my feet. (*MB* 18)

Tonally close to Cohen's last two or three albums, Merwin's most recent poems offer a memorial to time/age/times rather than to persons or things sunk back into the past, for the past, if we accept the Nietzschean idea, is already eternal and will come back no matter if we will it or not. The "flame tree" will blossom again even when the poet is gone, and to assume this view of eternal return requires greater courage than facing one's own death. Indeed, late Merwin finds himself already in the realm of eternal return when he marvels at how he has survived all his old friends and even himself: "Ghosts of words / circle the empty room / where I was young" (*MB* 66). Hence the feeling of afterlife in these two books in which Merwin meditates on how to give himself completely over to time: "this morning the black Belgian shepherd dog / still young looking up and saying // Are you ready this time" (*MB* 112). The dog's question sends a friendly invitation to him to participate in the unilluminated side of existence—something other than the end and the beginning. Over the years in Maui, Merwin has acquired an intimacy with other species' time experience, and in this sense his "intimations of immortality" are more animistic and agnostic than manifestly Platonic or Christian. They call for a special hearing: an extrasensory "listening" to other forms of time consciousness beyond human subjectivity.

Urgently questioning the measurability of time, Merwin hopes to widen the discrepancy between mnemonic and sociohistorical processes toward a revelation of time as what is still *indeterminate* to us. Time remains unappropriated despite our belief in its linearity, its "progress."[13] Sometimes Merwin marvels at his own age: "Still not believing in age I wake / to find myself older than I can understand" (*GT*

63). The poet's surprise in seeing the centenarian face of time (his own face) tells all the mysteries of time, memory, and consciousness, and in a Nietzschean stroke he further questions the illusion of age taken as accumulative, personal time: "how can it be old when it is now" (*GT* 63). Bergson's philosophy understands that time within human memory is not clock time because the moments interpenetrate each other in consciousness to form a duration, a whole. Yet Merwin still wonders at time's famous speed: "Going too fast for myself I missed / more than I think I can remember" (*MB* 112). If time is that which always returns to us humans who know but do not directly *feel* its passing, then Merwin is fully entitled to ask about the realness of our concept of time: "Is it I who have come to this age / or is it the age that has come to me" (*GT* 5).

Related to time is the phenomenon of forgetting. Merwin's last poems are saturated with forgetting as a prelude to the unknown: "but we lay there forgetting / asleep and awake / forgetting a breath at a time / while the rain went on falling around us" (*GT* 60). The speaker is thus submerged in the deep strata of time stretching to Immemorial Past and Unforeseen Future, yet his staying awake in the rain also sharpens a sense of living right here and now. Jean-Louis Chrétien takes forgetting to be a deeper loss than losing things in the world: "What in myself is lost, what is erased and disappears there—if there is such a thing—is lost much more profoundly than any being in the world, which is always only mislaid or displaced, thus lost in the sense of not being there where I seek it" (40). Loss within memory, a mark of human weakness, is thus double loss since it "tears us from ourselves and mutilates us in our interiority, for to lose something in oneself is also, necessarily, to lose something of oneself" (41).

Late Merwin's lamentation of such a loss of power to remember finally takes on a cultural value, although he seems to be writing from the other side or outside of human civilization, being a voice from elsewhere. Given the uncannily disastrous world we find ourselves in (pandemic, refugees, wildfires), we would do well to heed Merwin's last message on collective forgetting. The immensity (it may not be readily recognizable if we are not familiar with his trademark "paleness") of

Merwin's late poems resides in a critique of human hubris from a quasi-divine point of view. In "The Latest Thing," Merwin unleashes the power of collective forgetting: "In the cities the birds are forgotten / among other things but then one could say / that the cities are made of absences / of what disappeared so they could be there" (*MB* 77). Instead of discussing what already exists, Merwin wonders what might have existed if history had taken the other course. After the woods are gone, and "the wood thrushes taking / their songs with them," we only hear "in the continuous sound of the city / one white note plays on to prevent memory." The ecological lesson here is unmistakable, yet Merwin would also like us to consider how memory could be "prevented" by the city's monotonic music, which is characterized by vanishing (or making things vanish): "it may be that the sound of a city / is the current music of vanishing / naturally forgetting its own song." Merwin in his final years still tries to help us remember the music of the city as the "forgetting [of] its own song," for to approach the vanished and the vanishing through poetry, and to understand ourselves as part of this reoccurring process (to recognize that it's not that we forget, we ourselves will be forgotten), is already a step toward doing anything positively about this vanishing.

CONCLUSION

Merwin's poetry, from the 1950s to the present, strikes readers as a vast, continuous incantation of the alternative realities that tend to disappear from the current technocratic society. Merwin conjures and interrogates the other side of the rationalized existence, searching for the pre-symbolic mode of life that has escaped the hegemony of human language and signification. "Merwin's poems assume that language cannot determine experience" (Biespiel 140). To resist the conscious control of the writing process, which he deems as the ramification of a technological society, Merwin resorts to the prototype of the biblical waif, the tradition of the troubadours, and other inspirational sources such as European surrealism and Asian Zenic poetry. The urge to enunciate the "dumb reality which is *das Ding*" (Lacan, *Seminar VII* 55), to evoke the ultraphenomenal and the spiritual continues to inform Merwin's writings after he settled down in Hawaii in the late 1970s. He has not compromised his desire to reach out for the "new dimension" of the world; his obsession with alterity has only been transferred to the female form, to the flora, and to ancestral origins. The poetic self clings to the timeless memory traces from childhood to counteract its sociohistorical determinations.

Merwin's struggle with the phallic function enters into his poetry through psychoneurotic mechanisms. Much of his work can be simply read as a symptom sent to the Other, not the symbolic, big Other founded on the Name-of-the-Father that confers identity within the familial-social system, but the *real* Other, the traumatic Thing which resists signification, which spellbinds the poet by its staging of appearance as disappearance. Through poetry Merwin seems to have maintained an impossible relationship with this pre-symbolic entity: "*Das Ding* is that which I will call the beyond-of-the-signified. It is as a function of this beyond-of-the-signified and of an emotional relationship to it that the subject keeps its distance and is constituted in a kind of relationship characterized by primary affect, prior to any repression" (Lacan, *Seminar VII* 54). Bruce Fink explains Lacan's sentence as: "[The Thing] is the object from which the subject keeps his or her distance, not getting too close or too far away either. The subject comes into being as a defense against it, against the primal experience of pleasure/pain associated with it" (95). If the subject gets too close to the Thing, his symbolic world will collapse in excessive jouissance; if too far, he will be reduced by the symbolic order to a mere automaton deprived of subjectivity.

This study indicates that Merwin prefers a closer, thus more precarious, relation with the Thing. The basic message we hear from Merwin's corpus is that the speaker refuses to compromise on the question of desire by having a fixation of libido on the primal trauma of a non-understandable alterity. Merwin's infantile confrontation with the external stimuli that he can neither comprehend nor master disrupts his integration of the symbolic order and triggers psychoneurotic symptoms in his poetry afterward. Reliving the primal scene throughout his entire poetic career, Merwin attempts to subjectivize the Other's desire, to "assume the place of the cause" (Fink 62) and becomes what he has always already been: a poet of "what is not there." The constant projection of the self is effectuated by the discovery of an anterior otherness that keeps returning to disrupt as well as organize the poet's subjectivity. Byers's comment that Merwin compels readers to "envision relationships to the other . . . that are grounded in the value of its difference from us" (*What I Cannot Say* 114) thus can be supplemented by the observation that the constitutive difference/otherness arouses in the poet a psychic process of finding and refinding the Lacanian object.

Refusing to totalize or thematize the experiential world under the phallic function—the function of signifiers, the dubious "power" of words—Merwin has nevertheless subjected himself to the unsignifiable Other which miraculously resides in the self but cannot be contained by the self. Obsessed by this uncontainable, phantasmal otherness surging from the inside, Merwin takes on the responsibility to articulate the Other's primal absence that nevertheless constitutes one's subjectivity. Poetry for Merwin thus resembles an urgent cry at finding oneself "penetrated," as it were, by a knowing yet unknowable infinite Other who has already withdrawn from the horizon, so the self and Other, as we have seen in Merwin, Levinas, and Lacan, do not form a totality but a diachronic or displaced non-relation. It is exactly this interplay of contact and noncontact, interiority and exteriority, proximity and distance, that creates the kinesis in Merwin's writings. Byers's summary that Merwin "seeks a place for the self . . . in an essentially nonhuman order" (*What I Cannot Say* 105), which represents critics' consensus on Merwin's poems of the 1960s, thus seems to have missed the kaleidoscopic fantasies in his staging of the sublime quest for what is other than the dichotomy of human/nonhuman.

Merwin's poetic endeavors have been so unpredictable, unprogrammatic, and so narrowed down to the essentials that Edward Brunner's claim that "Merwin appears to have no style at all, or to take on whatever style suits the moment" seems fully justified (*Poetry* 286). If "to live with the unknown . . . is to enter into the responsibility of a speech that speaks without any form of power" (Blanchot, *Infinite* 302), then the elimination of any dominative style would coincide with a passive exposure of the self before the Other when exteriority, the void-Thing, overtakes, pierces, and suffuses the speaking subject. Such a Levinasian-cum-Lacanian irruption of exteriority precludes the heavy mediation of style. Assertive style, directed by instrumental reason, runs the risk of miring one deeper in what Merwin calls the "ego-bound, historical, culturally brainwashed, incredibly limited moment" (*RM* 329). Rather, Merwin has come to adopt a transparent style (or a nonstyle), an impersonal, "suspended regard" in order to evoke the "inexorable splendor," "the processions of an immeasurable continuum" ("Preface," xii, xiii). The luminosity of Merwin's poetic space and its chiaroscuro of light and shade originate from his desire to capture the ephemeral, to let the hallowed Other, which keeps withdrawing after the first encounter, shine again in its "inexorable splendor": rivers, lakes, creatures, flowers, lovers, parents, forebears, and origins. As McCorkle says, "[Merwin's] vision has an emergent corollary: the counterpunctual epiphany of a numinous world" ("Merwin" 1044). This transparent style is problematized, however, by the ego's traumatic fissuring when it is confronted with the infinite revelations and illuminations from the numinous world.

In the field of translation, Merwin has also followed Ezra Pound's advice to "Try to get as close to the original as possible," for "translating will teach you your own language" (ST 287). Since the late 1940s Merwin has produced an astonishing body of translation, more than twenty books, across more than ten languages, bringing dozens of other (Eastern and Western) poetic sources—including many occult, anonymous verses—into the reverberations of English. In a sense, Merwin's first encounter with poetry is an encounter with language as the numinous Other. Translating, techniques aside, first requires being "aware of the living resonance before it has words," as it also "impels one to be wary of any skill coming to shadow and doctor the source" (ST 11). Even though the original/source remains "as desirable, as indispensable but as elusive as ever," as Merwin admits, translation still strives to "represent, with as much life as possible, some aspect, some quality of the poem which made the translator think it was worth translating in the first place" (ST 291, 170). This seemingly circulatory reasoning redefines poetic quality as that which originally and timelessly prompts a translator to venture into the original language's "rudiments of form," which, though it cannot be matched with any equivalents in the other language, attract the force from that language: "The imaginative force which they [rudiments of form] embody, and which single words embody in the context, may suggest convocations of words in another language that will have a comparable thrust and sense" (ST 168).

Seeking this intuitive "thrust and sense," Merwin conceives poetic process, translations included, as contrary to the paternal function, for it seldom comes by authorial design. Poetry and translation happen in an unduplicatable, tremendous moment as chance work, a *tuché* with the "unframed originals," as one of his memoirs is titled. Merwin would agree with Alain Badiou, "The poem presents itself as a thing of language, encountered—each and every time—as an event" ("Language" 233). Under the proximity of the infinite moment, poetry, as a highly cathected movement of words, approximates the point where all motion becomes stasis, just as Merwin exclaims: "I really want a poem to make the world stop, for a matter of a few seconds" (*CW* 106). A poem thus evokes what resides in the self but can no longer be contained by that self—a surging, propelling desire/drive to respond to the present moment. Poets are those who are possessed by words and, more importantly, by a conation that words can only approximate. In "On Open Form" (1969), Merwin elaborates form as "the setting down of a way of hearing how poetry happens in words" and "testimony of a way of hearing how life happens in time" (*RM* 299). Such happenings are not to be circumscribed, categorized, or thematized but only recorded as testimony to the latent forces emerging from the fissures of a given socio-symbolic system. Far from an expected, rationalized discourse, poetry originates from the contact with exteriority, from an event that re-coordinates one's fantasy-frames and symbolic relations with other beings.

Suspicious of any human manipulation of signifiers to solidify ideology, Merwin would disagree with Victor Shklovsky's equation of art with technique. If art strives to give full liberation to human desire, drive, Eros, and spirit, it then refuses to be aligned with repressive mechanisms such as teleological design of forms found in academic poetry prevalent in the United States in the 1950s. Rhetoric in general, as Merwin sees it, "has been a dirty word in the discussion of poetry in the language for several decades" because its function is to "impose" an end in art, not to "question" it (*RM* 314). Paring away ostentatious impositions and persuasive ornaments, Merwin in his middle and later periods has brought poetry back to its naked condition, "where it touches on all that is unrealized." If in his early phase Merwin was still under the grip of formalism, since *The Moving Target* he has rejected the closed form and

significantly reduced his control of the writing process by relinquish-
ing punctuation, which according to him "assume[s] an allegiance to
the rational protocol of written language" (*SF* 1). Even in some of his
later books that obviously resort to a structured poetic—for instance,
Finding the Islands (1982) which employs haiku-like tercet, *The Vixen*
(1996) and *The Folding Cliffs* (1998) which use long, open-form lines
suitable for epic narratives—Merwin still intends to "let [the] words
find their own / places" (*V* 69), calling up the mythical, primordial, invisible forces that animate the structured lines.

Does Merwin still seem to be controlling of the poetic process
compared with other eco-poets like A. R. Ammons, Gary Snyder,
and Wendell Berry? Merwin's nature writings are motivated by a deep
metaphysical need to touch the hidden dimensions of the world (the
psychic Real), to approach alterity. Merwin's poetry, especially his later
work, only seems to be more nostalgic, having more to do with ancient
memories that return to haunt the poetic space. In other words, Merwin
seems more driven by *what is not there*—the obliterated and the unsub-
stantiated. Probing into the uncanny core of the poetic process, Merwin
evokes presentations from the unconscious, and as he said in a 1981
interview, he never got away from that "spooky feeling about poetry,"
without which poets are just playing "intellectual games" (*RM* 347). He
surely does not intend to denigrate human intellect that fosters poetic
sensibility but simply insists on the origin of poetry as the impersonal
spirit that "no one knows where it goes" (*RM* 295). Rather than intel-
lectualize or domesticate the alien spirit in the self, a poet follows that
spirit, calls upon it repeatedly, even obsessively, and finally, to incarnate
the spirit. Merwin rewrites the modernist imperative to make it new as
a returning to the locus where poetry renews itself: "True originality has
to do not with trying to be new but trying to come from the place from
which all renewal comes. The meaning of originality has to do with origin, the place where something comes from" (*CW* 106). Repetition and
spontaneity are united in that each *tuché* with the creative spirit opens
up a new horizon yet at the same time repeats or reinscribes the former
efforts in a differed/deferred way.

How do we evaluate this poetics of infinite obsession with the Other, this sublime hunger that does not call for satisfaction but its own starvation? What can this devotion to the unnamable Other make happen in a civilization characterized by global technocracy and military power? How can we imagine a radical passivity toward the Other without ironically turning it into a drama of victimization and self-glorification? Postwar American poetry has been a highly contested area for the ethical and political issues apropos of the ambiguous status of the Other. A full discussion of these questions exceeds the boundaries of the present study, and I will simply mention the Confessionals and the Beats—two groups manifestly engaged in transcending the Name-of-the-Father—in contrast with Merwin's own project to bring out a poetics of infinite opening.

Poets in the confessional mode, Sylvia Plath and Anne Sexton, for example, resort to an aesthetic of antagonism by depicting the Other as phallocentric and even crippling (for example, Plath's "Daddy," Sexton's "Her Kind"). Their efforts at transcending the Name-of-the-Father are compromised by dramatization and a symptomatic love-hate relationship between self and Other. Relying on the father figure as the conferrer of identity, though in a negatively deterministic way, Plath and Sexton still cling to the Name-of-the-Father by "ingesting" it. Despite their violent protestations, both are reluctant to abandon the liaison with the phallic function, which is seen in their employment of a rhetorical/authorial poetics to achieve persuasively pathetic effects. Their poetic spaces open more toward antagonistic tensions than anonymous exteriority: "Daddy" ends with a cursed deliverance from the father, and "Her Kind" constructs the speaker's ideal ego as opposed to a traditionally defined femininity. Concentrating on victimized experiences, Plath and Sexton have exploited their deeply troubled relationships with the paternal function in order to bring out a feminist subjectivity. Admittedly, one cannot reduce a poet's lifelong work to one poem, and there are moments when Plath, for example, does achieve a poetics of infinite opening—for instance, in "Ariel," Plath feels that "Something else / Hauls me through air" (239)—it is also clear that her poetic space, particularly her work from 1959 to 1963, is organized around the agonized question of the father (sometimes projected onto Ted Hughes), which boils down to the question of how to be a woman poet in a male culture.[1]

Another direction at transcending the Name-of-the-Father is offered by the Beat poets, Allen Ginsberg for instance, who displays a Whit-manian all-embracing attitude toward multiplicity. Ginsberg's equal-itarian gesture, however, to borrow Jonathan Culler's observation on Whitman, "constitute[s] the object as another subject with whom the poetic subject might hope to strike up a harmonious relationship" (qtd. in Byers, *What I Cannot Say* 111). For Ginsberg, personal freedom is based on the belief in the self's ability to choose among different ob-jects of representation for the more or less politically oriented agenda. The anti-cultural and anti-intellectual engagement, on one hand, affords Ginsberg raw materials for his incantations and denunciation of capi-talistic society while, on the other hand, it orients his poetry toward the same antagonistic tendency that characterizes the Confessionals. In a sense, both Ginsberg and Plath have politicized or antagonized the poetic space to achieve authenticity, a historical exigency Merwin him-self had felt and responded to with his own "visionary hopes" (*SF* 2) during the 1960s and 1970s.

Contrasted with Ginsberg and Plath, however, Merwin seems more withdrawn from the public realm, being less sure of his own orienta-tion. (Is Merwin therefore more *feminine* than Plath?) Merwin has his moment of fierceness, yet it does not consist in openly condemning the Name-of-the-Father but in the continuous exploration of what has es-caped the paternal function and signification, what he names "the other side of despair." He therefore tries to touch on all that is unrealized rather than criticize what is already realized as sociohistorical data. Merwin's imagination is basically nonantagonistic; even in his overtly political poems of the 1960s, readers still feel a psychotic detachment from pres-ent reality when the speaker confesses that "I found untouched the des-ert of the unknown, / Big enough for my feet. It is my home" (*SF* 16). Making one's home in "the desert of the unknown" entails a radical rup-ture with one's social, cultural, and ideological conditions.

The preoccupation with psychic process and constant becoming, which invalidates naming, would endow Merwin's poetics, quite unexpectedly, with a unique political potential. Incessantly undermining the bedrock of ideology—the belief in sameness—Merwin compels us to imagine the other side of the signified that keeps sliding away from our perceptual apparatus. Merwin's message comes from either an immemorial past or a distant future, or traversing both in the blink of an eye. Forming a picture of that fleetingness from memory traces, contemporary readers are able to evoke the primordial happiness and thus to reflect upon the distance between their present life and prehistoric origins. Contemporary life, marked by the market and overshadowed by pandemic and nuclear weapons, may begin to investigate its own worsening logic and examine how the very language we use has participated in consolidating this logic. Unlike Plath and Ginsberg, Merwin does not defy the father's name; he recognizes it, respects it, and plays it down at his own emotional cost. What the paternal function cannot tolerate is not open defiance but *the exclusion of its very structure.*

Merwin's writings are so diversified in their styles and concerns that any single approach may seem reductive. My psychoanalytic and philosophical readings, while revealing the essential dynamics, have left unsaid other important aspects such as his practice of Zen Buddhism, which shapes his later poetry toward Eastern spirituality, and the way his aesthetics of the open form relates to other contemporary poetics—for example, the projective verse of the Black Mountain practitioners. Definitely, eco-poetics with all its recent dynamics should be added to this list. My examination of the desire and infinity in Merwin's works points to the larger question of spirituality or aurality in contemporary poetry and its psychological, ethical, and political implications. Becoming more mindful of the unarticulated, unrealized side of existence, we may come to stay with a poetry that aims not only at a "criticism of life" but also at impossible creations and pure fascination.

NOTES

INTRODUCTION

1. Byers draws the vital distinction between Whitman and Merwin, arguing that "Whitman's encounters with nature often involve dominance and submission" while Merwin holds "a belief in the intrinsic value of that which is different from us" (*What I Cannot Say* 82, 84).

2. Merwin's deconstructive use of poetic language has been a shared discovery among his critics. See Nelson, "Resources of Failure" 78–121; Kalaidjian, "Linguistic Mirage" 198–223. Also see Byers, *What I Cannot Say* 79–110.

3. In "For A Coming Extinction," Merwin not only laments the animals/species that are dying out (whales, sea cows, the Great Auks, the gorillas) as "our sacrifices" but also indicates that humans will not likely survive this extinction because we are on same the track to The End, the "great god" (*SF* 122–23). Merwin's vision of eschatology should be distinguished from Francis Fukuyama's proposition of the predominance of Western liberal democracy as "the end of history." Merwin's vision in the 1960s rather prophesies a total collapse of human civilization.

4. For a detailed treatment of Merwin's essential disagreements with Emerson and Whitman, see Byers, *What I Cannot Say* 79–110.

5. For a detailed discussion on the loss of languages as the result of the loss of species in Merwin's poetry, see Moe 93–115.

6. We may note that, whereas René Descartes's concept of the Infinite is derived from the Christian concept of God, Levinas's idea of infinity refers to the absolute otherness of the Other, who is not necessarily the biblical God. The Levinasian notion of infinity is thus more metaphysical than theological. This nontheological infinity as pure transcendence in Levinasian ethics is exactly what Alain Badiou, in an attack on Levinas, has missed or obscured in order to advance his own version of "ethics of truth" similarly based on the evocation of the Immortal/the Infinite in humans. See Badiou's *Ethics: An Essay on the Understanding of Evil* (2012).

7. Lacan translated Freud's *Trieb* (drive) as *pulsion* (*Seminar XI* 162), which comes very close to Levinas's "propulsion." The Latin root *pellere* means "to drive forward."

8. Much of Levinas's later work is devoted to "glorification of the infinite" through the concepts of "trace," "proximity," and "obsession." See Levinas, *Otherwise than Being* (1998).

9. "Ex-timate" is a neologism Lacan uses in describing the relationship between the subject and object of desire, meaning "external intimacy" or "what is in the subject more than subject," "object in subject" (*Seminar XI* 263–76; Žižek, *Sublime Object* 180–82).

10. The word "absence" has been used to describe Merwin from the 1970s to the present; it was first thematized by Charles Altieri. See Altieri, "The Struggle with Absence: Robert Creeley and W. S. Merwin," *Enlarging the Temple: New Directions in American Poetry during the 1960s* (Lewisburg: Bucknell University Press, 1979), 170–224. (The section on Merwin was later revised and included in *W. S. Merwin: Essays on the Poetry*, ed. Cary Nelson and Ed Folsom.) Also see Sean Joseph McDonnell, "I with No Voice: Absence, Presence, and Intersubjectivity in the Poetry of W. S. Merwin" (2003).

11. The most conspicuous are Altieri 159–97; Lieberman, "Church of Ash" 96–105; Nelson, "Resources of Failure" 78–121; Byers, *What I Cannot Say* 79–110.

12. For instance, see Altieri 159–97; Hoeppner, "A Nest of Bones" 262–84.

13. See Folsom, "Strange Country" 224–49. Folsom's essay presents Merwin's criticism of American expansionism and his endorsement of Thoreauvian humility before the natural world.

14. Further studies might examine the deep intertwinement of human subjectivity (Dasein, memory, fantasy) and the natural world, for example Merwin's encounters with Deep Time and Deep Ecology, his poetic jouissance as a catharsis of ecological anxiety, his poetizing of the bodily transformations of animals and plants as explored by Aaron M. Moe in *Zoopoetics* (2014), his kinship with "the Chthonic" in the wake of Donna J. Haraway's *Staying with the Trouble* (2016), and his contributions to "the scalar discrepancies of the Anthropocene" as conceptualized in Lynn Keller's *Recomposing Ecopoetics* (2017), and so on.

CHAPTER ONE

1. For example, see Mark Christhilf's *W. S. Merwin the Mythmaker* (1986).

2. In "Rimbaud's Piano," a poem in *Travels* (1993), Merwin narrates Rimbaud's youth rebellion against home and his "penniless" wanderings in Europe (17), which mirrors Merwin's own experience in his twenties.

3. For an elaboration on "subjective destitution," see Žižek, *Metastases* 167–72.

4. For instance, see Hoeppner, "Shadows and Glass" 323–30.

5. It is no accident that the new edition of Merwin's *First Four Books of Poems* (Copper Canyon Press, 2000) adopts the painting *Floating Iceberg* by Frederic E. Church as its

cover. In the picture, the fatal iceberg appears as harmless as a drifting cloud, still and white, against the gray sky. Leaning slightly to one side, the iceberg is exactly "dog-hunched" as Merwin describes in the poem.

6. In *Moby-Dick,* some other unfathomable, mysterious objects are also likely the candidates for the Thing—for example, Queequeg's tattoo, which he inscribed onto his coffin: "And this tattooing, had been the work of a departed prophet and seer of his island, who, by those hieroglyphic marks, had written out on his body a complete theory of the heavens and the earth, and a mystical treatise on the art of attaining truth; so that Queequeg in his own proper person was a riddle to unfold; a wondrous work in one volume; but whose mysteries not even himself could read . . ." (Melville 558–59). I am indebted to Aaron Moe for this idea.

7. This is exactly how Lacan defines "sublimation": "It raises an object . . . to the dignity of the Thing" (*Seminar VII* 112).

8. Riggs Alden Smith provides an interesting connection between the death of Palinurus and his ancestor Iasius who had once affronted Neptune (33–36), but Palinurus may have been sacrificed for counseling Aeneas to land in the shores of Eryx, thus impeding the fleet's sailing toward Italy. See Virgil, *Aeneid* 5.1–35.

9. A legendary book explaining the nature of wild beasts in terms of biblical lessons, *Physiologus* can actually be traced to a Greek manuscript composed in second-century Alexandria. See *Physiologus: A Medieval Book of Nature Lore,* trans. Michael J. Curley (Chicago: University of Chicago Press, 2009).

10. Žižek usefully summarizes three types of Other: imaginary, symbolic, and real. The imaginary Other are "my fellow human beings with whom I am engaged in the mirror-like relationships of competition, mutual recognition, and so on," whereas the real Other refers to "the impossible Thing, the 'inhuman partner,' the Other with whom no symmetrical dialogue . . . is possible" (*Did Somebody Say Totalitarianism* 163).

11. Alice Benston clearly saw Merwin's painstaking effort to solve "the problem of solipsism," but her dismissal of "all change" as an "illusion" seems only too hasty (186), for this epic poem on self-transformation has radicalized the constitutive otherness of subjectivity and clearly transcends solipsism conceived as the question or denial of the existence of the Other.

12. Merwin's lines are comparable with Shelley's famous "Ozymandias." Whereas Shelley only mocks the vanity of kings, Merwin is more concerned with the inherent traumatic ahistoricity of the "vain" historical processes.

CHAPTER TWO

1. In Judaism, "the holiness of the holy" refers to the most holy in the sanctuary, separated from the holy by a veil or a curtain, see Exodus 26.31, 33. Derrida explains that

Levinas's phrase can be read both theologically and ethically, as it may mean holiness of the sanctuary and holiness of the other person (*Adieu* 4).

2. For example, from an eco-critical point of view, Jane Frazier reports that Merwin's poetic vision, like that of Thoreau, is firmly grounded in nature and its representations. See Frazier's *From Origin to Ecology* (1999).

3. Merwin's skepticism on the matter of the holy, due to his unwillingness to assign the holy a name, contrasts with Allen Ginsberg's sarcastic numerations of the "holy" objects and sanctification of human parts in the footnote to *Howl* (1956).

4. Brunner likewise regards Merwin's "Notes for a Preface" from the 1960s as an analysis of "the limitations of contemporary culture" even though it "explores the connection between a cultural crisis and the rediscovery of the essentially poetic" (*Poetry* 137).

5. In Latin, conjunctions of sibilance and long vowels (diphthongs) are common because of the particular morphology and the declensions of the language. In St. Fortunatus's well-known hymn "Lingua Gloriosi Proelium Certaminis," we witness the divine triumph over human weakness in a manner similar to Merwin's poem, delivered in an intricate sound system containing sibilant fricatives and vowels that could be read with much emphasis: "Pange lingua gloriosi prœlium certaminis / Et super crucis tropæo dic triumphum nobilem, / Qualiter Redemptor orbis immolatus vicerit."

6. See Libby, "W. S. Merwin" 19–40; Lazer 262–84.

7. For Derrida, any naming process necessarily involves "originary violence of language" (*Grammatology* 112); here Merwin agrees with Derrida in cautioning us against the ethnocentric/anthropologic use of the proper name.

8. In an alternative reading, the poem might suggest Christ's own "journey into the wilderness," although the naturalistic, impersonal tendency of the poem seems to contradict Christ's prayer to God the Father.

9. In the preface to his translation of the French poet Jean Follain (1903–1971), Merwin notes that Follain's works all share a "suspended regard," and it is the "evocation of this 'impersonal,' receptive, but essentially unchanging gaze [that] often occupies, in Follain's work, the place of the first person" ("Preface," xii). In "The Dream Again" and other Zenic poems, Merwin's lyric self, as can be found in various mystical practices, is not only *erased* but also *replaced* by an unchanging, divine, vantage.

10. Here the poem "How We Are Spared," in its immense, immersive imagery, exemplifies Aaron Moe's astute observation about "the weight of the language as it moves across the line breaks" (104).

11. Merwin has worries in adapting Hawaiian history to his purpose: "I was very dubious about writing anything about Hawaii, because I didn't want to start exploiting the Hawaiian material. That's tacky, and I felt very cautious about that. But the story kept nagging me. Finally, after most of ten years, I thought it probably had to be poem" (*CW* 143). The verse form fits because it's more memorable and enduring than prose.

CHAPTER THREE

1. A cursory comparison of Robert Lowell's "To Speak of Woe That Is in Marriage" with Merwin's "Fable" reveals the two poets' different approaches toward sexual desire. Lowell employs a confessional mode to lament the coarseness of desire while Merwin uses allegories to reveal fantasies in desire.

2. Eros, the love-drive, which aims at establishing unities, and Thanatos, the death-drive, which destroys organic unities, could not work independently. In Freud's formulation, the two basic drives "work against one another or combine with one another" (*Penguin Freud Reader* 5).

3. Both Merwin's "Canso" and Dante's *La Vita Nuova* (1295) follow the tradition of "courtly love" in presenting the essence of love as spiritual or divine.

4. Following Heidegger and Lacan, Bruce Fink explains "ex-sistence" as "'an existence which stands apart from,' which insists as it were from the outside; something not included on the inside, something which, rather than being intimate, is 'extimate'" (122).

5. Merwin's imagery might come from Robert Graves's *The White Goddess* (originally published in 1948), which traces Western poetic inspirations to a mythic White Goddess associated with the worship of the moon.

6. Merwin gives a full account of his meeting with Pound in St. Elizabeth's Hospital in the opening pages of *The Mays of Ventadorn*. Pound advised young Merwin to translate "the Provençal" and Spanish *Romancero* and to "get as close to the original as you can" (*MV* 8). Pound famously advised young Merwin: "Read seeds not twigs" (*MV* 10).

7. "Cino" opens with "Bah! I have sung women in three cities, / But it is all the same; / And I will sing of the sun"; in a dramatic monologue, the poem goes on to mourn the lost "lips," "words," "dreams," and "nights" when Cino the Italian Don Juan raves along the open road (Pound 6).

8. In "Noah's Raven," the animal-speaker laments: "Why should I have returned? / My knowledge would not fit into theirs. / I found untouched the desert of the unknown, / Big enough for my feet" (*SF* 16).

9. By foreclosing the Name-of-the-Father, the paternal function, subjects will obtain excessive jouissance from delusions and fantasies. Lacan proposes the foreclosure of the Name-of-the-Father as the fundamental mechanism of psychosis in *Seminar III: The Psychoses* (1955–56).

10. Michael Clifton has similarly noticed that "Merwin's mother also represents for him the unconscious," stressing how the "elusive essence of Merwin's relationship with his mother" has structured the poet's visionary imagery (74). This is surely not to dismiss the influence of other figures such as his father, his girlfriends, and even nature in Merwin's love poetry—all could be determinative; the mother image here simply makes clear one major phase in Merwin's work. Critics tend to consider the lovers in

Merwin's poetry as "provid[ing] the mirroring function of the eternally present mother" (McDonnell 118). For a full explication of Merwin's mother as the lost love object in his later poetry, see McDonnell 102–30.

11. "And [Jacob] dreamed, and behold a ladder set up on the earth, and the top of it reached to heaven: and behold the angels of God ascending and descending on it" (Genesis 28. 12). In Jewish mysticism, stairs and rungs essentially symbolize spiritual growth, as in the title of Martin Buber's *Ten Rungs* (1947), which points at the levels of religious consciousness and practice. Merwin's erotic narrative here, however, only dimly echoes the biblical legend.

12. Merwin's epic narrative *The Folding Cliffs* (1998) similarly recounts European merchants' perilous grabbing for sandalwood, a precious plant, in nineteenth-century Hawaii: "but some died there among the trees some on the trails some reached / home for a while as the demand for the wood quickened / and the debts mounted and it is legend that the cutters / pulled up every sandalwood seedling they could find" (*FC* 78).

13. Manini is another name for Don Francisco de Paula Marín (1774–1837), an avid Spanish horticulturist known for introducing many plants to Honolulu.

14. See Gary Snyder's preface to *No Nature: New and Selected Poems* (1992): "There is no single or set 'nature' either as 'the natural world' or 'the nature of things.' The greatest respect we can pay to nature is not to trap it, but to acknowledge that it eludes us and that our own nature is also fluid, open, and conditional" (v).

CHAPTER FOUR

1. A recent "mock" debate between Mark Halliday and Michael Theune on the value of Merwin's *The Shadow of Sirius* (2008) centers neither on historical nor ecological issues but on whether or not Merwin has really achieved "a condition of transcendent awareness of Essential Being" (Halliday and Theune 150). Though drawing opposite conclusions, both authors seem to agree that in late Merwin the problematic "radical simplicity of timeless archetypes" clearly predominates over other less enduring concerns (160).

2. The most vehement attack on Freud's formulation of "family romance" perhaps comes from Deleuze and Guattari's 1972 *Anti-Oedipus: Capitalism and Schizophrenia*, which argues for a productive, rather than prohibitive, interpretation of human desire. Deleuze and Guattari consider Freud's "tripartite formula"—"the Oedipal, neurotic one: daddy-mommy-me"—as a limited structure that has ignored ideological and social formations of the primal scene (*Anti-Oedipus* 23). Literary critics, Shoshana Felman and Mieke Bal for example, have consequently focused on the problematic conjunction of literature (textual structure) and psychoanalysis (Oedipal structure). In an early reappraisal essay, "To Open the Question" (1977), Felman proposes that "the notion of *application* would be replaced by the radically different notion of *implication*: bringing analytical

questions to bear upon literary questions, *involving* psychoanalysis in the scene of literary analysis" (216). Following Felman's implication procedure, Mieke Bal urges psychoanalytically informed literary criticism to gain "surplus information" in textual analysis and thus to "contribute to the rethinking of the subject in the socio-cultural sciences" rather than confirming psychoanalytic discourse (87).

3. Freud discovers that children are largely bisexual and may treat both parents as love objects. In *Three Essays on the Theory of Sexuality* (1905), Freud ventures the view that humans have an original predisposition toward bisexuality.

4. This line recalls an earlier poem, "Separation," in which the loss of the beloved is expressed through a haunting presence that conveys melancholic jouissance: "Your absence has gone through me / Like thread through a needle. / Everything I do is stitched with its color" (*SF* 15).

5. Is Merwin's mourning for his father usurping his grief for the planet? It would be very hard to disentangle ecological concerns, family issues, and questions about memory and time in Merwin's late writings. Here, I am merely highlighting one aspect, that is, his father complex, as the nodal point.

6. In the story "Blackbird's Summer," Merwin portrays a local wine merchant named Blackbird, who, similar to Merwin's grandfather, stands outside the local morals due to his fascination with wine and negligence to the church service. Blackbird knew the curative power of water and retained a spiritual rapport with mysterious nature. See Merwin, *LU* 157–307.

7. In different places in his later poetry, Merwin admits that his heart had been "caught by what was never there" (*RS* 112), or "when I went looking for what I thought I remembered / as anyone could have foretold it was not there" (*V* 3), or "reaching into the blindness that was there" (*SS* 45).

8. For instance, Merwin's speaker often becomes fearless by transforming himself into an enduring entity, as in "A Contemporary": "From the beginning I would be older than all the animals / and to the last I would be simpler / frost would design me and dew would disappear on me / sun would shine through me / I would be green with white roots / feel worms touch my feet as a bounty / have no name and no fear" (*FH* 12).

9. "Wands of the auroras," in a Stevensian overtone, visualize our desire for the infinite hyperobject: the far, shadowy light, inaccessible, uncontainable, dancing, beckoning, withdrawing.

10. M. P. Jones observes that "[u]sing the bleakness of silence to look forward, Merwin is able to experience loss without a sense of nostalgia"; "Merwin's silences contain multitudes, from lost objects to lost friends" (49, 51).

11. Žižek usefully distinguishes "loss" from "lack" for their different relations with desire: "Lack is co-substantial with desire, while loss designates the moment at which desire loses its dialect . . . by being transfixed by some positive object which is missing. . . . The subject possesses [the lost object] in the very mode of loss" (*Plague* 195).

12. M. P. Jones makes a wonderful point in including the loss of Merwin's dog as part of the mythology of the Dog Star: "The relationship between Merwin's Koa [one of his dogs] and the dog star elevates his personal loss to the mythological level" (59).

13. Recent theoretical formulations of speculative realism, for example, Quentin Meillassoux's concept of hyper-Chaos, could shed some light on the question of temporality in Merwin's last poems. Peering into the hyper-Chaos, we see "a rather menacing power—something insensible, and capable of destroying both things and worlds, of bringing forth monstrous absurdities, yet also of never doing anything, of realizing every dream, but also every nightmare, of engendering random and frenetic transformations. . . . We see something akin to Time" (Meillassoux 64). For late Merwin, time similarly causes vertigo rather than bringing experience, knowledge, or assurance.

CONCLUSION

1. See, for example, the chapter "Poetry and Survival" in Susan Bassnett's *Sylvia Plath: An Introduction to the Poetry* (2005).

WORKS CITED

Alaimo, Stacy. *Undomesticated Ground: Recasting Nature as Feminist Space.* Ithaca, NY: Cornell University Press, 2000.

Altieri, Charles. "Situating Merwin's Poetry since 1970." In *W. S. Merwin,* ed. Nelson and Folsom, 159–97.

Andersen, Kenneth. "The Poetry of W. S. Merwin." *Twentieth Century Literature* 16.4 (1970): 278–86.

Badiou, Alain. *Ethics: An Essay on the Understanding of Evil.* Trans. Peter Hallward. London: Verso, 2012.

———. "Language, Thought, Poetry." In *Theoretic Writings,* ed. Ray Brassier and Alberto Toscano, 233–41. New York: Continuum, 2004.

Bal, Mieke. *On Meaning-Making: Essays in Semiotics.* Salem, OR: Polebridge Press. 1994.

Barthes, Roland. *Le degré zéro de l'écriture.* Paris: Seuil, 1972.

———. *A Lover's Discourse: Fragments.* Trans. Richard Howard. London: Penguin, 1990.

Bassnett, Susan. *Sylvia Plath: An Introduction to the Poetry.* New York: Palgrave Macmillan, 2005.

Beach, Christopher. *The Cambridge Introduction to Twentieth-Century American Poetry.* Cambridge, UK: Cambridge University Press, 2003.

Benjamin, Walter. *Illuminations: Essays and Reflections.* Ed. Hannah Arendt, trans. Harry Zohn. New York: Schocken, 1968.

———. *Reflections: Essays, Aphorisms, Autobiographical Writings.* Ed. Peter Demetz, trans. Edmund Jephcott. New York: Schocken, 1978.

Bennett, Jane. *Vibrant Matter: A Political Ecology of Things.* Durham, NC: Duke University Press, 2010.

Benston, Alice. "Myth in the Poetry of W. S. Merwin." In *Poets in Progress,* ed. Edward Hungerford, 179–204. Evanston, IL: Northwestern University Press, 1962.

Biespiel, David. "Iron Man." *Poetry* 187.2 (2005): 137–42.

Blanchot, Maurice. *Desperate Clarity: Chronicles of Intellectual Life, 1942.* Trans. Michael Holland. New York: Fordham University Press, 2014.

———. *The Infinite Conversation.* Trans. Susan Hanson. Minneapolis: University of Minnesota Press, 1993.

Bloom, Harold. "Introduction." In *W. S. Merwin,* ed. Harold Bloom, 10–16. New York: Chelsea House, 2004.

Bly, Robert. *American Poetry: Wildness and Domesticity.* New York: Harper & Row, 1991.

———. *Selected Poems.* New York: Harper & Row, 1986.

Bowers, Neal. "W. S. Merwin and Postmodern American Poetry." *Sewanee Review* 98.2 (1990): 246–59.

Brunner, Edward. "*Opening the Hand:* The Variable Caesura and the Family Poems." In *W. S. Merwin,* ed. Nelson and Folsom, 276–95.

———. *Poetry as Labor and Privilege: The Writings of W. S. Merwin.* Urbana: University of Illinois Press, 1991.

Bryson, J. Scott. *The West Side of Any Mountain: Place, Space, and Ecopoetry.* Iowa City: University of Iowa Press, 2005.

Burt, John. "History and Narrative in Merwin's *The Folding Cliffs.*" *Raritan* 19.3 (2000): 115–34.

Byers, Thomas B. "The Present Voices: W. S. Merwin since 1970." In *W. S. Merwin,* ed. Nelson and Folsom, 250–75.

———. *What I Cannot Say: Self, Word, and World in Whitman, Stevens, and Merwin.* Urbana: University of Illinois Press, 1989.

Carroll, Paul. *The Poem in Its Skin.* Chicago: Big Table, 1968.

Chrétien, Jean-Louis. *The Unforgettable and the Unhoped For.* Trans. Jeffrey Bloechl. New York: Fordham University Press, 2002.

Christhilf, Mark. *W. S. Merwin the Mythmaker.* Columbia: University of Missouri Press, 1986.

Clifton, Michael. "Breaking the Glass: A Pattern of Visionary Imagery in W. S. Merwin." *Chicago Review* 36.1 (1988): 65–83.

Contoski, Victor. "W. S. Merwin: Rational and Irrational Poetry." *Literary Review* 22.3 (1979): 309–20.

Davis, Cheri. *W. S. Merwin.* Boston: Twayne, 1981.

Dean, Jeanie S. "Re-seeding the Burnt Wasteland: W. S. Merwin's *The Rain in the Trees*." In *Passions of the Earth in Human Existence, Creativity and Literature*, ed. Anna-Teresa Tymieniecka, 81–100. Dordrecht, Netherlands: Kluwer Academic Publishers, 2001.

Deleuze, Gilles. *The Fold: Leibniz and the Baroque*. Trans. Tom Conley. Minneapolis: University of Minnesota Press, 1993.

———. "The Simulacrum and Ancient Philosophy." In *The Logic of Sense*, ed. Constantin V. Boundas, trans. Mark Lester and Charles Stivale, 253–79. New York: Columbia University Press, 1990.

———, and Félix Guattari. *Anti-Oedipus: Capitalism and Schizophrenia*. Trans. Robert Hurley, Mark Seem, and Helen R. Lane. Minneapolis: University of Minnesota Press, 1983.

———, and Félix Guattari. *A Thousand Plateaus: Capitalism and Schizophrenia*. Trans. Brian Massumi. Minneapolis: University of Minnesota Press, 1987.

Derrida, Jacques. *Adieu to Emmanuel Levinas*. Trans. Pascale-Anne Brault and Michael Naas. Stanford, CA: Stanford University Press, 1999.

———. *Of Grammatology*. Trans. Gayatri Chakravorty Spivak. Baltimore: Johns Hopkins University Press, 1997.

———. *Of Spirit: Heidegger and the Question*. Trans. Geoffrey Bennington and Rachel Bowlby. Chicago: University of Chicago Press, 1987.

———. *On the Name*. Trans. David Wood, John P. Leavey Jr., and Ian McLeod. Stanford, CA: Stanford University Press, 1995.

———. *Sovereignties in Question: The Poetics of Paul Celan*. Ed. Thomas Dutoit and Outi Pasanen, trans. Thomas Dutoit et al. New York: Fordham University Press, 2005.

———. *Writing and Difference*. Trans. Alan Bass. London: Routledge, 2001.

Eliot, T. S. *Collected Poems, 1909–1962*. New York: Harcourt Brace, 1963.

Felman, Shoshana. *The Claims of Literature: A Shoshana Felman Reader*. Ed. Emily Sun, Eyal Peretz, and Ulrich Baer. New York: Fordham University Press, 2007.

Fink, Bruce. *The Lacanian Subject: Between Language and Jouissance*. Princeton, NJ: Princeton University Press, 1995.

Folsom, Ed. "'I Have Been a Long Time in a Strange Country': W. S. Merwin and America." In *W. S. Merwin*, ed. Nelson and Folsom, 224–49.

———, and Cary Nelson. "Introduction." In *W. S. Merwin*, ed. Nelson and Folsom, 1–18.

Frazier, Jane. *From Origin to Ecology: Nature and the Poetry of W. S. Merwin*. Cranbury, NJ: Associated University Press, 1999.

Freud, Sigmund. *The Penguin Freud Reader.* Ed. Adam Phillips. London: Penguin, 2006.

———. *Three Case Histories.* Ed. Philip Rieff. New York: Simon & Schuster, 1996.

———. *Totem and Taboo.* Trans. James Strachey. London: Routledge, 2008.

Geyskens, Thomas. *Our Original Scenes: Freud's Theory of Sexuality.* Leuven, Belgium: Leuven University Press, 2005.

Ginn, Franklin, et al. "Introduction: Unexpected Encounters with Deep Time." *Environmental Humanities* 10.1 (2018): 213–25.

Ginsberg, Allen. *Howl and Other Poems.* San Francisco: City Lights, 1959.

Goethe, Johann Wolfgang von. *Selected Poems.* Ed. Christopher Middleton. Vol. 1 of *Goethe: The Collected Works.* Princeton, NJ: Princeton University Press, 1994.

Grigg, Russell. *Lacan, Language, and Philosophy.* Albany: State University of New York Press, 2008.

Gross, Harvey. "The Writing on the Void: The Poetry of W. S. Merwin." *Iowa Review* 1.3 (1970): 92–106.

Guy, Sandra M. "W. S. Merwin and the Primordial Elements: Mapping the Journey to Mythic Consciousness." *Midwest Quarterly* 38.4 (1997): 414–23.

Hallberg, Robert von. "Authenticity." In *The Cambridge History of American Literature,* vol. 8: *Poetry and Criticism 1940–1995,* ed. Sacvan Bercovitch, 123–59. Cambridge, UK: Cambridge University Press, 1996.

Halliday, Mark, and Michael Theune. "*The Shadow of Sirius:* A Critical Conversation." In *Until Everything Is Continuous Again: American Poets on the Recent Work of W. S. Merwin,* ed. Jonathan Weinert and Kevin Prufer, 137–72. Seattle: WordFarm, 2012.

Haraway, Donna J. *Staying with the Trouble: Making Kin in the Chthulucene.* Durham, NC: Duke University Press, 2016.

Harp, Jerry. "All of Memory Waking: Word and Experience in W. S. Merwin's *The Shadow of Sirius.*" In *Until Everything Is Continuous Again: American Poets on the Recent Work of W. S. Merwin,* ed. Jonathan Weinert and Kevin Prufer, 173–83. Seattle: WordFarm, 2012.

Heidegger, Martin. *Being and Time.* Trans. John Macquarrie and Edward Robinson. New York: Harper & Row, 1962.

———. *Hölderlin's Hymn "The Ister."* Trans. William McNeill and Julia Davis. Bloomington: Indiana University Press, 1996.

———. *On the Way to Language.* Trans. Peter D. Hertz. New York: Harper & Row, 1971.

———. *Poetry, Language, Thought*. Trans. Albert Hofstadter. New York: Harper & Row, 1971.

Hix, H. L. "'This Simple Test': A Thematic Continuum in Merwin's Middle Period." In *Many Mountains Moving*, ed. Irwin, 68–74.

———. *Understanding W. S. Merwin*. Columbia: University of South Carolina Press, 1997.

Hoeppner, Edward Haworth. "A Nest of Bones: Transcendence, Topology, and the Theory of the Word in W. S. Merwin's Poetry." *Modern Language Quarterly* 49.3 (1988): 262–84.

———. "Shadows and Glass: Mirrored Selves in the Poetry of W. S. Merwin and John Ashbery." *Philological Quarterly* 65.3 (1986): 311–30.

Homer, Sean. *Jacques Lacan*. London: Routledge, 2005.

Howard, Richard. *Alone with America: Essays on the Art of Poetry in the United States since 1950*. Enlarged ed. New York: Atheneum, 1980.

Irwin, Mark. "A Conversation with W. S. Merwin." In *Many Mountains Moving*, ed. Irwin, 47–52.

———, ed. *Many Mountains Moving: A Tribute to W. S. Merwin*. Boulder, CO: Many Mountains Moving, 2001.

Jones, M. P. "Silence and the Lyric-Epic: Merwin's Hybrid Ecopoetics in *The Shadow of Sirius*." *Merwin Studies* (2013): 47–65.

Kalaidjian, Walter. "Linguistic Mirage: Language and Landscape in W. S. Merwin's Later Poetry." In *W. S. Merwin*, ed. Nelson and Folsom, 198–223.

Keller, Lynn. *Recomposing Ecopoetics: North American Poetry of the Self-Conscious Anthropocene*. Charlottesville: University Press of Virginia, 2017.

Lacan, Jacques. *Écrits: A Selection*. Trans. Bruce Fink. New York: Norton, 2002.

———. *The Seminar of Jacques Lacan, Book III: The Psychoses*. Trans. Russell Grigg. New York: Norton, 1997.

———. *The Seminar of Jacques Lacan, Book VII: The Ethics of Psychoanalysis*. Trans. Dennis Porter. New York: Norton, 1992.

———. *The Seminar of Jacques Lacan, Book XI: The Four Fundamental Concepts of Psychoanalysis*. Trans. Alan Sheridan. New York: Norton, 1998.

———. *The Seminar of Jacques Lacan, Book XX: On Feminine Sexuality, The Limit of Love and Knowledge*. Trans. Bruce Fink. New York: Norton, 1999.

Lazer, Hank. "For a Coming Extinction: A Reading of W. S. Merwin's *The Lice*." *ELH* 49.1 (1982): 262–85.

Levinas, Emmanuel. *Collected Philosophical Papers*. Trans. Richard A. Cohen. Dordrecht, Netherlands: Martinus Nijhoff, 1987.

————. *Entre Nous: Thinking-of-the-Other.* Trans. Michael B. Smith and Barbara Harshav. New York: Columbia University Press, 2006.

————. *Ethics and Infinity: Conversations with Philippe Nemo.* Trans. Richard A. Cohen. Pittsburg: Duquesne University Press, 1985.

————. *Existence and Existents.* Trans. Alphonso Lingis. The Hague: Martinus Nijhoff, 1978.

————. *God, Death, and Time.* Trans. Bettina Bergo. Stanford, CA: Stanford University Press, 2000.

————. *Otherwise than Being: Or Beyond Essence.* Trans. Alphonso Lingis. Pittsburg: Duquesne University Press, 1998.

————. *Time and the Other.* Trans. Richard A. Cohen. Pittsburg: Duquesne University Press, 1987.

————. *Totality and Infinity: An Essay on Exteriority.* Trans. Alphonso Lingis. The Hague: Martinus Nijhoff, 1979.

Libby, Anthony. "Merwin's Planet: Alien Voices." *Criticism* 24.1 (1982): 48–63.

————. "W. S. Merwin and the Nothing That Is." *Contemporary Literature* 16.1 (1975): 19–40.

Lieberman, Laurence. "W. S. Merwin: Apotheosis of the Lepers." *American Poetry Review* 41.2 (2012): 41–48.

————. "W. S. Merwin: Church of Ash." In *Many Mountains Moving,* ed. Irwin, 96–105.

Marcuse, Herbert. *Eros and Civilization: A Philosophical Inquiry into Freud.* 1955. Boston: Beacon, 1966.

Marion, Jean-Luc. *The Visible and the Revealed.* Trans. Christina M. Gschwandtner et al. New York: Fordham University Press, 2008.

McCorkle, James. "Merwin, W. S." In *The Greenwood Encyclopedia of American Poets and Poetry,* ed. Jeffrey H. Gray et al. Vol. 4: 1044–48. Santa Barbara: Greenwood Press, 2005.

————. *The Still Performance: Writing, Self, and Interconnection in Five Postmodern American Poets.* Charlottesville: University Press of Virginia, 1989.

McDonnell, Sean Joseph. "I with No Voice: Absence, Presence and Intersubjectivity in the Poetry of W. S. Merwin." PhD diss., University of California, Davis, 2003.

Meillassoux, Quentin. *After Finitude: An Essay on the Necessity of Contingency.* Trans. Ray Brassier. London: Bloomsbury, 2008.

Melville, Herman. *Moby-Dick.* New York: Penguin, 2012.

Merwin, W. S. *The Book of Fables*. Port Townsend, WA: Copper Canyon Press, 2007.

———. *Conversations with W. S. Merwin*. Ed. Michael Wutz and Hal Crimmel. Jackson: University Press of Mississippi, 2015.

———. *The Ends of the Earth: Essays*. Washington, DC: Shoemaker & Hoard, 2004.

———. *Finding the Islands*. San Francisco: North Point Press, 1982.

———. *The First Four Books of Poems*. 1975. Port Townsend, WA: Copper Canyon Press, 2000.

———. *Flower & Hand: Poems 1977–1983*. Port Townsend, WA: Copper Canyon Press, 1997.

———. *The Folding Cliffs: A Narrative*. Port Townsend, WA: Copper Canyon Press, 1998.

———. *Garden Time*. Port Townsend, WA: Copper Canyon Press, 2016.

———. "Introduction." In *Twenty Love Poems and a Song of Despair*. By Pablo Neruda, trans. W. S. Merwin, vii–xviii.

———. *The Lost Upland: Stories of Southwest France*. New York: Knopf, 1992.

———. *The Mays of Ventadorn*. Washington, DC: National Geographic Society, 2002.

———. *The Moon Before Morning*. Port Townsend, WA: Copper Canyon Press, 2015.

———. "Preface." *Transparence of the World*. By Jean Follain, trans. W. S. Merwin, xi–xiv. Port Townsend, WA: Copper Canyon Press, 2005.

———. *Present Company*. Port Townsend, WA: Copper Canyon Press, 2005.

———. *The Pupil*. 2001. New York: Knopf, 2002.

———. *The Rain in the Trees*. 1988. New York: Knopf, 2008.

———. *Regions of Memory: Uncollected Prose, 1949–82*. Ed. Ed Folsom and Cary Nelson. Urbana: University of Illinois Press, 1987.

———. *The River Sound*. New York: Knopf, 1999.

———. *The Second Four Books of Poems*. Port Townsend, WA: Copper Canyon Press, 1993.

———. *Selected Translations 1948–2011*. Port Townsend, WA: Copper Canyon Press, 2015.

———. *The Shadow of Sirius*. Port Townsend, WA: Copper Canyon Press, 2008.

———. *Summer Doorways: A Memoir*. Washington, DC: Shoemaker & Hoard, 2005.

———. *Travels*. 1993. New York: Knopf, 2003.

———. *Unframed Originals: Recollections.* 1982. Washington, DC: Shoemaker & Hoard, 2005.

———. *The Vixen.* 1996. New York: Knopf, 2006.

Moe, Aaron M. *Zoopoetics: Animals and the Making of Poetry.* Lanham, MD: Lexington Books, 2014.

Molesworth, Charles. "W. S. Merwin: Style, Vision, Influence." In *W. S. Merwin,* ed. Nelson and Folsom, 145–58.

Morton, Timothy. *Dark Ecology: For a Logic of Future Coexistence.* New York: Columbia University Press, 2016.

———. *Ecology without Nature: Rethinking Environmental Aesthetics.* Cambridge, MA: Harvard University Press, 2007.

———. *Hyperobjects: Philosophy and Ecology after the End of the World.* Minneapolis: University of Minnesota Press, 2013.

———. "Queer Ecology." *PMLA* 125.2 (2010): 273–82.

Nelson, Cary. "The Resources of Failure: W. S. Merwin's Deconstructive Career." In *W. S. Merwin,* ed. Nelson and Folsom, 78–121.

——— and Ed Folsom, eds. *W. S. Merwin: Essays on the Poetry.* Urbana: University of Illinois Press, 1987.

Neruda, Pablo. *Twenty Love Poems and a Song of Despair.* Trans. W. S. Merwin. London: Penguin, 2004.

Newman, Amy. "Radiance and Regret in W. S. Merwin's 'One Story.'" In *Many Mountains Moving,* ed. Irwin, 124–29.

Olson, Charles. "Projective/Verse." In *The Norton Anthology of Modern and Contemporary Poetry,* vol. 2, ed. Richard Ellmann et al., 1053–61. New York: Norton, 2003.

Otto, Rudolf. *The Idea of the Holy.* Trans. John W. Harvey. London: Oxford University Press, 1936.

Perkins, David. *A History of Modern Poetry: Modernism and After.* Cambridge, MA: Harvard University Press, 1987.

Perloff, Marjorie. "Apocalypse Then: Merwin and the Sorrows of Literary History." In *W. S. Merwin,* ed. Nelson and Folsom, 122–44.

Pinsky, Robert. *The Situation of Poetry: Contemporary Poetry and Its Traditions.* Princeton, NJ: Princeton University Press, 1976.

Plath, Sylvia. *The Collected Poems.* Ed. Ted Hughes. New York: HarperPerennial, 1992.

Plumwood, Val. *Feminism and the Mastery of Nature.* London: Routledge, 1993.

Pound, Ezra. *Personae: The Shorter Poems of Ezra Pound.* Ed. Lea Baechler and
A. Walton Litz. New York: New Directions, 1990.

Ramke, Bin. "Returning to the Place of Loss." In *Many Mountains Moving,* ed.
Irwin, 133–36.

Ramsey, Jarold. "The Continuities of W. S. Merwin: 'What Has Escaped Us We
Bring with Us.'" In *W. S. Merwin,* ed. Nelson and Folsom, 19–44.

Rilke, M. R. *The Selected Poetry of Rainer Maria Rilke.* Trans. Stephen Mitchell.
New York: Vintage, 1989.

Rueckert, William H. "Rereading *The Lice:* A Journal." In *W. S. Merwin,* ed.
Nelson and Folsom, 45–64.

Scholes, Robert. "Reading Merwin Semiotically." In *W. S. Merwin,* ed. Nelson
and Folsom, 65–77.

Scigaj, Leonard. *Sustainable Poetry: Four American Ecopoets.* Lexington: University Press of Kentucky, 1999.

Smith, Riggs Alden. *The Primacy of Vision in Virgil's Aeneid.* Austin: University
of Texas Press, 2005.

Snyder, Gary. *No Nature: New and Selected Poems.* New York: Pantheon Books, 1992.

Stepanchev, Stephen. *American Poetry since 1945: A Critical Survey.* New York:
Harper & Row, 1967.

Stewart, Susan. *The Poet's Freedom: A Notebook on Making.* Chicago: University
of Chicago Press, 2011.

Toliver, Carl Clifton. "W. S. Merwin and the Postmodern Environment." PhD
diss., University of Texas, Austin, 1997.

Trakl, Georg. *Poems and Prose: A Bilingual Edition.* Trans. Alexander Stillmark.
Evanston, IL: Northwestern University Press, 2005.

Vendler, Helen. *Part of Nature, Part of Us: Modern American Poets.* Cambridge,
MA: Harvard University Press, 1980.

Virgil. *The Aeneid of Virgil.* Trans. Allen Mandelbaum. New York: Bantam, 1981.

Watkins, Evan. "W. S. Merwin: A Critical Accompaniment." *boundary 2* 4.1
(1975): 186–99.

Westover, Jeff. "Story, Discourse, and the Voice of the Other in W. S. Merwin's
The Folding Cliffs." *Genre* 52.1 (2019): 51–75.

Wilson, Reed Daniel. "Words on a Journey: Vision and Religion in the Poetry
of W. S. Merwin." PhD diss., University of California, Los Angeles, 1988.

Yeats, W. B. *The Collected Poems of W. B. Yeats.* Ed. Richard J. Finneran. New
York: Simon & Schuster, 1996.

Zahavi, Dan. *Husserl's Phenomenology.* Stanford, CA: Stanford University Press, 2003.

Žižek, Slavoj. *The Abyss of Freedom.* Ann Arbor: University of Michigan Press, 1997.

———. *Did Somebody Say Totalitarianism? Five Interventions in the (Mis)use of a Notion.* New York: Verso, 2001.

———. *Enjoy Your Symptom: Jacques Lacan in Hollywood and Out.* New York: Routledge, 2008.

———. *The Fragile Absolute: Or, Why Is the Christian Legacy Worth Fighting for?* New York: Verso, 2000.

———. *The Metastases of Enjoyment: Six Essays on Women and Causality.* New York: Verso, 2005.

———. *On Belief.* London: Routledge, 2001.

———. *Organs without Bodies: Deleuze and Consequences.* New York: Routledge, 2004.

———. *The Plague of Fantasies.* New York: Verso, 1997.

———. *The Sublime Object of Ideology.* New York: Verso, 1989.

———. *The Ticklish Subject: The Absent Centre of Political Ontology.* New York: Verso, 1999.

———. *Violence: Six Sideways Reflections.* New York: Picador, 2008.

———. *The Žižek Reader.* Ed. Elizabeth Wright and Edmond Wright. Malden, MA: Blackwell, 1999.

INDEX